SOCIAL MEDIA
IN HIGHER EDUCATION

Social Media in Higher Education

Case Studies, Reflections and Analysis

Edited by Chris Rowell

OpenBook
Publishers

Acknowledgements

I would like to thank all the authors who have contributed to this book, especially Andy Horton, who helped me with the referencing. The Open Book Publishers team of Alessandra Tosi, Lucy Barnes and Liam Etheridge gave excellent guidance, advice and expertise in bringing this book to completion. Special thanks to Dr Tom Saunders and Martin Bennell for their unique perspectives on social media. The book would not have happened without the support and encouragement of Harriet Gill. And finally, thanks to Rosalie Kerr for being a cool daughter.

Contributors

Timos Almpanis is a Senior Lecturer in Teaching, Learning and Professional Development at the University of Greenwich, UK, with a long career in Education and a particular focus on staff development. He holds a BEd in Philosophy and Education (Aristotle University of Thessaloniki, Greece), an MSc in Computer-based Learning and Training (University of Southampton, UK) and a PhD in E-Research and Technology Enhanced Learning (Lancaster University, UK). He is a qualified teacher for the secondary and the tertiary sectors and a Senior Fellow of the Higher Education Academy (SFHEA). His research interests include academic staff development needs for blended and online learning; ways technology can be used pedagogically to enhance learning; curriculum design; learning theories; Open Educational Resources (OER); the future of online learning. Twitter: @timos75 LinkedIn: https://www.linkedin.com/in/timosalmpanis

Sam Aston is a Librarian working in learning development at The University of Manchester Library. Sam designs and delivers a broad range of teaching activities from innovative, credit-bearing, assessed units to development of academic skills support within programmes for students and staff. Sam has a flair for creating effective learning environments and encouraging creative active learning interactions, and has a keen interest in developing the groups with whom she works. Her areas of specialist interest are: skills development during transition into higher education, and the application of digital pedagogy. She is a Senior Fellow of the Higher Education Academy and the Call for Papers Officer for the Librarians Information Literacy Annual Conference, and you can find her at @manclibrarian on Twitter.

Alex Avramenko is Lecturer in Management in the Dundee Business School at the Abertay University. Alex is a business and management professional with particular interests in enabling effective teaching and learning in higher education. He has worked extensively with active and experiential learning methods within a spectrum of traditional and online programmes in the higher education sector. His current research focuses on lateral pedagogy.

Sue Beckingham is a National Teaching Fellow and Principal Lecturer in Business Information Systems and Technology at Sheffield Hallam University. Her research interests include the use of social media in higher education, and technology-enhanced learning and interpersonal communication; she has published and given keynotes on this work both nationally and internationally. She can be found on Twitter as @suebecks and blogs at https://socialmediaforlearning.com/

Jennie Blake is the Learning Development Manager at the University of Manchester Library and has been working in education for over twenty-five years, teaching in schools and universities in the US and UK. At Manchester, Jennie led on the development of the Library's multi-award-winning My Learning Essentials, and she contributes to university-wide work around teaching, curriculum design and research in higher education. She is particularly interested in how curriculum design and pedagogy can explicitly address inequality and enable student success. She is a Senior Fellow of the Higher Education Academy, has an MA in Education from the University of California at Berkeley and delivers talks across the UK on pedagogy, student engagement and curriculum design. You can find her on Twitter @jnyrose, and she is always up for a chat.

Rachel Challen has been passionate about the use of learning technology to support solid pedagogical curriculum design for over fourteen years in private, Further and Higher Education sectors and in that time has achieved Senior Fellowship of the Higher Education Academy, Certified Membership of the Association for Learning Technology (CMALT) accreditation, an MSc in Multimedia and eLearning and gives back to the community as an editor of the ALT blog (https://altc.alt.ac.uk/blog). Rachel is currently the Head of the Learning and Teaching Support Unit within the School of Arts and Humanities at Nottingham Trent

University and is an active member of the Nottingham Trent Institute for Learning and Teaching with membership of the ePortfolio Steering Group and the Digital Technologies Users Group; she also chairs the Flexible and Online Learning User Group. Jisc named Rachel as one of the top fifty Further Education social media users to follow and she can be found on Twitter @RKChallen or on her team blog https://ntuhum-ltsu.blog/

In twenty-five years teaching in schools, colleges and universities in the UK and overseas, **Martin Compton** has witnessed a shift from overhead projectors to digital projectors; from gigantic TVs on wheels to YouTube; and from cut-and-paste with scissors and glue to its electronic equivalent. History will telescope this era and describe what has happened as a digital revolution, but to live it is to see how slow change can be; especially in terms of technology for teaching and learning. When it comes to tech use, Martin likes to think of himself as a bit of an 'edupunk' (despite his age) and looks beyond the monolithic institutional tech systems for inspiration. Much of this is tangential to his actual role which is as a Senior Lecturer in teaching, learning and professional development at the University of Greenwich. His research interests include training lecturers in Trans-National Education settings and unorthodox approaches to the observation of teaching and learning. Twitter: @uogmc

Serena Gossain is a creative professional and lecturer in Advertising and Branding. She has worked in the UK and US and holds an MA in Communication Design from Central Saint Martins, and a PGCHE from the University of Westminster. She has over twenty years of industry experience, working as a senior creative for ad agencies and design consultancies and has developed a passion for teaching and learning in the creative field. Serena is currently an Associate Lecturer at the London College of Communication, University of the Arts London and teaches on their BA Advertising course. She is also a lecturer on branding, design management and luxury brand management in other universities. She loves all things design and enjoys creating images and finding the extraordinary in unexpected places. Her Twitter name is @sgdesign5 and you can find her on LinkedIn at https://www.linkedin.com/in/serena-gossain-64a98/

Julie Hall is Deputy Vice Chancellor at Southampton Solent University, a National Teaching Fellow and Professor of Higher Education. Julie's research has focused on pedagogic practices in HE, widening participation, managing change in universities and closing attainment gaps. Julie has worked on a number of projects in partnership with Jisc, HE Academy and HEFCE. Twitter: @julieh8

Andy Horton is currently a library manager at BPP University and enjoys delivering training to law and health students at London Waterloo and Cambridge and in partner centres overseas. In his previous role at Regent's University London, Andy won the prestigious Credo Digital Information Literacy award, collaborating with Chris Rowell to create the Twelve Apps of Christmas online course. Before this, he worked at The Inns of Court School of Law, and at Middle Temple library. Andy is passionate about the role of librarians as educators. He is a Fellow of the Higher Education Academy and former Training Officer for the Business Librarians Association. He also serves on the committee of the Alumni Libraries Forum. A graduate of King's College London, Andy studied librarianship at London Metropolitan University, where he captained the University Challenge team. Twitter: @fechtbuch. LinkedIn: https://www.linkedin.com/in/andy-horton-83b03945/

Paul Kawachi is Professor of Instructional Design at the Open University of China, with thirty years' experience teaching in higher education mostly in Japan. Currently he works in materials development, teacher training and undertakes research at the Open University of China. He is a lifelong student with a wide range of research interests in teaching English and using learning technologies. He is the editor of the *Asian Journal of Distance Education*, and has published prolifically throughout the world in books and leading academic journals. LinkedIn: https://www.linkedin.com/in/paul-kawachi-8612a415/

Suzan Koseoglu is an Academic Developer (research and development in technology enhanced learning) at Goldsmiths, University of London. Suzan holds a MEd and PhD in learning technologies. Her area of expertise is online learning with an emphasis on open and networked scholarship and socio-cultural aspects of learning in further and higher education contexts. Her recent research focuses on openness in education, exploring power and pedagogy in hashtag communities. Suzan occasionally blogs at https://wordpress.com/stats/day/different readings.com and can be found on Twitter: @SuzanKoseoglu

Donna Lancos is an anthropologist working with ethnographic methods and analysis to inform and change policy in higher education, in particular in and around libraries, research, physical and digital spaces, and teaching and learning practices. Between 2009 and 2018 she was the Library Anthropologist at the University of North Carolina, Charlotte. She has conducted anthropological research in libraries at University College London as well as at UNC Charlotte, and regularly delivers workshops and talks on issues of digital practices, leadership, and institutional change. She co-led the iterations of Jisc's Digital Leadership Course in 2017 and 2018, and has also conducted a study of teaching practices in Higher and Further Education on behalf of Jisc. She writes about these and other projects at www.donnalanclos.com, and you can also find her on Twitter @DonnaLanclos.

Pat Lockley started out in WordPress at the University of Nottingham as a blogger. He then went to work at the University of Oxford as a developer on WordPress OER projects, before moving to the University of London, where amongst other things, he helped redesign their blog. For the last four years, he's been self-employed running Pgogy Webstuff and doing a lot in WordPress. You can see more on his WordPress profile https://profiles.wordpress.org/pgogy or on Twitter at @pgogy

Margy MacMillan (@margymaclibrary) is a librarian and professor recently retired from Mount Royal University in Calgary, Alberta, Canada. Her areas of interest are information literacy, the scholarship of teaching and learning, social media use by academics and the barriers students face in reading academic materials. She is enjoying retirement exploring Vancouver Island, developing an interest in photography, and catching up on all the academic and not-so-academic projects she didn't get to while still working. She stays connected to her academic communities and is active on Twitter @margymaclibrary, working in various capacities for Teaching & Learning Inquiry (http://tlijournal. com), and serving as an Advisor-at-Large for Project Information Literacy (http://www.projectinfolit.org).

Andrew Middleton is Head of Academic Practice & Learning Innovation at Sheffield Hallam University and a National Teaching Fellow. As Chair of the UK Media-Enhanced Learning Special Interest Group he has led innovation through the scholarly development and sharing of good practice in relation to digital and social media pedagogies since 2008 when the SIG was established. He is known for his pioneering work on developing audio feedback, smart learning, future learning spaces and digital placemaking. He has recently published *Reimagining Spaces for Learning in Higher Education* (2018) which proposes the development of innovative hybrid learning space reflecting the disruption of formal-non-formal and physical-digital spatial binaries in higher education. Andrew has been instrumental in organising the UK Social Media in Higher Education Conference over three years.

Chris Millson is eLearning Manager for The University of Manchester Library. He oversees the Library's eLearning output including the open source, open access online resources for My Learning Essentials. He is leading development of the Library's approach to using the social writing platform Medium for learning, currently implemented in two courses: Open Knowledge in Higher Education (aimed at staff), and Digital Society (aimed at undergraduates). He has been a tutor and course leader on both, helped develop the former, and led a successful redevelopment of the latter. Chris has a PG Cert in Academic Practice and is a Fellow of the Higher Education Academy. He has been Chair and Vice Chair of the Centre for Recording Achievement. He is passionate about learning, technology, and their intersection. His work has led to two Blackboard Catalyst Awards. He is @asameshimae on Twitter and is always happy to chat.

Dave Musson is editor-in-chief of The Native – a hub of inspiring resources for education and youth marketers – as well as the lead social media strategist at Natives Group. His colleagues sometimes call him a social media 'guru', but he gets embarrassed when it happens. Before joining Natives Group, Dave led on social media at the University of Warwick. He also spent two years as co-chair of the Council for the Advancement and Support of Education (CASE) Europe Social Media and Community Conference. Outside of work, he hosts not one, not two, but three podcasts. Twitter: @davemusson LinkedIn: https://www.linkedin.com/in/davemusson85

Chrissi Nerantzi (@chrissinerantzi) is a Principal Lecturer in Academic CPD in the Centre for Excellence in Learning and Teaching at Manchester Metropolitan University. Chrissi's area of interests are creativity and openness in learning and teaching and she has co-founded a range of innovative professional development opportunities fuelled by cross-boundary collaborations and community engagement. She used to be a computer programmer in the Greek Navy, teacher of Modern Foreign Languages, and a literary translator, and loves photography, writing stories for children and making stuff. Visit Chrissi's LinkedIn profile at https://www.linkedin.com/in/chrissinerantzi and her website at https://chrissinerantzi.wordpress.com/

Jane Norris is interested in digital theories of time, materials and objects and the narratives we build around design. She is currently writing on post-enlightenment ways of relating to materials: *How Materials Speak*. She has an essay 'Touching Knowledge' in *Meet Us in The Now*, a collaborative Royal College of Art book, as well as a short story, 'Re-Pairing' in the *Virtual Futures Vol. 1* anthology. She has written a regular *Dictionary of Craft* column in the Crafts Council *CRAFTS* magazine and opinion pieces for design magazine *Fiera*. Her piece 'A View from the Throne' was published in the 'Toilet' issue of *Dirty Furniture*. She recently completed post-doc research in the Critical Writing department of the Royal College of Art. Jane works as an Associate Professor in the School of Liberal Arts at Richmond University the American University in London. Twitter: @janeviatopia

Lawrie Phipps' current portfolio contains work in student experience, technology-enhanced learning, digital research practice, digital leadership and change management. He developed Jisc's Digital Leaders course and continues his research around digital leadership. His previous work includes social media in education, institutional efficiency, and accessibility for disabled students. Lawrie is Fellow of the Higher Education Academy, and is a Senior Codesign Manager working in the Jisc research and development directorate. He is a facilitator, coach and mentor around all things digital. Prior to his current role, Lawrie worked as a learning technologist, a telecommunications engineer and served in the Royal Navy. You can find him on line at www.Lawriephipps.co.uk and Twitter @lawrie

Chris Rowell is an Academic Developer in Digital Enhanced Learning at London South Bank University. Previously he was Learning Technology Manager at Regent's University in London, a Lecturer in Economics (1990-2005) and a Lecturer in Education (2005-2010) at the University Centre Croydon. Currently he is studying for a doctorate in Education at the Institute of Education, UCL. His research interests are all to do with learning technology, more specifically the use and evaluation of social media by staff and students in Higher Education. He is also editor of the Association for Learning Technology's (ALT) blog. He lives in Camberwell, London and is interested in things to do with cycling, photography, travel, politics and London. You can find him on Twitter @chri5rowell and blogging at https://totallyrewired.wordpress.com/

Santanu Vasant leads the Learning Technology Team in the Centre for Excellence in Learning and Teaching at the University of East London. He has over fifteen years' experience in education having previously worked at Brunel University London, Imperial College London and City, University of London and as a secondary school teacher of ICT. His current work involves investigating the impact of classroom technologies and mobile technologies (including the use of social media) on learning, and the design of teaching and learning spaces. He is also a school governor at the Northwood School in North West London and reviewer for the Association for Learning Technology's *Journal Research in Learning Technology*. Twitter: @santanuvasant

Mark Warnes is a Research Fellow in Anglia Learning & Teaching at Anglia Ruskin University. As part of his wide portfolio of pedagogic research--related activities, he has delivered an online course of Twitter for academic purposes since 2014. Mark manages ARU's Learning and Teaching Project Award scheme, mentoring pedagogic researchers through an 18-month-long project, and co-organising the annual Learning and Teaching conference at which they present. Mark also manages the Good Teaching Exchange, identifying colleagues engaged in good teaching practice, and capturing their expertise using video interviews and case studies. Mark manages the Pedagogic Research Directory, an online repository of outputs from pedagogic activities at ARU. Mark further supports the Pedagogic Research Community by co-facilitating monthly meetings and biannual writing retreats.

Twitter: @MarkWarnes2. LinkedIn: https://uk.linkedin.com/in/mark-warnes-81b72229

David Webster is Head of Learning & Teaching Innovation / Principal Lecturer in Religion, Philosophy & Ethics at the University of Gloucester. He works on the intersection of popular culture, religious belief and philosophical reflection. He is interested in how these all impact on the way we choose to live, and the choices we make in relation to our fellow sentient beings. He studied his PhD with Professor Peter Harvey at the University of Sunderland, in Buddhist Studies. As well as working for the Open University, and a variety of adult education providers and universities, David has been at Gloucestershire since 2000. He teaches a range of topics, as well as publishing and speaking in a range of settings. Twitter: @davidwebster

Neil Withnell is Associate Dean, Academic Quality Assurance, at the University of Salford. A qualified mental health nurse, Neil has worked in higher education for the past fifteen years and is a Senior Fellow of the Higher Education Academy. He is the author of *Family Interventions in Mental Health* (2012) and his research interests include therapeutic horticulture and social media in healthcare. Neil is active on Twitter and can be found under @neilwithnell

PART ONE
INTRODUCTION

1. From a Tweet to a Blog, to a Podcast, to a Book

Chris Rowell

This book brings together a variety of different people working in higher education (HE) who use social media; academics, researchers, senior managers, academic developers, learning technologists and librarians. That this has not been done before is surprising given the amount of interest there is in this topic. The book also gives a voice to those in the sector who are not academics or researchers. Many of the book's contributors are used to writing and publishing in academic journals or books, but for some this is a new experience, since they are more used to writing in the newer forms of communication, such as blog posts or tweets.

It has become apparent for both staff and students working in colleges and universities that the teaching and learning experience is changing. Smartphones and mobile devices are now ubiquitous. Students study and learn using a variety of digital equipment, resources and software. HE staff are also expected to engage with virtual learning environments, electronic forms of assessment and digital modes of communication. Some staff have seen this as an opportunity to develop more open and networked practices, whilst others find the balance between such openness and the maintenance of individual privacy difficult to strike. Still others are curious about these affordances and would like to know more before they change their own practice. Consequently, this book aims to be a guide for those working in academia who are seeking

 https://doi.org/10.11647/OBP.0162.01

inspiration or for those who are just looking for ways of doing things differently.

This book also critically evaluates the impact that social media is having in HE. Several themes have emerged from the varied contributions. All of the chapters accentuate the positive aspects of social media but they also highlight some more difficult and contentious issues regarding this mode of communication, such as sexism, racism, homophobia, the pernicious presence of trolling and the abuse of power in these spaces. If institutions are expecting staff to engage with social media in their professional practice how should they be supported? What happens if things go wrong or a mistake is made? These are some of the questions this book aims to answer, and to inspire others to further research and debate.

What is Social Media?

Given the growing variety of social media apps and websites, is it possible to actually define what social media is? A good starting point is Merriam-Webster's (2019) dictionary definition, 'forms of electronic communication (such as websites for social networking and microblogging) through which users create online communities to share information, ideas, personal messages, and other content (such as videos)'. This broad definition is further refined by the inclusion of some defining features that social media incorporates. Social media sites and apps have resulted from Web 2.0 technologies that have seen the Internet environment become more dynamic, interactive and participatory. Indeed, the very lifeblood of social media is the user-generated content, such as messages, posts, comments, images, photos and videos. As this content is shared, users create their own profiles, which in turn adds to their online identity both in a personal and professional capacity. These separate features come together to allow social media users to connect and network with others, sometimes individually but often with groups at a global level (Obar & Wildman, 2015). The scale of the increase in the use of social media in recent years has been phenomenal. As of December 2018 there were 2.32 billion active users of Facebook per month (Statistica, 2019a). To put this in some sort of perspective this is greater than a third of the world's population. Similarly, at the end of

2018, Twitter had 231 million users per month (Statistica, 2019b), which is higher than the population of the United States. Both at a global and UK level this trend shows no signs of decreasing.

This book looks at the application of these social media sites, focusing on some of the most widely used in the UK higher education sector: Facebook, Twitter, Snapchat, WhatsApp, Medium, and YouTube. The only chapter that some would argue does not fit neatly into this definition of social media is the chapter on podcasting. However, as the podcast itself does generate user content, and they are shared widely on podcasting platforms enabling further discussion and interactions to take place, they exhibit many of the features of social media.

It is also important to acknowledge the number of chapters in this book that focus fully or partially on Twitter. Indeed, there is a small but growing collection of research literature led by authors such as Georges Veletsianos and Royce Kimmons (2016) and Bonnie Stewart (2015) focusing on the use of Twitter in HE. There are a number of reasons for this popularity. Firstly, its simplicity: a new Twitter user can create their own account, profile and 'handle', and be interacting with colleagues in a few minutes. It might take some time to understand the more advanced features of Twitter, but initially at least a new user can be 'up and running' very quickly. It doesn't require a lot of instruction and support to use Twitter, and the user's account is not linked directly to the institution. Secondly, whilst many HE professionals use Facebook to connect for their personal lives, Twitter makes it very easy to be found and to find others in professional networks. It is very 'outward-facing' platform that makes networking and sharing information very easy to do. Thirdly, Twitter has reached a 'critical mass' or 'tipping point', which means that it is fully established in the sector. If you wanted to find an academic, librarian or profession working in HE they are probably more likely to be on Twitter than any other social media site. Given this, it doesn't make sense to look anywhere else. Finally, Twitter is one of the most synchronous and spontaneous of the social media platforms. Quick-fire discussions can spark up on any number of topics, from aspects of teaching, leaning, research, academic life, conferences, picket-line activity or just the state of the weather! All of these factors make it ideal for use by many professionals in this sector.

Why This Book Is a Bit Different

This book is about social media, but it was also created by social media. Once I had had the initial idea for the book I sent out a tweet to my followers asking if they were interested in contributing a chapter, using the hashtag #SocMedinHE. If at this stage the response had been indifferent, or even negative, I don't think I would have pursued the project. However, I received an overwhelmingly positive response so I then directly invited others to contribute, again using Twitter to send a Direct Message (DM) to certain individuals who work in this field. Within a week I had enough contributors, so I posted a blog post about my book project and gathered more interest. I was using my own social media networks to 'crowd-source' contributions to the book. After I received each contributor's chapter I interviewed the authors and produced a series of podcasts that accompanies this book (see Chapter 1.2). Here the authors talk through the development of their ideas, giving further context for their use of different types of social media. The final stage was to edit the book and group together the chapters into the relevant themes.

The style of the book also aims to reflect the type of writing seen on social media. All the chapters are relatively short for an academic book (3,000–4,000 words). The language used in the chapters aims to be accessible for a general reader who is not a specialist in this area of research. However, while some of the chapters have an 'open' style or are reflections on practice, similar to a blog post, all the contributors have connected their practice to relevant learning theory or an appropriate educational context. References have been kept deliberately short and aim to direct the reader who wants to pursue the topic in more detail to other similar projects or relevant sources of information.

This book is arranged into thematic sections that are outlined below, but in addition there are several hashtags (#) at the start of each chapter that will help the reader find a route though the book. All the chapters have at least one of the following hashtags; #Beginner, #Intermediate or #Advanced. The #Beginner hashtag assumes the reader has little knowledge about the use of social media. They might have downloaded social media apps onto their devices, such as Twitter or Instagram, and perhaps used these a few times, but they are not sure how these tools could be used in a professional context. The #Intermediate hashtag assumes some working knowledge of at least one or two social media platforms; they might even have used them in an HE context. Consequently, they will be familiar with using an interactive networking platform and the associated terminology that goes with it. There are a few chapters with the #advanced hashtag. These are aimed at the more experienced social media user and they assume a high degree of knowledge and understanding of social media apps (especially Twitter) and how they can be used in a HE context. There are also hashtags to describe the topics and different types of social media covered in the chapter, e.g. #identity or #instagram.

Although the writing style of all the chapters aims to be accessible, there is a glossary of social media words and phrases included at the end of the book.

Thematic Organisation of the Book

In addition to the hashtagging system outlined above, this book is divided into six broad themes that reflect the diverse use of social media in HE. Part Two of the book looks at the 'Professional Practice' of academics in HE. Sue Beckingham's opening chapter explores the type of online identity that HE professionals want to project. This identity may not be stable and may change over time, or even between different social media platforms. Once the identity is established, Sue argues that the benefits of sharing information on social media will create discussion, interactions and informal learning. This can, in turn, lead to a 'networked participatory scholarship' in which HE professionals can further develop their professional identity, promote their own research or develop opportunities to collaborate with others working in their field. Sue also gives lots of practical information about how to set up, develop and maintain this professional online persona.

The second chapter in this section, by Timos Almpanis and Martin Compton, outlines how academic developers can use 'cloud-based tools' and social media apps to improve the training that lecturers receive. They suggest that we need to move away from a 'one-size-fits-all' transmissive style of training to more transformative types of continuing professional development (CPD). Their two case studies look at the benefits of introducing social media apps that academics can immediately try, experiencing them from the learner's perspective. Similarly, Mark Warnes's chapter on the 'Ten Days of Twitter' describes the process of running an online course for staff working at his university. After a brief description of the course content and how 'digital badges' were introduced, Mark assesses the impact of the course using the Twitter analytics tool and a course satisfaction survey. As the course was created with a Creative Commons licence it is freely available and has now been run by several other universities.

In the last chapter in this section, Susan Koseoglu explores the emergence of open and networked scholarship. She notes that social media can have a positive impact on an individual's ability to build Personal Learning Networks (PLN) through Twitter chats, but there can also be tensions between personal, professional and institutional use. She argues that academics need to have an understanding of networked structures and recognise that these structures often mirror the inequalities and prejudices that exist in society at large. She also highlights the power issues inherent in online networks and questions the premise these that open networks are in fact empowering or a force for change.

Part Three of this book focuses on how social media impacts the teaching and learning sphere in HE. Alex Avramenko and Chrissi Nerantzi's chapter 'Exploring the use of Social Media in a Higher Education Classroom' is based on their own research into how final year students use smartphones in lecturers and seminars. Within the scope of this small-scale study they noted that all students in their study had used, and continued to use smartphones during classes to access various social media platforms. This is unlikely to surprise those currently teaching in HE and has led some tutors to ban mobile devices in lectures or tutorials. The authors make several practical recommendations for practitioners on how to approach and reengage these students in the learning process. Similarly, Serena Gossain's chapter discusses how she introduced specific social media tools into her teaching. The case study shows how she used Instagram and Pinterest with students studying a BA in Advertising at the London College of Communications. She explains the rationale of these changes and relates them to contemporary theories of education and learning.

The next chapter by Paul Kawachi takes a slightly different perspective. Paul shows that social media can help students establish a social presence on their course, but once that role has been created it can be a distraction from engaging in collaborative learning activities. Paul makes reference to social and virtual presence to explain why the use of Facebook has led to improved learning in some case studies, but less learning in others.

The chapter entitled 'Bursting Out of the Bubble: Social Media, Openness and HE', written by three members of staff at the University of Manchester, provides an excellent insight into the blogging platform Medium. The authors discuss the reasons why they chose Medium as opposed to other more conventional blogging platforms and then give some reflections on the experience of delivering the course through this form of social media. The final chapter in this section is by Zoetanya Sujon's on 'Cambridge Analytica, Facebook, and Understanding Social Media Beyond the Screen'. It has a different emphasis as Zoetanya aims to contextualise some of the learning challenges of teaching social media in the classroom. The study uses Facebook's interactions with Cambridge Analytica to explore the importance of personal data collection in social media and 'surveillance capitalism'. It gives practical advice, and examples of different approaches to teaching these topics that other lecturers will find useful.

Part Four focuses on how social media is used by teams and managers in leadership positions in universities. Julie Hall is Deputy Vice Chancellor at Southampton Solent University. In her chapter 'Leadership and Social Media' she argues that good leadership in universities requires effective communication and this includes the use of social media. University staff in a leadership role can use social media to broadcast information to their staff and students, raise the profile of the university and build both external and internal relationships. Julie also outlines how such public engagement can create uncertainty and fear as it 'fractures' the more traditional modes of communication.

Donna Lanclos and Lawrie Phipps approach the issue of leadership from a different perspective. They have both organised several iterations of Jisc's Digital Leadership course, which brings together leaders in HE to discuss how the digital impacts on their own personal practice and how they can make effective use of social media. They discuss the usefulness and limitations of visual mapping frameworks such as the Visitors/Residents continuum, as well as summarising their own mapping of digital engagement. Like others in this book they note that engagement in social media is beneficial but it can also mirror and even amplify societal issues of racism, sexism, bullying and other issues related to the abuse of power.

Part Five contains three chapters on building networks and creating cohesion amongst students. David Webster's chapter considers the role of social media in fostering cohort identity on a Religion, Philosophy & Ethics course at the University of Gloucestershire. Initially a blog was set up to provide a noticeboard and area for debate for the course. This was followed by a course Facebook group, Twitter account and video blog. This short case study shows that social media can reinforce the sense of the communal experience, but it also has ethical concerns that affect minority groups who might experience abuse or troubling interactions. Rachel Challen's chapter describes how her university used Facebook Live to help new students gain a sense of belonging and orientation before they arrived and during their induction week. Students who had already accepted a place on a course could watch the Deputy Dean of School conducting a tour of the campus and facilities, introducing them to key members of staff and allowing students to ask questions about their course, or related issues. With over 6000 views of the event and really positive feedback from the students, they plan to repeat the virtual tour at the start of the next academic year.

The next chapter in this section by Margy MacMillan and Chrissi Netantzi discusses how they used Twitter first to connect with one another and then to develop a relationship around their shared interest in phenomenography. Chrissi was using phenomenography as her research methodology in her PhD and initially sent out a tweet asking for help. Margy responded, sent Chrissi some links to related articles and then the conversation took off! This 'conversational' chapter is very different in style from the other contributions to the book and is a particularly good example of how social media enables academics to meet those working within their research field in other institutions or even on different continents.

Pat Lockley's chapter describes the process of setting up a Twitter conference called #pressedconf2018. During the conference presenters would tweet out their presentation, in a series of tweets over fifteen minutes, which was followed by a Twitter conversation with participants from all around the world. There have been similar conferences, but his was the first with a focus on the use of WordPress in education. Pat shows that this type of conference has many of the benefits of physical conferences but without some of the drawbacks, like travelling to the destination or the cost of the venue/accommodation. The rest of the chapter gives some detailed quantitative data on the participants' Twitter activity during the conference. This striking innovation has the potential to be replicated by others in HE in years to come.

Part Six has several chapters on how social media can produce innovative forms of learning in HE. The chapters in this section are very different from one another but they do have one common connection in that they attempt to move seamlessly between the online and physical environments. Dave Musson provides a fascinating insight into how podcasting is being used in HE. First he describes the recent popularity of podcasting and outlines its potential benefits to the HE sector, before highlighting some exceptional examples of how universities are using podcasts both here in the UK and the United States to show off their expertise, showcase their research, provide a window on campus life, or even to celebrate their past students' achievements.

Jane Norris's chapter on 'Etiquette for the Anthropocene' is about discovering new way of teaching and engaging with students about global warming and the Anthropocene without increasing their anxiety levels. Jane uses what she calls 'para-fictional' objects that move from the physical to the digital realm, as a way to explore digital memes. As part of her project she made and distributed physical badges and then asked participants (mainly her students) to send her photos of themselves wearing the badges, which were then collated on an Instagram site. Jane outlines her rationale for this project and describes the student response, which was not altogether enthusiastic.

The next two chapters look at how social media can be used to explore spaces on and around the university campus. In Andrew Middleton's chapter he explains what a 'Twalk' is, how to design effective Twalks, and why they create useful and rich learning environments. Drawing on his experience organising several Twalks, Andrew set out some emerging issues that should be considered by academics interested in using and developing such novel, blended social media learning spaces, especially if personal learning technologies are used. Santanu Vasant develops similar themes when discussing academics' attitudes and practices in relation to learning spaces. Starting with some clear definitions of Twitter chats, Twalks and learning spaces, Santanu outlines how social media can be introduced to raise awareness about the importance of teaching and learning spaces. Twitter chats such as the #LTHEchat bring together developers, academics and learning technologists from different institutions and widen the debate about the spaces we use for learning within the institution.

Finally Part Seven has two chapters that detail the personal experiences of two HE practitioners. It is often quite difficult to separate out personal and professional use of social media. For many working in HE, the merging of the personal and professional is a new and unwelcome development, whilst others have embraced the trend. Like many librarians working in Higher Education, Andy Horton was an early adopter of using Twitter in his professional practice. He describes its benefits at conferences where he developed his networks though his use of conference hashtags and then later engaging in Twitter chats both in relation to gaming and teaching and learning. These activities led in turn to further collaborations delivering online courses to develop digital literacy skills for both academic and professional staff in the university. Andy does not separate his personal and professional identity on Twitter and his followers are just as likely to receive a tweet on a business law journal as they are on the result of his latest softball game. Neil Withnell traces a similar journey in his use of Twitter and other types of social media, but his emphasis is on the public/private sphere within the healthcare sector. Neil outlines the guidelines produced by professional healthcare associations. He also discusses the personal and professional divide in social media and notes that often, healthcare professionals sharing information as 'private' posts compromises their professional roles. Neil notes that the guidelines given by professional associations are closely related their codes of conduct. The online behaviour and conduct of healthcare professionals are governed by these codes of conduct, just as they are in the 'real' world.

For more information follow #SocMedinHE or check out my blog at https://totallyrewired.wordpress.com/

References

Merriam-Webster Dictionary (2019). 'Social media', https://www.merriam-webster.com/dictionary/social%20media

Obar, Jonathan A. and Wildman, Steve (2015). 'Social media definition and the governance challenge: An introduction to the special issue', *Telecommunications Policy*. 39:9, pp. 745–50, https://doi.org/10.1016/j.telpol.2015.07.014

Statistica (2019a). *Number of monthly active Facebook users worldwide as of 4th quarter 2018 (in millions)*, https://www.statista.com/statistics/264810/number-of-monthly-active-facebook-users-worldwide/

Statistica (2019b). *Number of monthly active Twitter users worldwide as of 4th quarter 2018 (in millions)*, https://www.statista.com/statistics/282087/number-of-monthly-active-twitter-users/

Stewart, B. (2015). 'Open to influence: What counts as academic influence in scholarly networked Twitter participation', *Learning, Media, and Technology*, 40, pp. 287–309.

Veletsianos, G. and Kimmons, R. (2016). 'Scholars in an increasingly open and digital world: How do education professors and students use Twitter?', *The Internet and Higher Education*, 30, pp. 1–10.

2. Social Media in Higher Education – The Podcast

Chris Rowell

After all the authors had contributed their chapters, I interviewed them and asked them questions about what they had written. Each of the following podcasts gives further information about where they work, the types of jobs that they do and the way they use social media:

Professional Practice

Developing a professional online presence and effective network:

DELcast #8
Interview with Sue Beckingham
https://doi.org/10.11647/OBP.0162.24

Re-engineered CPD and modelled use of cloud tools and social media by academic developers:

DELcast #9
Interview with Martin Compton
https://doi.org/10.11647/OBP.0162.25

      https://doi.org/10.11647/OBP.0162.02

Teaching and Learning

Exploring the use of social media in the higher education classroom:

DELcast #18
Interview with Alex Avramenko
https://doi.org/10.11647/OBP.0162.26

The use of social media tools and their applications for creative students:

DELcast #13
Interview with Serena Gossain
https://doi.org/10.11647/OBP.0162.27

Cambridge Analytica, Facebook, and understanding social media beyond the screen:

DELcast #12
Interview with Zoe Sujon
https://doi.org/10.11647/OBP.0162.28

Leadership

Leadership and social media:

DELcast #7
Interview with Julie Hall
https://doi.org/10.11647/OBP.0162.29

Leadership and social media — challenges and opportunities:

DELcast #4
Interview with Lanclos and Phipps
https://doi.org/10.11647/OBP.0162.30

Building Networks

Creating a sense of belonging and connectedness for the student arrival experience in a School of Arts and Humanities:

DELcast #16
Interview with Rachel Challen
https://doi.org/10.11647/OBP.0162.31

Joint reflections on Twitter, phenomenography and learning friendships:

DELcast #17
Interview with Chrissi and Margy
https://doi.org/10.11647/OBP.0162.32

Innovation

Expertise in your ears — why you should jump on the podcasting bandwagon:

DELcast #1
Interview with Dave Musson
https://doi.org/10.11647/OBP.0162.33

Etiquette for the Anthropocene:

DELcast #14
Interview with Jane Norris
https://doi.org/10.11647/OBP.0162.34

Ten days of Twitter:

DELcast #2
Interview with Mark Warnes
https://doi.org/10.11647/OBP.0162.35

Learning to Twalk — an analysis of a new learning environment:

 DELcast #11
Interview with Andrew Middleton
https://doi.org/10.11647/OBP.0162.36

Academics' understanding of learning spaces: attitudes, practices and outcomes explored through the use of social media:

 DELcast #3
Interview with Santanu Vasant
https://doi.org/10.11647/OBP.0162.37

The Personal Journey

Somewhere in between — my experience of Twitter as a tool for continuous personal development:

 DELcast #6
Interview with Andy Horton
https://doi.org/10.11647/OBP.0162.38

The 'healthy academic', social media, and a personal and professional journey:

 DELcast #5
Interview with Neil Withnell
https://doi.org/10.11647/OBP.0162.39

PART TWO
PROFESSIONAL PRACTICE

3. Developing a Professional Online Presence and Effective Network

#Identity #Beginner #LinkedIn #Twitter

Sue Beckingham

Introduction

This chapter considers the significance and value of students and educators using social media to develop an online presence. Such a presence can allow both groups to showcase their professional and academic achievements and provide an opportunity to demonstrate both student learning gain and teaching excellence. There are a variety of different ways to present academic work; social media can be used in a professional context to maximise reach and engagement, thus contributing to the success of this work. This chapter explores how an online presence can be utilised to network with others and how this can open 'virtual doors' to CPD and informal learning, potential scholarly collaborations, new job opportunities or work experience. Furthermore, a framework is introduced to illustrate the important areas on which to focus when developing an online presence.

Social Media

Over the last decade there has been seismic change in the way we communicate socially and professionally. In addition to mastering

   https://doi.org/10.11647/OBP.0162.03

face-to-face communication and email, we have had to grapple with the use of social media, which has pervaded our lives and provided a new medium to navigate. Social media has empowered individuals to become digitally-connected social creators and curators, communicators and collaborators, conversationalists and critics (Beckingham, 2013). Within these social spaces individuals share not only information, but also their social identities.

Through participating openly in online activities, individuals develop an online presence. This is also referred to as a 'digital footprint' as contributions leave a trail that can be seen by others. Understanding what this looks like, and how to make it personally valuable, can be beneficial to educators, students and future graduates alike.

However, despite the general popularity of social media, some have not embraced its use in a professional context: that is, they have not purposefully developed a work-related online presence and an effective network. Whilst the categories are not black and white, we can consider three types of social media users: the advocates, the dabblers and the unengaged. It may be argued that there is a transition between the first two, if the user has a social media profile but initially might not interact in this space very often. It is also possible to be an advocate in one social space, a dabbler in another and totally unengaged or even unaware of other social spaces.

- Advocates: well developed profile; active user; connected; sharing and collaborating.

- Dabblers: sporadic visits; low contribution; profile may only be partially set up.

- Unengaged: unaware of potential; not using social media.

It is important to note that once an individual creates an online profile, this forms part of their online presence, irrespective of whether they go on to use the social media space or not.

What is a Professional Online Presence?

Taking a step back, it may be helpful to define what is meant by an online presence. Simply put, this is the collective existence online of any individual (or organisation). This may be as a result of having a presence on a website, social networking site or other digital space; having a profile within that space; or interacting with the online presence of others.

A professional online presence refers one's online existence in a professional context, and also gives consideration to conducting oneself professionally within any online space. Having a negative or improper online personal presence can have a damaging effect on one's professional reputation and digital identity.

How Do Others Perceive Your Online Presence?

Bozkurt and Chic-Hsiung (2016) refer to the conscious awareness of being present within digital environments as an important part of identity formation. Being aware of what your online presence portrays is therefore important. Yet, for some, the following may still come as a surprise. Just as you use Google (or any other search engine) to find out a vast array of information, so people could be searching to find out more about you. Whilst your name in isolation may bring up multiple entries, few of which are related to you (unless you have an uncommon name), when it is coupled with your institution the number of entries which refer directly to you is significantly increased. Potentially this search will not only locate your institution profile page, but may also find any open social media profiles you have, for example your LinkedIn profile. For most people this shouldn't trigger any warning bells; however, if you have vague memories of a profile you created on the fly and you can't remember when you last revisited it, then this is your prompt to do so now. Just because you are not monitoring your social profiles, doesn't mean to say that others aren't looking at them. Whoever is searching for you (this could include current and prospective students, their parents and your peers) will click on the link to your profile. As we know, first impressions count, so it is important to understand how others perceive you. At a basic level, an incomplete profile left without having been proofread can look unprofessional. However a profile showcasing your practice and research has the potential to shine a bright light on your achievements.

Other social media profiles may also come up in this search. Keeping abreast of changes in security settings can ensure that your 'social'

Facebook feed is kept for the eyes of your immediate network of friends and family. If you use Twitter, the search will not only bring up your profile (assuming it matches your name), it will also present the latest few tweets you have posted within the Google search.

A further consideration is that unless you are presenting a clear identity there is a danger that you could be mistaken for someone else who happens to share your name. As the online presence of your digital doppelgänger could be misconstrued as your own, it is a good idea to use a professional photo in your profile to replace the standard avatar, as it will help to verify who you are.

Blurring of the Boundaries

Considering what persona you wish to present, as well as understanding what you are *actually* presenting, are key steps the development of a professional online identity. Seargeant and Tagg (2014) suggest that 'Identity is not a stable, pre-determined property of an individual, but rather a set of resources which people draw upon in presenting and expressing themselves via interaction with others'. An individual may construct and re-construct different aspects of their self, thereby potentially sharing multiple facets of their identity and personality. This may include aspects from both their social and professional lives.

It is therefore important to reflect on your current identity and reputation. How do others perceive you? Do you need to better emphasise your professional skills and values in the eyes of the world? Once you clearly identify these you can start planning for your future reputation — who you want to be known as. Socrates is reputed to have said, 'The way to gain a good reputation is to endeavour to be what you desire to appear'. I'd argue that presenting an authentic representation of yourself is important, but don't undersell yourself. Writing and talking about your own achievements can be difficult; however, nothing is gained from hiding under a bushel!

When developing and optimising your professional identity, consider the following:

1. *Identity* — *who you are*
   When thinking more deeply about your identity as a
   professional, you may wish to reflect on what it is that you

do within your role, the skills you have, what you value about your career, and what it is that others might value.

2. *Networks — who you know and who knows you*
   Your strong ties (immediate friends and colleagues) are part of your everyday network, and in the main provide a source of readily accessible knowledge. There are also benefits to developing weak ties through networking, as they can both connect you to new ideas and help others to find you.

3. *Knowledge — what you know*
   Demonstrating your knowledge may start with details of your education and qualifications. Also include concrete outcomes of your work, such as projects, publications, awards or successful funding bids. Being clear about what the focus of your specialism or research is will help others discover this experience.

Professional Social Networks

LinkedIn (originally to be named 'Colleaguester') was one of the earliest social networking sites created in 2002, and whilst not adopted at the rate Facebook was (launched two years later in 2004), it has gone on to be considered as the leading *professional* social network. Having now surpassed over 562 million members in over 200 countries, and boasting that two new members join every minute (LinkedIn 2018), it may be useful for professionals and students in higher education to revisit the affordances this site offers.

Knowledge sharing	Knowledge finding
Answering questions	Raising questions
Networking	Recommendations
Feedback	Discussions
People search	Company search
Job opportunities	Recruitment opportunities

Fig. 3.1 Sue Beckingham, Affordances within LinkedIn (2018), CC BY 4.0

In addition to LinkedIn, there are other social media that can be used in a professional context. These include blogs (WordPress, Blogger, Tumblr), microblogging (Twitter), social bookmarking (Diigo, Mendeley) and social networks (Facebook — and specifically intended for academics — ResearchGate and Academia.edu). Multimedia may be used to augment the written word. These might include video (YouTube, Vimeo), audio (SoundCloud, AudioBoom) and images (Flickr, Instagram). All of these contain powerful search functions and the opportunity to activate comments.

The Value of Sharing

Kramer (2016) argues that 'We share for many reasons — some self-serving and some not — but I firmly believe that our need to share is based on a human instinct not only to survive, but to thrive'. Sharing is enhanced by: visibility in social spaces, an informative profile, social connectedness, mutual interests, active listening, interactive dialogue and a dash of serendipity. When these elements are in place and you become an active sharer, reciprocity tends to follow. Others not only start to share your work, but interact with you, opening opportunities for informal learning, discussion and feedback.

In an academic context, Veletsianos and Kimmons (2012) refer to networked participatory scholarship, and describe this as the 'emergent practice of scholars' use of participatory technologies and online social networks to share, reflect upon, critique, improve, validate and further their scholarship'. Not only does this practice help to convey our professional identity, the process opens opportunities for social learning and personal development. In this context users are not simply consumers of information, they are adopting the technology that allows them to participate with others in dialogues about their scholarship. Pasquini et al. (2014) reinforce this by outlining the benefits of using social academic tools to share their online presence and professional profile, links to research, and also opportunities for collaboration.

As previously mentioned, reflecting on your digital footprint is an important exercise, one that needs revisiting over time. Boyd (2011) raises four important points in relation to the affordances created by self-expression and interactions between people online:

- online expressions are automatically recorded and archived;
- content made out of bits can be duplicated;
- the potential visibility of content in networked publics is great;
- content in networked publics can be accessed through searches.

We need to be mindful that whilst open profiles can portray individuals positively, a glib comment could be taken out of context and perceived negatively if care is not taken.

Working Out Loud

A further useful approach to help you develop both a professional identity and a network is 'working out loud', coined by John Stepper (2014; 2015). He describes this as follows:

> Working Out Loud starts with making your work visible in such a way that it might help others. When you do that — when you work in a more open, connected way — you can build a purposeful network that makes you more effective and provides access to more opportunities.

In 2016 Stepper revisited the five elements of working out loud as: relationships, generosity, visible work, purposeful discovery, and a growth mindset. These are presented as a sketchnote in Figure 3.2.

Providing visibility for your work might include developing your professional profile, a website or blog, and sharing outputs using Twitter, LinkedIn or SlideShare. In addition to presenting polished summaries, it can also be valuable to share the ongoing process. As your network develops there is scope to receive feedback, for others to ask questions, and ultimately the means to develop and improve. Equally you can provide value, help and support by reaching out to others who are working out loud. This process can lead to meaningful discussion both online and face to face.

Fig. 3.2 Tanmay Vora, *Five Elements of Working Out Loud* (2017), http://qaspire.com/2017/01/26/5-elements-of-working-out-loud-by-johnstepper/

Celebrating Student Learning Gain and Teaching Excellence through Online Networks

As educators in higher education, we can become important role models through using our online presence effectively. This might include adding projects, publications or awards to a LinkedIn profile; interacting in online discussions or writing a blog. Moreover, once you are actively present online, it becomes possible to engage with the information posted there. This can be done through simple acknowledgements, such as likes, shares or retweets. To add further value, adding a question or comment has the potential to open a dialogue or provide feedback. All of these avenues provide opportunities to actively recognise and celebrate the achievements of students and staff.

Taking Practical Steps

In order to build a network you can engage with, you need to take the practical steps of creating your online presence. Table 3.3 provides a summary of four key areas to focus on.

Developing a professional online presence		
1. Creating an online presence	Choosing online spaces	There is clearly a wide variety to choose from and whilst multiple spaces can be beneficial, it is better to be active in one rather than not active in many. Examples might include LinkedIn, an e-portfolio in the form of a website or blog and Twitter to engage in conversations.
	Your profile	Add a photo to all your profiles as this helps to identify who are, along with a concise bio. Brevity is key given the limited word or character allocation so focus on what you want others to know about you professionally
	Interconnectedness	Link your profiles by adding the URL to other spaces you are using and want people to visit. For example your blog, website or university profile.

2. Maintaining an active online presence	Updating your profile	Keep your profile up to date and current. This includes role changes (promotions / secondments, placements / internships), but also adding projects, publications, presentations and other outputs that demonstrate personal achievements.
	Working out loud	Consider sharing what you are doing — not just the outputs but reflections on the journey you have taken and what you have learned.
	Proactive interactions	To develop an effective network, your online contributions should include interacting with others. Share and comment on others' work.
3. Evaluating your online presence	Public view	Perform a regular Google search on your name. If you get limited results, add keywords people might use to locate you. Which social media profiles are visible on the first page? Do these results portray your professional self?
	Engagement	Responses to your online contributions such as likes, reposts and comments on what you share indicate interest. Question whether these interactions portray you in the best light.
	Analytics	Utilise the social media analytics offered by the space you are using to identify a more detailed summary. Track mentions of your name by setting up a Google Alert or using Mention.com
4. Protecting your online presence	Security settings	Regularly check the settings options and adjust to meet your needs. These vary but range from a public profile, shared with names users, or private only viewable by yourself.

Fig. 3.3 Sue Beckingham, Developing a professional online presence (2018), CC BY 4.0

Motivations for Developing an Online Presence

Reaching out to my own network, I asked the following question of educators and students: 'How have you used social media in a professional context where it has contributed positively to the development of your online presence and professional identity?'

What was clear from the extended conversations was that confidence, and a valued network, were not developed overnight, but through incremental steps and interactions, the participants benefited from richer opportunities in the longer term. The responses in Table 2.1.3 demonstrate that by using social media spaces to share content, the individuals have extended their network, and this has led to new opportunities they are unlikely to have experienced otherwise.

My LinkedIn profile allows me to display my work examples, which helps people to discover my online presence.	Using Twitter chats allows me to develop my online presence in terms of demonstrating my skills and knowledge when replying to questions.
Although I use other social media platforms I would say that Twitter has been the main area that has impacted most significantly on my professional development and online identity.	My Flickr photo stream allows me to display my photographs and allows others to like and comment on them, bringing more people to my Flickr site and developing my online presence.
Social media helped in supporting my confidence in sharing ideas and practices from my teaching and learning.	I use LinkedIn posts, as well as blog posts and Twitter (in combo) to give my work greater exposure.
I have a WordPress blog that has helped me connect with others in my field as people have stumbled across my blog through the link on my Twitter profile.	Joining the #LTHEchat on Twitter for example has helped me to build a network with educators, enabling us to learn together and work together.
A colleague was approached by *The Guardian* a few years ago as a result of his Twitter presence as he was seen as a knowledgeable source in his field on the basis of his tweets.	Writing a blog gave me a space to demonstrate my knowledge. Creating YouTube videos and adding these how-to guides to posts was noticed by an employer, leading to a job interview.

Engaging with Twitter chats such as #LTHEchat and sharing my experience of social media use has led to engagement with a number of eminent individuals in learning and teaching. This has subsequently led to inclusion in the #SocMedHE17 conference and being asked to become a facilitator on the recent #BYOD4L course. My inclusion and activity in both of these events has enhanced my online presence and professional identify, opening up additional opportunities.

Fig. 3.4 Sue Beckingham, Developing an online presence: contributing factors (2018), CC BY 4.0

Final Thoughts

Developing a professional online presence and an effective network is an iterative process. Both need to be tended as carefully as a garden: quality should be prioritised over quantity with regards to the information shared and nature of your connections. Taking the time to update your profile and interact with your network can pay dividends. However, the rewards are only as good as the effort you put in. This can be best managed by short but regular engagement with your networks and chosen professional social spaces.

References

Beckingham, S. (2013). 'Social media and the digital scholar' [PowerPoint presentation] University of Roehampton, https://www.slideshare.net/suebeckingham/scholarship-and-social-media

Boyd, d. (2011). 'Social network sites as networked publics: affordances, dynamics, and implications', in Papacharissi, Z. (ed.), *A Networked Self: Identity, Community and Culture on Social Network Sites*. Abingdon: Routledge.

Bozkurt, A. and Chic-Hsiung, Tu. (2016). 'Digital identity formation: Socially being real and present on digital networks', *Educational Media International*, 53:3, pp. 153–67, https://doi.org/10.1080/09523987.2016.1236885

Kramer, B. (2016). *Shareology: How Sharing is Powering the Human Economy*. New York: Morgan James Publishing.

LinkedIn (2014). 'Our Story', https://ourstory.linkedin.com/

Pasquini, L., Wakefield, J., Reed, A., and Allen, J. (2014). 'Digital scholarship and impact factors: methods and tools to connect your research', in T. Bastiaens (ed.), *Proceedings of World Conference on E-Learning*. New Orleans,

LA: Association for the Advancement of Computing in Education (AACE), pp. 1564–69, https://www.learntechlib.org/primary/p/148918/

Seargeant, P. and Tagg, C. (2014). *The Language of Social Media: Identity and Community on the Internet*. London: Palgrave Macmillan.

Stepper, J. (2015). *Working Out Loud: For a Better Career and Life*. Chicago: Ikigai Press.

Stepper, J. (2016). *The Elements of Working out Loud (revisited)*, http://working outloud.com/blog/the-5-elements-of-working-out-loud-revisited

Veletsianos, George and Kimmons, Royce (2012). 'Networked participatory scholarship: Emergent techno-cultural pressures toward open and digital scholarship in online networks', *Computers & Education*, 58, pp. 766–74, https://doi.org/10.1016/j.compedu.2011.10.001.

Vora, T. (2017). *5 Elements of Working Out Loud by @JohnStepper* [Sketchnote], http://qaspire.com/2017/01/26/5-elements-of-working-out-loud-by-johnstepper/

4. Re-Engineered Continuing Professional Development and Modelled Use of Cloud Tools and Social Media by Academic Developers

#Intermediate #Twitter #CPD

Martin Compton and Timos Almpanis

Transforming Lecturer Practice and Mindset

Academic Developers (a.k.a. Lecturers in Education, Teaching Fellows or Educational, Faculty or Staff Developers) may work in discrete units, within faculties, from within a broader education faculty or closely aligned to Human Resources or Quality departments. Their own values and the organisational structures and culture they work within will likely lead them to exhibit a particular 'orientation' such as 'internal consultant', 'modeller-broker' or 'managerial' (Land, 2001). Despite the growth of the role during the 1990s from a position of obscurity to the norm in most institutions today, the varying orientations and frequent restructuring in many higher education institutions can stifle the role of the Academic Developers and lead to a focus on teams rather than individuals and is rooted in scholarship rather than perceived deficits (Gibbs, 2013). As a new 'tribe' in academia (Bath and Smith, 2004) Academic Developers often work in a delicate environment, balancing the competing demands of senior managers against their own values

   https://doi.org/10.11647/OBP.0162.04

and negotiating the inevitable tensions that exist when working with busy academics (Brew, 2011), especially those that do not see teaching as their first priority. In a complex and varied world there is one thing that unites Academic Developers and that is a commitment to notions of change. One such change is the (often vague) notion that teaching academics should be doing more with technology.

This vagueness is part of the problem, what exactly should lecturers be doing with technology in their teaching? Bayne (2015) argues that the complex interrelationships between technology, society and education are not clearly understood or articulated. It is difficult to simplify what Technology Enhanced Learning (TEL) means and should seek to achieve:

> ...technology in TEL tends to be black-boxed, under-defined and generally described in instrumental or essentialist terms which either subordinate social practice to technology, or subordinate technology to social practice. (Bayne, 2015)

We are often told that we are or should be in a 'post-digital' age but some higher education providers are still battling with limited Wi-Fi and insufficient computer access (Newman and Beetham, 2017). Likewise, conferences and publications dazzle us with innovative practices that mask the mass of laggards or, at best, late-adopters that perfectly illustrate Rogers' (2003) famous diffusion of innovations model.

We have previously argued (Compton and Almpanis, 2018) that this mixed impression is exacerbated by common models of continuing professional development (CPD) in relation to the use of technology in HE. The CPD is too often standardised and follows a one-size-fits-all model that exhibits the inadequacies of 'transmissive' training rather than the desired 'transformative' development opportunity (Kennedy, 2011).

We nevertheless accept that there is a need to continue to educate academics who teach and those with student-facing roles about the digital capabilities for teaching, learning and assessment, as well as the impact such capabilities could have on their wider professional roles. We argue, though, that many traditional approaches to hastening the pace of change are flawed. Institutional systems (e.g. Virtual Learning Environment, lecture capture) are often conflated in the minds of teachers with all teaching and learning technology. However, we distinguish these from social, collaborative downloadable apps and cloud-based educational and productivity tools designed for education or productivity purposes. It is those that we use to enhance our own programmes and use as vehicles to support pedagogy-focussed CPD.

We believe tools that enable collaboration, interaction and enhancement are the perfect vehicle to illuminate the practical potential of better student engagement. In many ways, the general productivity tools serve our goals best. They are designed not with teachers and lecturers in mind, but professionals, or anyone else who wants to interact online. A secondary impact of training people in the use of these tools is that its embeds digital skills into their practice and enhances their employability. When these tools are used alongside social/collaborative tools, they provide lecturers with an opportunity to focus on concepts such as digital professionalism, data protection, and e-safety. Academic developers often have a uniquely pan-institutional vista that affords them the opportunity to witness, harness and disseminate actual applied practices (in contrast to the technical or theoretical) which then, in turn, feed into the practice of others. The following two case studies illustrate how we, as academic developers, use these tools and how we interpret the 'social' in social media through re-engineered CPD and modelled use on the PGCert HE programme.

Case Study 1: Re-engineered CPD

A common issue is that much institution-wide CPD (from one-off sessions to pan-institutional teaching and learning conferences) is voluntary. In the case of TEL-based CPD, it is the early adopters and not the *hard-to-reach* that participate. To address these issues we continue to offer a menu of one-off sessions and promote our conferences; but we are also working with key faculty members to engage the harder to reach. For example, we support 'lunch and learn' initiatives, seek invites to whole department or faculty meetings and ensure we are available for faculty-level conferences. Undoubtedly, this is aided and driven by senior management and the culture within which we work, but it can also happen from the bottom up if enthusiastic individuals invite us to such events.

More importantly, we argue that one-size-fits-all, training style CPD sessions are often flawed because they focus on the tool rather than pedagogy and follow a training rather than a discovery format

(Compton and Almpanis, 2017). Thus, the sessions we offer draw on some core principles:

1. We are explicit about the distinction we make between the institutional systems and CPD on offer. We show value in these systems and make clear the centrality of their role whilst allowing space and acceptance for the frequent gripes about the VLE (navigation, clunkiness, un-intuitiveness) or, for example, lecture capture software (challenge to autonomy, implications for practice).

2. We seek to distinguish our sessions from the common experience of the 'follow the trainer' model and aid participants in embracing the idea that they are not in a step-by-step or 'how to' session.

3. Challenging expectation and mindset is partially achieved by the use of 'quick win' openers that illustrate the philosophy of 'easy, free and fit for purpose' as outlined below. For example a Tweet Wall or 'backchannel' is displayed for in-session interaction and after asking participants to contribute, say, their expectations, they are then challenged to set up their own backchannel for their own teaching (done collaboratively where needed, but usually independently). The opportunities and challenges of using such social interaction methods in their own teaching contexts are then naturally discussed.

Pedagogical needs or the nature of the lecturer-student interaction frames the CPD event, rather than the capabilities of the tools themselves. Thus, in the training session we look at co-creating presentations, focussing on cloud-based presentation tools that have collaborative and social functionality, e.g. Haiku Deck and Prezi and how to organise questions in lectures. A large part of the training session models the use of three or four student response systems and finishes with participants choosing one and creating a resource. We have also designed sessions around the long-established concept of the 'advance organizer' (Ausubel, 1978) to illustrate ways in which relatively simple technologies can be used to ask questions in the classroom and draw students into core concepts through reflection or discussion.

Attendees asked 35 questions
with a total number of 33 likes

91% of questions were asked anonymously

What were
the most popular questions?

👤 Anonymous   6 👍   0 👎

Yes, we should make lectures interactive but how can we ensure students are going to interact?

👤 Anonymous   4 👍   0 👎

What if the student doesn't have a device?

👤 Anonymous   3 👍   0 👎

Keeping large numbers of students engaged is difficult, even with interaction because the quiet ones still escape! How can the quiet ones become engaged?

👤 Anonymous   2 👍   0 👎

Should we go to the pub?

👤 Anonymous   2 👍   0 👎

How do you get students to sit at the FRONT of the lecture theatre?

Fig. 4.1 Martin Compton, Backchannel[1] screenshot (2018), CC BY 4.0

---

1   Backchannel Chat is an app designed to enable teachers to facilitate online discussions about their subject.

4. As stated above, we are acutely aware of the difficulties
    many of those in teaching-facing roles have with core
    technology. Part of the rationale for our approach is to show
    that there are more accessible entry points and that by using
    apps and cloud tools as alternatives to built-in VLE functions,
    for example, the VLE itself can be enhanced. Of course,
    ease of use is relative so we ensure that there are a range of
    entry points and that at least one of the ways the pedagogic
    concept can be addressed with an app or cloud-based tool is
    very simple. We often highlight the notion that the two core
    technical skills are 'typing stuff in boxes' and 'copying and
    pasting web links'.

5. The notion of 'free' is complicated by so-called freemium
    software or by the implications of an advertising model
    with adverts appearing alongside resources used. The latter
    point seems largely immaterial with regard to the ubiquitous
    YouTube which has normalised this type of advertising,
    so we simply ensure that participants are alert to limits
    on freemium tools and the implications of the advertising
    model.

6. The most important aspect is utility, or a tool's 'fitness for
    purpose'. To emphasise this point, we refer back to the
    underpinning pedagogy and encourage participants to
    recognise their own expertise and contextual pedagogic
    knowledge. One of the biggest criticisms we have
    encountered in the past is that academics are unable to
    connect tools and approaches to their own practice. We
    pre-empt this challenge by acknowledging it up front,
    challenging them to find a way to utilise a tool and to share
    back, at a later date, their experience so that their successes,
    or even 'magnificent failures', might aid colleagues in or
    beyond their faculties.

By extending the offer of CPD and by following the principles
above, we are seeing a quickening in adoption of social, collaborative
and interactive technologies by lecturers and others with teaching
responsibilities in the university. In these sessions, we model their use

by embedding them within the sessions themselves wherever possible, thus providing the opportunity to witness our claims of ease of use. We argue that the best way to challenge cynicism, reluctance or outright fear is to respect the existence of these fears and to host CPD events that are open to them whilst simultaneously challenging them in design and delivery. Our goal is to generate momentum and enthusiasm by addressing head-on some of the obstacles to change that apply not only to use of social media but to all aspects of development in pedagogic practices in our institution.

Case Study 2: PGCert in Higher Education (HE)

The PGCert in HE is delivered in a blended mode with some face-to-face contact and substantial online elements, both synchronous and asynchronous. UK-based participants spend four study days on campus, spread over the duration of the year, whereas international participants are visited by the lecturers twice a year. The rest of the programme takes place online, using a combination of institutionally-supported platforms and cloud-based tools.

Moodle is the backbone of the online component of the course, as all core materials are uploaded and/or linked from it; furthermore, the Moodle discussion forums are used extensively by participants and the course team to discuss weekly topics and peer-review each other's group work in a safe environment. Beyond the walled gardens of the VLE, however, a range of other communication and collaboration tools is used in order to utilise the best tool for each task. This also enables us to demonstrate and model the pedagogically effective use of a range of cloud-based tools and enhance participants' digital capabilities.

This approach begins early in the programme. As part of the induction, participants are encouraged to post a short description about themselves and mention the reasons why they are doing the programme in a Moodle forum, titled 'about me'. They are also encouraged to reply on other participants' posts and comment on common interests. A cloud-based wall is used to collate participants' responses on their initial feelings and experiences of what it is to be a student again.

Additionally, free cloud-based presentation software is used for an ice-breaker activity where participants are asked to create one slide each saying something about themselves and asking a question or using their own ice-breaker activity. This way we offer an alternative way of interacting with others on the programme and help to build a community of learners, but also to model some of the ways participants can help their own new students to settle in and build relationships with each other. A screenshot of a slide from this activity is shown in Figure 4.2 below.

Describe yourself as a horse...

...might be an icebreaker I would do with my equine students...are you a fine, fiery Thoroughbred? Do you work steadily like an Irish cob, or perhaps you're more like a German warmblood, needing patience & understanding, what colour would you be, & where do you see yourself? At a show, in a field on Snowdonia, winning Hickstead?

Of course as a an icebreaker on this page this isn't an awful lot of good, so I'll simplify (sounds a bit like the tv program The Cube....).

What animal would you be, & why......?

I'd be a rag and bone man's weary nag, still going but with a constant wary eye out.

This is a great idea- and can be specialist or, as you have done here, generalisable.

If I were a horse, I would like to be a black strong horse with curly long hair who usually wins at shows.

I would be a lion because it's in my name :)

I would be a dog: loyal, fun, inquisitive, cuddly and protective

Fig. 4.2 Martin Compton, Screenshot of an ice-breaker activity using cloud-based presentation software (2018), CC BY 4.0

Later in the programme, many participants use the same cloud-based presentation software as a basis for their group task on developing a short, narrated presentation on an allocated learning theory.

While asynchronous communication tools offer flexibility regarding the time when a participant can read and respond to a comment, synchronous online communication can further enhance the feeling of belonging in a learning community and motivate participants further during seminar-type activities that take place at predetermined times. During the first module of the PGCert Programme, which covers theory of teaching, learning and assessment, an hourly webinar, which is conducted twice for flexibility in participation, aims to focus participants' learning around a certain topic and promote discussion around it. The webinars are initiated by two course tutors who frame the weekly topic and pose relevant questions, encouraging participation and the sharing of views and experiences among the group.

Webinars are recorded and made available from Moodle for revision purposes, but also in order to make sure that any participants unable to attend the recordings are not disadvantaged.

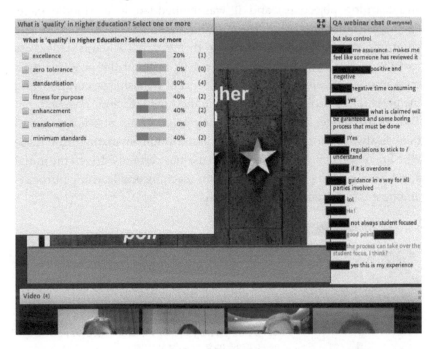

Fig. 4.3 Martin Compton, Screenshot of the web conferencing system in use (2018), CC BY 4.0

The web conferencing system is also used for group tutorials at pre-arranged times negotiated between the personal tutor and their group; during these, further, tailored advice and support is provided and participants have an opportunity to ask questions and discuss any potential issues with their assignments, or other aspects of the course.

The use of free, real-time online collaboration tools is also encouraged among study groups, so that participants can devise their plan on how to tackle their formative group tasks. Due to the limited licences associated with the main web-conferencing tool that we use, free, synchronous online collaboration tools are promoted; resources and support for such online group collaboration is provided by our 'online tutor' of the PGCert programme.

We used a social network curation service that allows for stories/timelines to be harvested using Twitter and other online media to bring together some tweets from the course leader regarding lesson planning and learning objectives, and it was embedded in a Moodle page. Participants discussed their lesson plans, aims and objectives in the safe environment of the Moodle forum. In this way, participants had access to Twitter content outside of Twitter itself without the need for their own account. It exposed them to the concept of hashtags, curation, and the potential for utilising these tools in their own teaching. We find that Twitter use ranges from 10–20% in any given group of academics and there is always a lot of prejudice and assumption emanating from those who are non-users. Nevertheless, this use has certainly driven the initial application and the extension of use for teaching and learning purposes amongst the academics we work with.

Martin Compton @uogmc · 30 Sep 2016
On the problem of assuming cognitive levels are somehow education level
specific vega.jeffco.edu/szak/handouts/... #1286plan

Martin Compton @uogmc · 30 Sep 2016
Replying to
or see the comments here for a nice range of views #1286plan
researchgate.net/post/What_is_T...

Martin Compton @uogmc · 30 Sep 2016
Replying to
or this extract from Heywood #1286plan

Fig. 4.4 Martin Compton, Curated content on Twitter which was subsequently
re-curated with other online resources and then embedded in the VLE
(2018), CC BY 4.0

Additionally, a Twitter aggregator is used to automatically share
relevant, pre-defined content on a daily basis to further aid participants'
understanding of the potential of this tool.

The Teaching, Learning and
Assessment Daily

Fig. 4.5 Martin Compton, Screenshot of Twitter content aggregator (2018),
CC BY 4.0

An online newsletter was used to collate some programme-related
resources regarding peer observations, which is an integral part of the

programme. The same online newsletter has also been used to outline the way various online tools enhance the course, either by adding interactivity or by creating multimedia content. We are thus using tools that have interactive potential to illustrate and exemplify other tools that do the same. Numerous participants have gone on to use their choice of these tools with their own students.

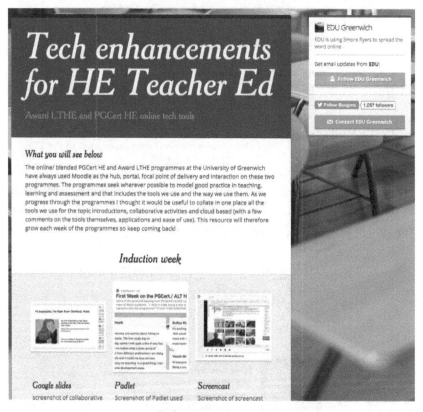

Fig. 4.6 Martin Compton, Newsletter for curation and exemplification with built in social media elements (2018), CC BY 4.0

It is important to note that all of the above tools were used in context to achieve our own teaching and learning goals on the PGCert programme as well as to raise participants' awareness of the possibilities of adopting some of these tools in their own teaching practice. The development of the digital capabilities of participants is also a side-benefit of the course, due not only to its online nature but the fact that TEL is discussed explicitly as one of the topics. We focus on the pedagogical effectiveness of TEL by modelling its use, rather than focusing on the technical aspects of the software, as there is often plenty of software solutions that can achieve similar outcomes and the lifecycle of free or freemium software has nowadays been significantly shortened.

Conclusion

Technology is embedded in all aspects of our lives including work and education and, for better or worse, it is one of the weapons in an academic developer's arsenal; while numerous studies have been published in the field of technology-enhanced learning, there is still some way to go before TEL becomes fully integrated into the student experience. From a staff development perspective, although there are certain minimum digital capabilities required in order for a lecturer to make good use of TEL, an open mind about the possibilities and a willingness to experiment to refresh one's practice are more important. This means that while training and support for institutional platforms may continue to be centralised, sharing knowledge about the pedagogically effective use of various cloud-based applications is very important too. Modified or re-engineered CPD opportunities offered to all staff as well as the Postgraduate Certificate in Higher Education or Postgraduate Certificate in Academic Practice (PGCert in HE/PCAP) course can be the vehicles for that, aiming to move TEL practices beyond the innovation and early-adoption stages.

Whilst it is virtually impossible to empirically measure the impact of the strategies we use, we are confident that the impact can be 'felt' when working with colleagues, and from the unsolicited comments and feedback we've received. A single CPD session in one faculty, for example, led to two attendees embracing one of the promoted social interaction tools. A recent visit to the same faculty's all-staff meeting found that the enthusiasm and willingness of those two relatively new lecturers to share examples in context have led to widespread take-up amongst colleagues who might be seen as 'hard to reach' as far as we, in the academic development team, are concerned. In terms of the PGCert, a 'TEL special issue' of our in-house journal featured contributions from three former participants who have used their experiences on the PGCert to embed social and interactive media in the face-to-face delivery of their programmes. They experienced it, they adapted it, they presented it at conferences and subsequently published about it. As part of a relatively small team, we highly value this evident cascading and the willingness to disseminate via both formal and informal mechanisms.

References

Ausubel, D. P. (1978). 'In defence of advance organizers: A reply to the critics', *Review of Educational research*, 48:2, pp. 251–57.

Bath, D., and Smith, C. (2004). 'Academic developers: An academic tribe claiming their territory in higher education', *International Journal for Academic Development*, 9:1, pp. 9–27.

Bayne, S. (2015). 'What's the matter with 'technology-enhanced learning?', *Learning, Media and Technology*, 40:1, pp. 5–20.

Brew, A. (2011). 'Foreword', in Stefani, L. (ed.) *Evaluating the Effectiveness of Academic Development: Principles and Practice*, New York: Routledge, pp. 127–32.

Compton, M., and Almpanis, T. (2018). 'One size doesn't fit all: Rethinking approaches to continuing professional development in technology enhanced learning', *Compass: Journal of Learning and Teaching*, 11:1.

Gibbs, G. (2013). 'Reflections on the changing nature of educational development', *International Journal for Academic Development*, 18:1, pp. 4–14.

Kennedy, A. (2011). 'Collaborative continuing professional development (CPD) for teachers in Scotland: Aspirations, opportunities and barriers', *European Journal of Teacher Education*, 34:1, pp. 25–41.

Land, R. (2001). 'Agency, context and change in academic development', *International Journal for Academic Development*, 6:1, pp. 4–20.

Newman, T and Beetham, H. (2017). *Student Digital Experience Tracker 2017: The voices of 22,000 UK Learners*. Bristol: Jisc.

Rogers, E. (2003). *Diffusion of Innovations*. 5th edn. New York: Free Press.

5. Ten Days of Twitter

#Intermediate #Twitter #ARU10DoT #RUL10DoT #UCD10DoT #LivUni10DoT #YSJ10DoT #10DOTTEL #HSLU10DoT #MMJC10DoT

Mark Warnes

Introduction

Much has been written about digital literacy since Prensky's (2001) (now debunked) *Digital Natives, Digital Immigrants*, and the importance of digital literacy in higher education was highlighted by the inclusion of Dimension K4 of the UK Professional Standards Framework which describes 'The use and value of appropriate learning technologies' as Core Knowledge (HEA, 2011).

In recent years, the concept of digital literacy has expanded to include the use of social media in higher education, and national events such as the *Social Media for Learning in Higher Education Conference* (#SocMedHE17) (Williams and Warnes, 2017) which has run at Sheffield Hallam since 2014, illustrate the importance of this development. Indeed, Jisc published their list of 'social media superstars' (Parr, 2017), including academics enhancing their teaching by incorporating social media such as Facebook, Instagram, YouTube, Snapchat, and, most frequently, Twitter.

It was to address staff development needs for the latter that Webster (@scholastic_rat) (2015) created 10 Days of Twitter (10DoT). The primary purpose of this is to gently introduce university staff to

    https://doi.org/10.11647/OBP.0162.05

the use of Twitter in bitesize chunks and, despite its reputation as a vehicle for celebrity gossip, how it might be used in a professional academic context. Following Webster's departure from Anglia Learning & Teaching (AL&T), the learning development unit at Anglia Ruskin University (ARU), I took over running the course and updating the content for each iteration due to regular software updates from Twitter.

The ARU version of 10DoT, #ARU10DoT (Webster and Warnes, 2017), has run once per semester (December and March) since November 2013, attracting around thirty-five participants each time. Content is presented via a WordPress blog (http://aru10dot.wordpress.com) with scheduled posts containing daily tasks. Participants follow the blog using their email address and there is no need to create a WordPress account (although participants may subscribe using an existing WordPress account). Delivered in ten-minute blocks over ten (working) days, #ARU10DoT supports participants as they create and use their Twitter account.

Access to #ARU10DoT is not restricted to ARU staff only and anyone can participate. The course thus operates as a mini-MOOC, which was easily manageable prior to the introduction of micro-credentialing (Educause, 2017) in the form of Digital Badges, in March 2017. However, due the amount of time required to monitor participants' progress, this model is not scalable and should the number of participants increase, access to the course will have to be restricted.

Ten Days of Twitter and Beyond

Course content is delivered via a series of blog posts, each dealing with a single aspect of Twitter. Each day's blog post is edited in advance and scheduled for publication on the appropriate day. The fortnight prior to delivery is spent reviewing the content against Twitter to identify and incorporate any changes that Twitter have made (such as the increase in the number of characters per tweet). Even without any changes, most of the embedded screenshots are replaced, primarily to maintain the currency of the content.

ARU staff are alerted to each delivery via a range of internal communication methods, including the fortnightly staff newsletter, announcements on the staff intranet, weekly faculty emails, inclusion on the 'Online learning' section of the AL&T website (http://arul.ink/ alt-10dot), and, of course, Twitter. In addition, #ARU10DoT is included in the schedule of CPD events delivered by AL&T. Although ARU staff are encouraged to register via the HR system, and their participation is checked at the end of the course, calculating exactly how many participants engage with the course is difficult as registration is not compulsory,

That said, on average, not including 'lurkers' who observe but do not actively contribute (Sun, Rau & Ma, 2014), the course attracts around 30 to 40 participants for each delivery using various access methods: subscription to the blog; bookmarking the blog; or simply following the hashtag or @ handle. At the time of writing, the blog has attracted 2,163 visitors who have viewed the 158 posts 9,195 times.

The WordPress blog posts are disseminated daily via email to those participants who subscribe. Notifications are also publicised via Twitter @ARU10DoT and @MarkWarnes2 (then retweeted by @AngliaLTA); Facebook (my personal account as AL&T does not currently have a page); Google+ (my personal account as AL&T does not currently have a page) further iterations will not use Google+ as this was shut down in April 2019; and LinkedIn (my personal account as the AL&T page does not currently permit this activity). Figure 5.1 shows the ways in which participants access the blog.

Subscription Type	n
WordPress.com	24
Email	111
Social media	831
Total	**966**

Fig. 5.1 Mark Warnes, ARU10DoT blog posts: types of subscription and number of followers (2018), CC BY 4.0

The total for social media combines the numbers of followers for Twitter (@markwarnes2 n=257, @ARU10DoT = 352) and LinkedIn (n=222). These numbers, however, represent potential rather than actual participants.

Digital Badges

After running the course in December 2016, the decision was taken to add a micro-credential to the course in the form of a Digital Badge. Digital Badges are available from a range of educational institutions including Lynda.com (2018), Instructure (Canvas LMS), John Wiley and Sons, and the Open University (OU). The OU (2018) offer twenty-six free Badged courses including *Digital Literacy: Succeeding in a Digital World*.

Digital Badges were first added to #ARU10DoT in March 2017. This meant a radical redraft of the daily tasks as, to qualify for their Badge, participants needed to record evidence that they had engaged with a task related to that day's post. This shifted the focus of the course from (mainly) passive to (optionally) active, although there remains no compulsion on participants to complete the tasks, other than the desire to qualify for a Digital Badge.

Each daily task covers a specific aspect of Twitter and each task should take no longer than ten minutes to complete. Consequently, if a participant misses a day (or two) it doesn't take long for them to catch up. Ideally participants should complete the course, including the tasks, during the period of delivery, but, acknowledging that some staff may find it challenging to do this, participants are given a further two weeks. Also, all blog posts, for all deliveries, remain available on WordPress, so that participants can work at their own speed.

Those participants who are seeking accreditation must post something either on Twitter or add a comment to that day's blog post:

Week 1

- **Day 1 — Setting up your profile**
  Today's Digital Badge activity is to tell me your Twitter handle using the 'Leave a reply' comment box on this blog post

- **Day 2 — Sending tweets**
  Today's Digital Badge activity is to tweet '*Joining in #ARU10DoT with @ARU10DoT and @markwarnes2*'

- **Day 3 — Following people**
  Today's Digital Badge activity is to post, in the comments section

below, the handles of three interesting people you think others should follow; let us know why you chose them!

- **Day 4 — Sending @messages**
  Today's Digital Badge activity is to send me an @message to tell me how it's going @markwarnes2

- **Day 5 — Retweeting**
  Today's Digital Badge activity is to edit three tweets to add #ARU10DoT and retweet them

Week 2

- **Day 6 — Hashtags and trending**
  Today's Digital Badge activity is to post a hashtag of a conversation you'd like to join in the comments section of this blog post

- **Day 7 — Pictures and videos**
  Today's Digital Badge activity is to tweet a picture. Take a picture of your desk, your colleagues, your building, anything you like, and share it with your followers. If you need inspiration then look at the pictures that the people you follow have tweeted. Just make sure you use the #ARU10DoT hashtag so we can all see it. And, if you're feeling adventurous, there's always video...

- **Day 8 — Managing people**
  Today's Digital Badge activity is to create a list and post the link to this blog page. You might want to try making a list of your colleagues on Twitter, or perhaps one for the professional and funding bodies you follow

- **Day 9 — Managing information**
  Today's Digital Badge activity is to choose a third party application that looks useful to you, and experiment with it — post below to let us know your thoughts and findings

- **Day 10 — The past and the future**
  Today's Digital Badge activity is to complete the Satisfaction Survey. OR (if you think that's just too cheeky!) Post a 100-word reflective summary of your experience of the course and whether it has had any impact on your practice

The process of checking that participants had completed the daily tasks proved to be more challenging to manage than originally anticipated, even though this required checking only two possible locations (except for the Satisfaction Survey on Day 10 which is hosted on SurveyMonkey). For one thing, some Twitter posts did not appear in the #ARU10DoT column in TweetDeck and it was necessary to check participant's tweets. In addition, some participants posted tweets that should have been blog comments, or sent a Direct Message rather than an @message, in which cases the wording of the task was edited for clarity. An additional blog post was published at the end of both the first and second weeks showing participants' progress at those points. Participants were invited to provide evidence in the form of screen shots of any activities I had missed.

As noted above, acknowledging that some participants might be unable to complete the course in the allotted time, they were allowed a further two weeks after the course had finished to complete any outstanding tasks, after which Digital Badges were issued to participants who had completed all ten tasks.

A number of Digital Badge platforms exist (Badge Alliance, 2017), such as Open Badges.me (2016), Mozilla's Open Badges.org (2016), and Credly (2018). Following a review of platforms in 2015, AL&T had selected Credly as most suited to their needs. The #ARU10DoT Digital Badges were created and issued using Credly. This involved creating the Badge image along with a course description, complete with a set of criteria confirming the awardee's achievement. Consequently, #ARU10DoT participants had to create a Credly account to accept and share their badges. Instructions for doing this are provided for participants on the Digital Badges page of the blog and, to date, no-one has raised this as an issue.

Digital Badges can be exported in a number of ways: downloaded in Open Badge format or as a printable PDF, embedded, shared as a link, shared to Open Badges, or shared to social media platforms such as Facebook and Twitter, and, possibly most importantly, LinkedIn. Digital Badges exported to LinkedIn appear in the Certifications area of the Achievements section of the profile, and are linked to the issuing institution.

The introduction of Digital Badges had some unintended consequences. For one thing, participants who had completed the course previously, many times in some cases, repeated the course simply to qualify for a Badge. A small number of previous participants asked for a retrospective Badge, hoping to avoid repeating the course, but these requests were denied on the grounds of fairness.

Another unexpected result was the increase in the number of blog hits, which during March 2017 more than doubled the typical traffic. This phenomenon was repeated in December 2017. Although this has not (yet) been systematically researched, it is reasonable to infer that participants were eager to qualify for their Badges.

As the course is open to external participants and its numbers cannot be restricted, it operates like a Mini-MOOC (Massive Open Online Course) (cf. edX, 2016; Coursera, 2018; FutureLearn, undated). However, should the number of external participants increase, it would become impossible to check that all daily tasks had been completed. Should this happen then access to the course would be restricted to ARU staff only.

Impact

The 10DoT format of daily, bitesize chunks has been adapted by colleagues at ARU for a range of courses including *TEL-ve Days of Christmas* (Williams and George, 2015), *5 Days of Digital Literacy #5DoDL* (Williams and George, 2016) and its successor, *5 Minutes of Digital Literacy #5MoDL* (Williams and George, 2017, http://arul.ink/ alt-5dodl), both of which offer Digital Badges, and which address ARU's *Digital Literacy Framework* (Kerrigan & Evangelinos, 2015), which is in turn based on the EU's DIGCOMP framework for Digital Competence (Ferrari, 2013).

In addition, Dr Toby Carter (Director of Learning, Teaching and Assessment for the Faculty of Science and Technology) has adapted #ARU10DoT into a module for his *MSc Communication Skills for Conservation* (Comm4Cons, #C4C10DoT). The module is delivered via the ARU Learning Management System, Canvas, and covers the same content but contextualised for the module (Warnes and Carter, 2016; Carter, 2017).

Twitter analytics also show the impact of @ARU10DoT which tweeted 29 times during December 2017 attracting 5,536 impressions (i.e. '[the number of] Times a user is served a tweet in timeline or search results' (Twitter, 2018) and 564 profile visits. One new follower in December brought 1,355 followers and another in January 2018 brought 2,912 followers, thus increasing the potential reach of the course.

Day Eleven of Ten

Although the course lasts only ten days, a final Day Eleven post is published on the Monday following the conclusion of the course. An eleventh day had been included in 10DoT from its inception but Carter and East (2017) rewrote the content for #C4C10DoT. This new content was such a significant improvement on the original text that it was incorporated into #ARU10DoT.

Topics include tweeting about new publications (with a link to an online version, where possible) and/or relevant new developments in a particular research area or academic subject; publicising events in advance and live-tweeting them on the day; use of hashtags to contribute to conversations; reaching out to new audiences such as government departments, NGOs, businesses, and so on; and monitoring funding sources.

Challenges and Opportunities

Occasionally, prospective participants have asked for face-to-face delivery, which somewhat defeats the object. That said, an exception was made for a specific purpose when Carter and I were invited to deliver a session on using Twitter for academic purposes for a Faculty CPD Day and we decided to run through #ARU10DoT in a single two-hour workshop slot (Warnes and Carter, 2018). This, however, proved to be a logistical nightmare, mainly due to the range of technological skills of the participants, and it was only possible to complete eight of the ten tasks in the session. Participants were given the opportunity to complete the course in their own time to qualify for a Digital Badge. However, only two staff members took the opportunity. That said, according to WordPress statistics, that day recorded the highest number of views of the blog in a single day (43 views from 16 visitors).

Satisfaction Survey

A link to the SurveyMonkey-hosted Satisfaction Survey (mentioned earlier) is sent via email to all individuals who registered for and/or participated in the course. However, rather than using a simple 'Happy Sheet' (CHRM, 2018) asking participants to rate the course in general, this survey is designed to collect specific data concerning the quality of the content and the impact of the course (Future Work Centre, 2015).

The first two questions invite respondents to explain why, having they registered for the course, they chose not to participate or, having started the course, why they chose not to complete it. Respondents' views on the quality of the daily content is captured using a 'Goldilocks' question (Pappas, 2015), *please let me know which topics have too much detail, which have too little, and which are just right*. This is followed by questions asking which topics should be abandoned and which are missing. The final question measures the impact of the course by asking if participants have changed the way they use Twitter and, if so, how and why.

Responses from the latest survey show that almost all topics are 'just right' with the exception of *Day 8: Managing People* and *Day 9: Managing Information*, which I shall expand ready for the next delivery. In addition, all participants agreed that the course demonstrated how Twitter can be used in a professional context.

Conclusions and Recommendations

While a great deal of attention has been paid to developing digital literacy for students (Jisc, 2015), this is an area that also involves staff (HEA, 2017). Only a few short years ago, staff digital literacy included little more than a working knowledge of email, word processing, and PowerPoint. The increasing pervasiveness of social media in everyday life has permeated into the classroom. University staff need to engage with the current milieu of information and communication opportunities, in order to both understand their students and to remain relevant in the twenty-first century. Universities must offer CPD that enables staff to expand their skills in this area.

#ARU10DoT helps academic staff to develop their competence using a social media tool for education and, in doing so, contributes to the requirements of ARU's Digital Literacy Framework. The sustained popularity of the course over five years is testament to its user-friendly mode of delivery, tone and pace, and the addition of Digital Badges has provided additional motivation for participants to fully engage with all aspects of the course.

As 10DoT was created with a Creative Commons license, it has spread throughout the sector and is running at a number of universities, both domestic and overseas, including Regent's University London (#RUL10DoT), University College Dublin (#UCD10DoT), University of Liverpool (#LivUni10DoT), York St John (#YSJ10DoT), University of Sussex (#10DOTTEL), Lucerne University of Applied Sciences and Arts (#HSLU10DoT), and University of Western Ontario (#MMJC10DoT). Any institution wishing to develop their own version can simply copy, paste and adapt the existing blog posts.

References

Badge Alliance (2017). 'Badge issuing platforms', http://www.badgealliance.org/badge-issuing-platforms/

Carter, T. (2017). '2017 MOD003368 TRI2 F01CAM: C4C10DoT overview', https://canvas.anglia.ac.uk/courses/2875/pages/c4c10dot-overview

Carter, T. and East, M. (2017). 'Eleventh day of #C4C10Dot: Beyond C4C10DoT: Twitter and research', https://canvas.anglia.ac.uk/courses/2875/pages/c4c10dot-day-11

Center for Digital Education (2017). 'Why micro-credentials are taking hold in universities', http://www.centerdigitaled.com/higher-ed/Why-Micro-Credentials-Universities.html

Community for Human Resource Management (2018). 'What is a Happy Sheet?', http://www.chrmglobal.com/Qanda/87/1/What-is-a-Happy-Sheet-.html

Coursera Inc. (2018). 'Take the World's Best Courses', https://www.coursera.org/

Credly (2018). 'What's your Digital Credential Strategy?', https://credly.com/

EDUCAUSE Learning Initiative (2017). '7 things you should read about microcredentialing/digital badging', https://library.educause.edu/~/media/files/library/2017/7/elir1704.pdf

edX (2016). 'Mooc.org', http://mooc.org/

Ferrari, A. (2013). *DIGCOMP: A Framework for Developing and Understanding Digital Competence in Europe.* Luxembourg: Publications Office of the European Union, http://ftp.jrc.es/EURdoc/JRC83167.pdf

FutureLearn (n.d.). Learn new skills, pursue your interests, advance your career, https://www.futurelearn.com/

Future Work Centre (2015). 'Beyond the happy sheet: Adopting an evidence-based approach to training and development evaluation', http://www.futureworkcentre.com/wp-content/uploads/2015/09/FWC_BeyondHappySheet.pdf

Higher Education Authority (HEA) (2011). 'The UK professional standards framework for teaching and supporting learning in higher education', https://www.heacademy.ac.uk/system/files/downloads/uk_professional_standards_framework.pdf

Higher Education Authority (HEA) (2017). 'Digital literacies', https://www.heacademy.ac.uk/knowledge-hub/digital-literacies

Jisc (2015). 'Developing students' digital literacy', https://www.jisc.ac.uk/guides/developing-students-digital-literacy

Kerrigan, M. and Evangelinos, G. (2015). 'Digital literacy framework (V.6)', Anglia Ruskin University, https://vle.anglia.ac.uk/sites/LTA/Course%20Documents/Digital_Literacy/Digital%20Literacy%20Definitions%20v6.pdf

Lynda.com (2018). 'Lynda.com certificates of completion — frequently asked questions', https://www.linkedin.com/help/lynda/topics/10083/10084/70176

Openbadges.me (2016). 'Design and issue Open Badges', https://www.openbadges.me/

OpenBadges.org (2016). 'Discover Open Badges', https://openbadges.org/

Open University (2018). 'Badged courses', http://www.open.edu/openlearn/get-started/badges-come-openlearn

Pappas, C. (2015). '6 tips to apply the goldilocks principle in eLearning', https://elearningindustry.com/6-elearning-tips-to-apply-the-goldilocks-principle-in-elearning

Parr, C. (2017). 'The top 10 UK Higher Education social media superstars of 2017', *Times Higher Education,* https://www.timeshighereducation.com/blog/top-10-uk-higher-education-social-media-superstars-2017

Prensky, M. (2001). 'Digital natives, digital immigrants part 1', *On the Horizon,* 9:5, pp. 1–6, https://doi.org/10.1108/10748120110424816

Sun, N., Rau, P. P. and Ma, L. (2014). 'Understanding lurkers in online communities: A literature review, Computers', *Human Behavior*, 38, September 2014, pp. 110–17, https://doi.org/10.1016/j.chb.2014.05.022

Twitter (2018). 'About your activity dashboard', https://help.twitter.com/en/managing-your-account/using-the-tweet-activity-dashboard

Warnes, M. and Carter, T. (2016). 'Ten days of Twitter and beyond', paper presented at 17th Annual Learning and Teaching Conference, Anglia Ruskin University, 23 June 2016, http://www.lta.anglia.ac.uk/annual.php/Session-Abstracts-and-Presentations-49/

Warnes, M. and Carter, T. (2018). 'Develop Your Use of Twitter', workshop delivered at ALSS CPD Day, 5 January 2018.

Webster, H. (2013). '#10DoT ten days of Twitter', https://10daysoftwitter.wordpress.com/

Webster, H. and Warnes, M. (2017). '#ARU10DoT ten days of Twitter', https://aru10dot.wordpress.com/

Williams, J. and George, J. (2015). 'TEL-ve days of Christmas', https://telvedaysataru.wordpress.com

Williams, J. and George, J. (2016). '5 days of digital literacy', https://5daysofdigitalliteracy.com/

Williams, J. and George, J. (2017). '5 minutes of digital literacy', https://canvas.anglia.ac.uk/courses/2224

Williams, J. and Warnes, M. (2018). '#SocMedHE17', https://www.anglia.ac.uk/blogs/socmedhe17

6. Open and Networked Scholarship

#Intermediate #Twitter #OpenEd #HEdigID #DigPed

Suzan Koseoglu

Affordances and Barriers

If you use the Internet on a regular basis, chances are you use social media to connect with friends, family and colleagues, and to dip your toes into the resources and information that constantly flow online. You might use YouTube to learn how to learn a new recipe, contact your family on Skype, check a friend's pictures on Facebook, or join a Twitter chat with colleagues from around the globe. The possibilities social networking tools offer are endless. They change the way we think about ourselves and our relationship with the world. Each tool is designed with certain properties but our everyday actions, the decisions we make with or without intent, constantly change these tools' potential and impact future design decisions.

Network Publics, the notion of public spaces constructed through digital technologies, their capabilities and potential, has created a significant shift in how publics and civic participation are experienced (Boyd, 2010) and has implications that are yet to be fully explored in Higher Education (HE) institutions. One visible change is that it is becoming increasingly common for institutions to open up their teaching and research practices to the public for various reasons ranging from widening participation and better outreach, to marketing. A parallel development, sometimes not so much in line with institutional

    https://doi.org/10.11647/OBP.0162.06

visions and practices, is the emergence of *open and networked scholarship* (Veletsianos and Kimmons, 2012). This might sound new or unfamiliar, yet it refers to activities that have increasingly become part of academic practice, such as teaching an open online course, publishing open access, or creating a wiki with fellow colleagues and students. It also includes practices that are not necessarily tied to formal education, such as blogging or participation in a hashtag community. For me, the most exciting dimension of open scholarship is 'learning with the web and on the web,' as Gardner Campbell (2015) would say. We learn with the web and on the web, because the Internet offers many tools to think with, to work with, and to further develop our practices. And we further shape these technologies with our habits, intentional choices, with the way we interact with people and information resources — all the things that make us human.

Whilst the possibilities of networked technologies are exciting, there are significant barriers to meaningful participation. The boundaries of teaching and learning have expanded so fast that institutional policies, pedagogic practices, tools, and organisational frameworks are often struggling to keep up with the pace. This is not to say institutional and organisational readiness means we are ready for change too. Sometimes when we are fully up-to-date with a technology and feel at ease with it, it goes through an 'upgrade' that make no sense to us, or worse, it disappears and a new one pops up with different functionalities. Sometimes we make conscious decisions to reject technologies because, at their core, they do not reflect the values we have. And sometimes the barriers are harder to describe, or be aware of, because they reflect societal issues that are deeply embedded in the structure and politics of everyday life, such as racism, classism, and sexism among many others.

If we are to *learn on the web and with the web*, how can we respond to the barriers for meaningful participation in a constructive and ethical way and nurture a more inclusive space for all? In this chapter, I explore these issues in the light of the work of scholars who have inspired me and my own professional practice in educational technologies. Most of the discussions in this chapter are based on my experiences and research on Twitter, as this is a platform where I have met many colleagues working on issues related to education and built partnerships with them; it is a platform that helped me complete my dissertation study and fuelled the energy for subsequent studies. I begin the chapter by discussing how open and networked scholarship changes the nature of academic practice, which is a shift that often creates a tension between professional and personal identities. I then argue that certain literacies we develop through formal education, but mostly through informal everyday practice, teach us how to go about online participation. Finally, I draw attention to power issues in online networks and question the premise of the open as an empowering or equalizing force of change.

Open Scholarship in Higher Education

The affordances of social media, their capabilities and potential, no doubt impact the way we go about professional practice, both at individual and institutional levels. The knowledge produced can reach a much bigger and diverse audience than in the pre-Internet era through online publications, open teaching, and with digital networks of practice. A connected and open platform like Twitter, for example, is often seen as a way to build personal learning networks, which makes it a thriving space for formal and informal professional development through the connections it affords (for an example see the invitation for participation in #HEdigID Twitter chat: a series of chats focusing on Networked, Digital Life in Higher Education, Fig. 6.1). In addition, we also see that scholars are increasingly turning to online networks to voice their concerns on issues that matter to them (for an example see Fig. 6.2). Indeed, Bonnie Stewart (2016) in her research on scholarly practices on Twitter noted that the platform has become a place for scholars who are 'isolated, disillusioned, marginalised, or junior in their institutional scholarship' to have a voice.

Yet, participation in open networks is always personal and negotiated, as Catherine Cronin (2017) showed in a research study on how and if staff at a HE institution engaged in open educational practices. Cronin found that striking the 'balance between privacy and openness' in open networks was a primary concern for most staff, noting: 'many [staff] wanted to avoid mixing streams of conversations about work with other conversations about family, social activities, sports, politics, etc.' The

Fig. 6.1 Susan Koseoglu, #HEdigID Twitter chat: a series of chats focusing on Networked, Digital Life in HE (2018), CC BY 4.0, https://twitter.com/laurapasquini/status/956978197438091264

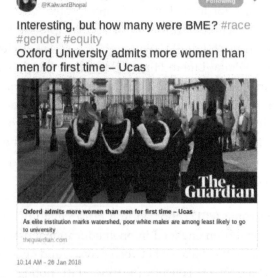

Fig. 6.2 Susan Koseoglu, Prof. Kalwant Bhopal's reaction to an article published by *The Guardian* (2018), CC BY 4.0, https://twitter.com/KalwantBhopal/status/956923189887754241

open and connected nature of social networking platforms even pushed some staff to work in closed learning environments, such as institutional virtual learning environments, because they felt safer and protected by boundaries. In my dissertation study, where I explored the different engagement patterns in an open online course, participants also often talked about the time it had taken for them to build relationships and make sense of connections in open spaces. It was clear that open practices like building a personal learning network or participating in an open online course required time, resources, energy, social support and perseverance. But finding the much needed resources, finding the time and energy to stay engaged and build relationships in networked spaces are problematic because open practices often occur outside of formal HE settings. As Maha Bali (2017) argued, most of open scholarship is 'based around volunteering models around people carving time outside of paid work.' Bali further argues that this is problematic and not sustainable because although these practices are important for professional development, often staff do not receive institutional recognition for their time and hard work. It is also true that the emerging venues for academic scholarship (such as publishing in independent open access journals, maintaining an educational blog) may not be seen legitimate paths for academic progression and tenure (in the US).

Going beyond the intersection of institutional and personal identities, we can also question what it means to be a 'scholar' in online networks, because in many social networks, ongoing participation in a community and shared practice define the extent to which one's voice is heard and further amplified. My view is that open scholarship is not, and should not be, limited to academic scholarship only. The academic community should be open to the views and experiences of everyone, regardless of their titles and earned ranks — informal should not mean less valued or less valid. The power of open and networked learning is that they can provide us a holistic understanding of learning that connects the formal with the informal, institutional spaces with community and home spaces. They can provide us a view of learning that connects geographies and the wealth of experiences across different generations and cultures. The pressing questions going forward concern how to create more sustainable models for open connections and learning, and how to better bridge formal and informal channels which exist on, and are enabled by, social networks. Finding the answers requires certain literacies.

Literacies for Meaningful Participation

Howard Rheingold, a scholar specialising in the socio-cultural implications of digital technologies, observed how students, regardless of their ages, need to have 'social media literacies' in order to make the best of the Internet (Rheingold, 2010). Students, he argued, often lack basic skills to separate the trustworthy from the 'crap', and the skills needed for focused attention, meaningful and purposeful learning online. Rheingold was one of the first to point to the importance of having network awareness in order to become a thoughtful and responsible citizen in a networked society: 'Understanding the nature of networks — technical and social — is essential. Doing so is not just a matter of engineering but also a question of freedom' (Rheingold 2010).

But this holistic understanding, especially the understanding of the social aspects of networks, is largely experiential. Most of our knowledge of the Internet comes from direct experience: unless we use the Internet and are present on its networks (even if that simply means listening to others' activities) we cannot develop a thorough understanding of what it means to be a citizen or a scholar in a networked society. We need to learn *when, how* and *why to participate* (or not to participate) in online networks, which is often a skill that is developed with active participation in online networks and with the relationships and connections we build on them. A thorough understanding of the 'social' also means an awareness of the ethical, cultural, political, and economic dimensions of social structures. I do not think this is easy to achieve considering the complexity of culture in online spaces, the ever-changing nature of online technologies, and our engagement with them.

But at the very least, as we become 'residents' (White and Le Cornu, 2011) in networked spaces, and as our online activities become increasingly controlled and monetised with social media tools and platforms, we can strive to act responsibly and ethically; we can seek meaningful connections and be on the lookout for the kinds of spaces and tools designed with a lack of sensitivity to people's agency and welfare. I believe this requires a critical understanding of the inequalities in networked spaces — the social construction of the digital and an understanding of why our response to networked spaces matters. This takes me to the last issue: the misuse of power and privilege.

Power and Privilege

There are deep issues with power and privilege that further complicate open online spaces. Although open practices in education are often posited as way to democratize education and 'level the playing field' in HE, there are many inequalities that are perpetuated in networked connections and work to exclude people from participation, especially marginalised and disadvantaged groups and people (this could be due to gender, ethnicity, social class, or disability among others). Bonnie Stewart (2016) notes: 'On networked platforms such as Twitter, users can lurk without making themselves visible but cannot connect with others without signalling some form of identifiable presence. Yet visibility has drawbacks: as networked platforms are increasingly recognised as sites of rampant misogyny, racism, and harassment'. Visibility also means the tracking, collection and use of participation as data.

Zeynep Tufekci writes about how social media often puts us into a vulnerable position as our engagement with networks becomes monetised through immense processes of data collection and analysis. We want to be seen and to see others in online networks without knowing, or ignoring, the fact that this very basic human desire is in fact tapped into by profit-oriented companies or organizations to make strategic decisions targeted towards gaining our attention, time, and other valuable resources. Critical approaches to education acknowledge that the curation of knowledge (for example, contents of a history textbook), the way in which it is organized and presented, is political; it serves the interests of a particular group of people at a particular point of time in history. The same holds true for the makings of the digital world, as can be seen in a recent interview by Mike Allen (2017) with Sean Parker, the founding president of Facebook:

> When Facebook was getting going, I had these people who would come up to me and they would say, 'I'm not on social media.' And I would say, 'OK. You know, you will be.' And then they would say, 'No, no, no. I value my real-life interactions. I value the moment. I value presence. I value intimacy.' And I would say, ... 'We'll get you eventually.' I don't

know if I really understood the consequences of what I was saying, because [of] the unintended consequences of a network when it grows to a billion or 2 billion people... it literally changes your relationship with society, with each other.

This is a striking comment because it reflects the (perceived) power held by the tech giants and the uncertainty of our future with these technologies, let alone the future of open scholarship. Power might also be held by institutions, organisations, governments and non-human agents, all of which might shape our actions directly or indirectly in open and networked platforms

A critical attitude is needed in any network setting to challenge pre-defined or imposed relationships on users (i.e. how the design architecture wants us to behave) and to reflect on our own assumptions and biases:

- Whose voice can be heard? Whose voice is missing? Who decides that?

- How does the network design impact our connection with others? The way we see them and the way we are seen?

- What is the labour involved here? Whose time and resources are used, and at what cost?

- What is my responsibility?

These are just some of the questions we might ask to better understand and reflect on open and networked scholarship. As Rheingold (2013) says, '[t]he future of digital culture — yours, mine, and ours — depends on how well we learn to use the media that have infiltrated, amplified, distracted, enriched, and complicated our lives and how well we respond to it.' In other words, it depends on how well we claim our citizenship in its complex and wondrous spaces.

References

Allen, M. (2017). 'Sean Parker unloads on Facebook: "God only knows what it's doing to our children's brains"' [Interview], https://www.axios.com/sean-parker-unloads-on-facebook-god-only-knows-what-its-doing-to-our-childrens-brains-1513306792-f855e7b4-4e99-4d60-8d51-2775559c2671.html

Bali, M. (2017). 'No me without us: Reflections after the UNIR #SelfOER #OpenTuesday webinar', *Reflecting Allowed*, https://blog.mahabali. me/whyopen/no-me-without-us-reflections-after-the-unir-selfoer-opentuesday-webinar/

Boyd, D. (2010). 'Social network sites as networked publics: Affordances, dynamics, and implications', in Z. Papacharissi (ed.), *Networked Self: Identity, Community, and Culture on Social Network Sites*, New York: Routledge, pp. 39–58.

Campbell, G. (2015). 'Thought vectors in concept space'. Plenary talk at the meeting of the 8th Annual Emerging Technologies for Online Learning International Symposium, Dallas, TX, http://olc.onlinelearningconsortium. org/conference/2015/et4online/thought-vectors-concept-space

Cronin, C. (2017). 'Openness and praxis: Exploring the use of Open Educational Practices in Higher Education', *The International Review of Research in Open and Distributed Learning*, 18:5, http://www.irrodl.org/index.php/irrodl/ article/view/3096/4301

Rheingold, H. (2010). 'Attention, and other 21st-century social media literacies', *EDUCAUSE Review*, 45:5, http://er.educause.edu/articles/2010/10/attention-and-other-21stcentury-socialmedia-literacies

Rheingold, H. (2012). *Netsmart*, Cambridge, MA: The MIT Press.

Stewart, B. (2016). 'Collapsed publics: Orality, literacy, and vulnerability in academic Twitter', *Journal of Applied Social Theory*, 1:1, pp. 61–86.

Veletsianos, G. and Kimmons, R. (2012). 'Networked participatory scholarship: Emergent techno-cultural pressures toward open and digital scholarship in online networks.' *Computers & Education*, 58:2, pp. 766–74.

White, D. S., and Le Cornu, A. (2011). 'Visitors and Residents. A new typology for online engagement', *First Monday*, 16:9, http://firstmonday.org/article/ view/3171/3049

PART THREE
TEACHING AND LEARNING

7. Exploring the Use of Social Media in the Higher Education Classroom

#*Beginner #Facebook #Instagram #LinkedIn #Pinterest*

Alex Avramenko and Chrissi Nerantzi

Introduction

Social media has been actively penetrating all aspects of modern life, including learning, and its influence over HE classroom activities is no exception. Today's learners in the United Kingdom are well armed with a range of the latest gadgets: smartphones, tablets, smart watches, health bracelets — to name but a few.

HE students carry these gadgets around with them, bring them into the classroom, and use them regularly throughout their sessions. Often smart gadgets are utilised by academics and other professionals who teach or support learning in higher education. Such activities may include searching for resources, creating opportunities for interaction, group work, projects and participation in large and small group sessions. This book includes examples of smart devices and social media being used effectively for such purposes. Further, growing research into the use of digital technologies suggests that there are a plethora of benefits for learners and academics (Beetham, 2018) since digital technologies, based on an informed pedagogical rationale, have the potential to enhance and transform learning in and outside the classroom to create new and stimulating learning experiences.

https://doi.org/10.11647/OBP.0162.07

In this chapter, the focus is on reviewing students' perceptions and behavioural patterns with respect to their use of smartphones during lectures and tutorials. We share some reflective guidance for HE practitioners to suggest that the use of smartphones by students can be a learning opportunity and contribute to students' learning journeys.

Smartphones and Classroom Dynamics

The array of amazing technology has an impact on students' behaviour and preferences beyond its immediate benefits (Duvalet et al., 2017). All these gadgets have in common a built-in sophisticated notification system, aiming to keep the gadget's owner abreast of any changes and updates. These notifications however, intentionally or not, have been facilitating certain behavioural modifications to their owners' lifestyle associated with 'connected' presence (Licoppe and Smoreda, 2005). Using another explanatory angle — classical conditioning — as a frame of reference (Melton, 2014), being unremittingly attentive to one's own smartphone is, de facto, the result of continuous reinforcement provided by notifications. In other words, when a notification arrives, the smartphone's owner seems to check up on its content almost mechanically, creating an intermittent but permanent distraction of attention. Despite the fact that notifications can be switched off, many smart device users seem to live in a state of being constantly connected or switched on.

Another angle to consider when reflecting on the use of smart gadgets and social media is social influence (Aronson et al., 2013), that is a self-alteration of behaviour governed by imaginary approval or disapproval of our physical surroundings — classmates in our case. Being able to glance at our own smartphone almost without limitations is an established social norm and it is being reinforced incessantly by peers and technology (Derks et al., 2015). One more influence that reinforces this intricate behavioural pattern is the myth of multitasking, especially among the so-called millennial generation. There is no definitive scientific verdict about it.

A study of the effects of multitasking in the classroom found the 'students performing multiple tasks performed significantly poorer on immediate measures of memory for the to-be-learned content'

(Hembrooke and Gay, 2003). While it is acknowledged that multitasking can rewire the brain, enabling a learner to deal with multiple tasks more rapidly (National Chamber Foundation, 2012), there is a trade-off — a capacity for thinking deeply and creatively suffers as a result. Hence, the multitaskers are 'more likely to rely on conventional ideas and solutions rather than challenging them with original lines of thought' (Carr, 2011).

Can this rather distracting phenomenon, in the context of learning and attention span, be reduced or even stopped, or do we have to learn to live with it and try to normalise the use of smart devices in the classroom, even if not used for learning? Is asking students to switch them off an option when we want them switched on to learning?

Here we aim to elicit new insights into students' use of social media, which is often perceived by academics as a distraction from classroom activities, and to articulate specific teaching strategies that have the potential to maximise students' engagement and participation while at the same time minimising, where possible, the distracting use of smart devices and browsing behaviour in the HE classroom.

Research Settings

A small-scale study was conducted at a UK HE institution, focussed within a Business School, with the following objectives: to identify the characteristics of the current use of smartphones in the classroom and propose interventions to mitigate the perceived distracting effect of random browsing of social media by students in these settings.

Gadamerian hermeneutics (Gadamer, 2004) was used to gain rich insights into the usage of smart devices during classroom learning. Thirteen students from several undergraduate Business and Management programmes, predominantly in the final year of study, volunteered to participate in this study through in-depth interviews using a convenience sampling method.

The interviews were followed by a questionnaire to obtain views of a larger student audience for the purpose of validating interview findings. The questionnaire was introduced via Blackboard to the group of thirty third-year students. It consisted of fifteen statements using the Likert scale with the choices: Never, Rarely, Sometimes, Quite Often, Almost Always.

The questionnaire was available to a mixed class of 29 Stage 3 students of different schools and programmes. Due to the timescale restrictions on this study it was open to responses for two weeks and had a 93% of response rate.

The respondents quotes used in this study have been anonymised and given a reference e.g. R1, R2, etc.

Results and Discussion

A number of findings emerged from the analysis of interviews based on the identified uses of smartphones during classroom activities, which are grouped here into the following themes that emerged during the interviewing stage: continuous connectedness, entertainment, educational drift and catch of advertisement. The findings from the interviews and questionnaire are brought together and discussed in themes.

Continuous Connectedness

One observation common to all the interviews is that students want to be constantly connected to their chosen cyberspaces. Students' connections to their virtual social surroundings are often closely monitored. One of the respondents summarises this connection as follows:

> the use of social media through mobile devices is almost a mild addiction [...] many students (including myself) would feel like something is missing if they did not have their phone on their person for an entire day. (R11)

This trend is also receiving prominence in research literature. According to Rosen (2017), a typical student actively engages in six types of social media several times a day due to the fear of missing out and/or the constant temptation of keeping up with others in their social networks. The questionnaire's results demonstrate that 100% of students indicated that they have been using their smartphones during classes for non-educational purposes with varying degrees of regularity: sometimes — 15%; quite often — 50%; almost always — 35%; with almost all respondents (85%) using Facebook during classes. It is interesting to note that only 11% of respondents indicated that using smartphones during classes is unacceptable, whereas 61.5% of respondents believe that using smartphones in the classroom is a new reality of the contemporary learning environment and hence, where educators fail to incorporate smartphones for educational use, they would be used for other purposes.

The influence of Facebook specifically extends beyond being a mere distraction in the classroom. Since group space within Blackboard's discussion forum, one of the dominant learning management systems in HE institutions, is not popular due to its limited functionality, the majority of participating students prefer to form a group file exchange and communication environment in Facebook.

> Facebook is a useful tool for group work however it was rare for me to make use of this during a lecture. My use of social media during lectures has definitely more to do with boredom or communicating with my friends, both in the lecture and outside the university. (R3)

Unlike social media, most learning management systems place greater emphasis on a formal curriculum than on the 'networking' element of social media (Cho and Cho, 2014). Therefore Facebook has filled this gap. Social media allows students to collaborate informally, and instrumental support from Facebook friends is found to have a positive impact on the learning process (Khan et al., 2014). 84% of respondents indicated that they prefer to use Facebook for group-work activities, and that raises questions about the effectiveness of learning management systems and investment in them by HE institutions.

Entertainment

Another common aspect of social media that was indicated by all participants is the immediate and often entertaining content available online: games, music, video and sharing of amusing textual and multimedia content.

> social media was used relatively often as a form of entertainment between my friendship group within lectures and content was shared between us [...] because there is plenty of interesting stuff there... (R12)

While the students do not commonly use social media for this purpose in tutorials or seminars because of *'respect for the tutor'* (R1), they might certainly do so in lectures, especially in large classes, as a way of dealing with boredom. Responding to the perceived monotony of lectures, students tend to improvise a short break to re-energise their focus on the lecture's content. This self-administered brief pause in a form of 'disconnect from class' or 'technological break' (Aagaard, 2015) is typically filled with surfing the web or checking on social media news or shared gags.

> I felt it was totally unacceptable to use a phone unless an emergency or for work in the context of a tutorial. I think there is a more personal connection in this setting than in a lecture and it would therefore be rude not to pay attention to the tutor. The underlying reason for this may be to do with morals instilled in me by my parents. Use of a mobile phone was always discouraged at the dinner table or in other more formal settings such as family/ friends visiting. (R4)

This view is supported by the majority of respondents, 69% do not mind using smartphones for entertainment purposes even during hour-long lectures as long as the lecture is deemed to be boring. This distribution of responses raises a number of questions, some rather controversial, regarding the need to make the delivery of the educational material as engaging as possible for all students. Is there a need for *'edutainment'* or for another type of radical change in higher education? What constitutes an engaging lecture in nursing, engineering, mathematics and other technical sciences? And there is a more enduring question concerning the essence of large-group teaching: are large groups intended to communicate content, or to be a learning opportunity of a new kind?

Educational Drift

The use of rapid-response applications to achieve more effective classroom engagement is becoming more common (Wang, 2015). These apps, such as Mentimeter or Socrative, enable tutors to connect with students to support their learning process, helping them to self-assess within the scope of prearranged activities and/or on-the-fly questions, and allowing tutors to gain an immediate insight into students' understanding of subject matter. They also encourage students to find out more about the information on slides provided in the apps.

 The respondents seem to appreciate the use of response applications but are also mindful of their distracting potential:

I think that [it would be good to use] a system where everyone in the lecture has their device assigned to their name and the system can tell if an individual has not responded to a question (this may already exist in the apps mentioned as I am not familiar with them). (R2)

I think that allowing or encouraging fellow students to use social media would help alleviate the desire to a use smartphone in lectures and thus remove the 'mental itch' of not using the device for the duration of a lecture. (R11)

The above excerpts show students' awareness of the potentially distracting power of smart devices when used for learning and teaching in the classroom. However, around 85% of the questionnaire's respondents are in favour of using in-class response applications for the purpose of active participation in classroom activities.

Catch of Advertisement

Despite a general trend in which advertisements on web resources and social media are ignored by users, marketing campaigns have been evolving to become more sophisticated, entertaining, and informative. Students are therefore increasingly finding themselves in the situation of being carried away by the interest of the moment, triggered by clever advertisements, particularly on the Pinterest platform.

When I go on Pinterest I almost always follow prompts and pop-ups as they are so creative and I'm getting a lot of ideas for my work [as a marketeer]. (R10)

Sometimes I would have to watch a snippet in order to get to the content I had chosen to watch and even forgot my original purpose for browsing. (R6)

According to the respondents, Pinterest is an effective platform in capturing their attention because it sends visual information (compilations of examples) to the registered users matching their interests. It sends these compilations every day, typically in two ways: as notifications to smartphones and as emails with a focused summary centred on users' interests. As a result, during the interview participants agreed that Pinterest is more interesting and effective in keeping attention of its users compared with Facebook, labelling it as 'captivating but addictive' (R1).

Recommendations (for HE Practitioners)

The authors have used a number of teaching interventions for embedding smartphones into teaching and learning processes with the aim of counteracting perceived boredom in large-group sessions. These include, but are not limited to: mood-setting starters; conversational dialogues; using multimedia material; changing the routine of the session regularly; allowing for students' questions and feedback using technology; and alternative no- or low-tech strategies to engage students in a variety of ways. These interventions require the attentive participation of students in classroom activities to varying degrees of success, depending on stimuli that would fuel different aspects of students' interest in learning as well as their curiosity and imagination. The use of rapid response systems, such as Mentimeter and Socrative, appears to be one of the most effective interventions in utilising for educational purposes the urge many students have to use their smartphones in the classroom. This suggestion is based on a personal observation that students normally respond to an invitation to use their smart devices for classroom activities quite enthusiastically.

Typically, such an activity can be organised in three steps. Initially, students are invited to use Mentimeter or Socrative to register their views in a tailor-made mini-quiz on a particular subject discussed in the lecture or tutorial. After the quiz, a sequence of browsing tasks aimed to encourage the discovery of specific resources (e.g. published articles or proven working solutions) can be introduced to give students an opportunity to explore the concept- or subject-related resources. Lastly, the lecturer can point out to students how the quiz and subsequent browsing tasks relate to a specific threshold or advanced concept within the lecture or tutorial. This allows students' attention to return gradually to the main subject of the session.

Such an approach offers a variety of things for the student to focus on, thus maintaining their attention and helps to develop their research skills. In practice, it was noticed that at the end of browsing tasks students often do a quick check of their social connections anyway, but this habit seems to be fading with time. Overall, embedding smartphones in the class activities helps to change the perception of smartphone use as forbidden (by tutors) or as an inappropriate activity. Similarly,

Wang (2015) has found that introducing new learning technology in the classroom results in a spike of enthusiasm from the students, and although this fades over time the students remain fairly engaged and motivated. The findings of this study also indicate that 81.4% of respondents would appreciate an opportunity to use in-class response applications as a form of active participation in classroom activities.

Conclusions

This review of the use of smartphones by higher-education students has identified certain challenges academics have been facing recently. It was established within the scope of this small-scale study that all respondents have used and continue to use smartphones during classes to access social media platforms (mainly Facebook and Twitter), with more than 60% of questionnaire respondents believing that this is a new reality in higher education and their tutors should find ways of using it.

It would appear that despite the omnipresent use of smartphones to access social media platforms in the classroom, certain approaches for regaining students' attention may prove to be sufficiently effective. A proven practical example, supported by 85% of student responses, is the use of rapid-response applications, such as Mentimeter or Socrative, to invigorate the academic involvement of students in classroom activities by appealing to their habit of using smartphones.

While the choice of student engagement strategies is fairly broad, it rests on a few assumptions to be considered in further studies. First, academics should try to recognise the presence of smartphones in the classroom as a learning opportunity and attempt to integrate them into the teaching process. Second, a large number of student comments that express the desire to have interesting sessions indicates the challenges higher education faces: none of the participating students were able to specifically articulate the key characteristics of an interesting lecture. What might these be? Is it the perceived appeal of the subject material, or its delivery, or another combination of yet-to-be-rationalised factors?

References

Aagaard, J. (2015). 'Drawn to distraction: A qualitative study of off-task use of educational technology', *Computers & Education*, 87, pp. 90–97, https://doi.org/10.1016/j.compedu.2015.03.010

Aronson, E., Wilson, T. D. and Akert, R. M. (2013). *Social Psychology*, Harlow: Pearson.

Carr, N. (2011). *The Shallows: What the Internet Is Doing to Our Brains*, New York: Norton & Co.

Beetham, H. (2014). 'Students' experiences and expectations of the digital environment', https://www.jisc.ac.uk/blog/students-experiences-and-expectations-of-the-digital-environment-23-jun-2014

Cho, J. Y., and Cho, M. (2014). 'Student perceptions and performance in online and offline collaboration in an interior design studio', *International Journal of Technology and Design Education*, 24:4, pp. 473–91.

Derks, D., Duin, D., Tims, M. and Bakker, A. B. (2015). 'Smartphone use and work-home interference: The moderating role of social norms and employee work engagement', *Journal of Occupational & Organizational Psychology*, 88:1, pp. 155–77, https://doi.org/10.1111/joop.12083

Duval, E., Sharples M. and Sutherland, R. (2017). *Technology Enhanced Learning*, New York: Springer.

Gadamer, H. G. (2004). *Truth and Method*. 2nd edn, London: Sheed and Ward Stagbooks.

Hembrooke, H. and Gay, G. (2003). 'The laptop and the lecture: The effects of multitasking in learning environments', *Journal of Computing in Higher Education*, 15:1, pp. 46–64, https://doi.org/10.1007/BF02940852

Khan, M. L., Wohn, D. Y. W. and Ellison, N. B. (2014). 'Actual friends matter: An internet skills perspective on teens' informal academic collaboration on Facebook', *Computers & Education*, 79, pp. 138–47.

Licoppe, C. and Smoreda, Z. (2005). 'Are social networks technologically embedded?: How networks are changing today with changes in communication technology', *Social Networks*, 27:4, pp. 317–35.

Melton, A. W. (2014). *Categories of Human Learning*, New York: Academic Press.

National Chamber Foundation (2012). 'The millennial generation: Research review', https://www.uschamberfoundation.org/sites/default/files/article/foundation/MillennialGeneration.pdf

Rosen, L. D. (2017). 'The distracted student mind — enhancing its focus and attention', *Phi Delta Kappan*, 99:2, pp. 8–14, https://doi.org/10.1177/0031721717734183

Wang, A. I. (2015). 'The wear out effect of a game-based student response system', *Computers & Education*, 82, pp. 217–27.

8. The Use of Social Media Tools and Their Application to Creative Students

#Beginner #Snapchat #Facebook #Instagram #Pinterest #LCCBad

Serena Gossain

Introduction

In this chapter I shall explore the use of social media to support and increase student knowledge on a BA (Hons) Advertising course. The following analysis will explore whether students were more engaged with the visual learning because they also took part in the construction of that learning using social media apps. The study I will be discussing took place at the London College of Communication (part of University of Arts London), with the kind cooperation of the Programme team headed by Dr Paul Caplan and Steve Spence. It is a critical study into student engagement and learning, using social media to support and increase student knowledge of design and advertising, particularly for visual learning and understanding.

On this BA programme, we teach the concepts and practice of advertising, to students mainly of the so-called millennial generation (which is widely agreed to be the people born between 1981 and 2000). Some of the students are from an era that has never known life without

https://doi.org/10.11647/OBP.0162.08

the Internet, apps, smartphones and all of their many benefits and distractions! Their generation are used to communicating far more widely and socially through their screens, via social media, Snapchat, Facebook, Instagram, YouTube and Twitter. They are very aware of their online presence and curate their own digital identity based on what they post, their preferences, likes and follows. With this in mind, the programme team decided to embed some of these social media platforms into their teaching to see if it helped with engagement, relevancy and even preference for their learning experience. As these tools were already familiar to the students, we were curious to see if they could adopt the new formats quickly and put them to work immediately.

This chapter will therefore focus on a new approach to teaching over one term, which incorporated social media tools, to determine whether their use enhanced the learning experience for students and assisted in their engagement with the subject of advertising. By focusing on the newly enrolled first-year BA(Hons) Advertising students at LCC, we could compare their learning and engagement with that of previous cohorts. This study was carried out from September 2017 until December 2017 at LCC and we introduced our own visual boards of Pinterest and Instagram pages. These two platforms provided the best visualisation and both are very familiar to, and popular with, many of our current students.

Background to the Course

As this is an advertising course, knowledge is gained through observing, engaging, doing, reviewing and reiterating (though not always in this order!) Creative work can be chaotic at times, but advertising provides a framework for this sort of expression as it is channelled and framed by a strategic business problem that needs solving. It is not art for arts' sake (unless, of course, art is the product that needs selling). Rather, advertising is all about selling. If the advertising does not help to sell or somehow promote the brand in a positive light, then it simply is not working. The challenge is to create meaningful advertising that surprises and engages the consumer, whilst meeting the specific objectives of the client's brief. The student has to master many strategic and creative skills in order to be successful on the course and then to secure a job within this competitive industry. The students need to build their knowledge rapidly, to be able to learn all about the various aspects and nuances of advertising so that they have enough time to develop a portfolio of work to take to job interviews once they have graduated.

Exploring the Related Learning Theories

The BA programme has been shaped and influenced by different theories of learning. A central learning theory that effects the design and curriculum on this course is the work of the Russian psychologist, Lev Vygotsky (1896–1934) who created the foundations of Constructivist learning. Vygotsky's theory asserts three major themes regarding: social interaction; the more knowledgeable other; and the zone of proximal development.

In Vygotsky's time, many schools traditionally held a *transmissionist* or *instructionist* model in which a teacher or lecturer 'transmitted' information to students. In contrast, Vygotsky's theory promoted learning contexts in which students played an active part in learning. The roles of teacher and student therefore shifted, as a teacher collaborated with his or her students in order to help facilitate their construction of meaning, and learning could therefore become a reciprocal experience. Constructivism, then, is the theory that learners construct their own meaning through their own social and interactive experiences.

The Cognitive learning approach is one based on students being involved in learning through memory, insights and problem solving. This theory was developed from Gestalt psychology, which held that students become more intelligent through information processing and memory. Creating memories through their experience of these key attributes of successful advertising, does play a large role on the Advertising course. Through the memory recall of past advertising campaigns (through the Pinterest page for example), students are provided with useful frameworks and support in their own creative development.

The main theories that this course employs are Constructivist theory and Constructive alignment. Fry, Ketteridge and Marshall (2010) noted that the idea of Constructivism is based on *'continuous building and amending of structures in the mind that 'hold' knowledge.'* This is far more student-centred and allows students to construct their own learning — building on their own knowledge and reconstructing it to augment their own understanding. The Constructivist approach is also known as 'scaffolding', allowing us to build on a student's existing knowledge by supporting them as they increase their understanding and make their own connections.

In the context of the BA Advertising course, the Cognitive and Constructivist approaches are being employed through the use of Instagram, as the students continuously update and review their Instagram feeds. One could also state that by actively encouraging students to look at more advertising via the Pinterest page, *students are potentially learning more by seeing more.* And they may learn at a faster rate. Students are encouraged to discuss what they have seen and add their own examples, thereby building their own personalised learning structure.

Within teaching and learning theory, it is well known that a wide range of different learning experiences should be utilised to capture more student engagement. Novotney (2010) discussed how to engage with the typical undergraduate learner: 'New research suggests that offering variety may be the best way to engage today's undergraduates.'

Some of our students may be kinaesthetic learners, who learn by doing, while others may be auditory or visual learners. Students may utilise a combination of their senses to take in information, but each will have a preference for how they learn. In order to help our students learn, we need to include as many of these preferences as possible. With the inclusion of social media platforms, we have encouraged students to engage with their learning from a familiar and comfortable space that they would typically inhabit daily in their personal lives. As a programme team we still have the traditional lectures and workshops, but the emphasis is always on interaction and encouraging students to join in with debates and demonstrate their learning through 'crits,' in which students present their work for everyone to see and accept feedback from their tutors and peers. The whole process prepares the student for an industry in which they will have to persuade senior creative teams, and ultimately the clients, to buy into their advertising ideas. Therefore, the practice of showing and telling is very common in most of the units on the Advertising course. Social media gives students another voice for this showing and telling, and it can also help them to organise their thoughts.

Connectivist theory (Siemens 2005) also helps us to understand the digital forms of communication within the course. It describes a process of acquiring knowledge that is rooted in digital connections and social media. Greenhow and Lewin (2016) argue that being more knowledgeable can consist of: the ability to nurture, maintain, and traverse network connections; the ability to access and use specialized information sources just-in-time; and the 'capacity to know more' rather than the individual's ability to construct meaning from prior knowledge, or 'what is currently known' (Siemens 2005).

The Study

At the beginning of the term the students were asked to create new Instagram accounts for their university work. These had to be completely separate from their personal ones. They were able to follow, respond and react to posts by tutors on the official LCC Bad Instagram page (See Fig. 8.1). Separately, within their own university Instagram accounts, the students were able to keep a visual record of their own work. They were required to use their accounts as digital sketchbooks, including captions as part of their reflective writing. As part of their summative assessments, the students had to use Instagram to showcase their thinking and creative work over the ten weeks of the course, whilst using the course hashtag to link their work back to the official page.

The work and the thought processes were then photographed and uploaded onto the site and the students used the hashtag #LCCBad so that their page would be linked to the official programme Instagram page. Currently, this is still live and the Instagram feed has 46 followers and 23 posts. All of our current Advertising students have their own university Instagram accounts, so there are approximately 300 users in total. Along with capturing their initial sketches, students also wrote captions as part of a reflective piece of work — therefore replacing their assessed short reflective essays with 10 to 12 entries of 25 words each. As formal essay writing is already a part of other units in the course, within the creative units the writing is kept to a minimum with a simple written reflection. This type of reflective writing is something that

Fig. 8.1 Serena Gossain, Screenshot of LCC Bad Instagram page (2018), CC BY 4.0

students often struggle with (since they have to switch from a more academic style of writing), but by including the reflective written work on Instagram, students were able to do this far more naturally, referring to their creative work there and then, as the weeks unfolded. This was also a more effective way for them to manage and speed up their work, and keep it organised in a weekly structure.

At the same time a Pinterest board (Fig. 8.2) was created and a large collection of ads were 'pinned' to the board for students to look at and comment on. At first it was set for private viewing only, but this proved difficult for students to view easily (because some students had not responded to the emailed invitation to follow the private board) so it was switched to public view. This allowed students (and members of the public) to view casually, without becoming followers.

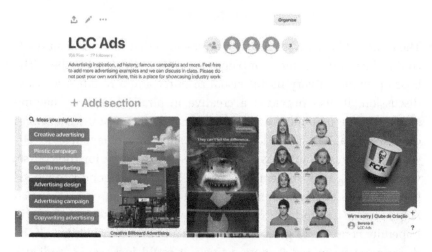

Fig. 8.2 Serena Gossain, Screenshot of LCC Ads Pinterest board (2018), CC BY 4.0

The online visual board was continuously populated over the term, with many advertising campaigns — mainly print ads — which were either award-winning campaigns, political ads or interesting or inspirational visually or through the copy. Students could go to the board without 'following' it and look at the many examples easily. They were also invited by email to become contributors to the board and therefore to become active followers. The board is still active and public, although you cannot contribute to it unless you are personally invited by email. At the time of writing the board has 26 followers and 168 posts; the board is also viewed by many other students who, for whatever reason, have not chosen to become followers (perhaps because they did not want to log in to the site).

The Results

After one complete term from September to December 2017, the newly introduced Pinterest and Instagram platforms were reflected upon. Was the introduction a success, what difficulties did we face and what could we improve upon to take us forward?

Pinterest

The Pinterest board was created with the idea that tutors and students could share advertising campaign examples with each other. The board provided a very useful visual resource and a resource for class discussion. It also provided a creative inspiration bank — helping students to become more aware of creative thinking, of the challenges of communicating a clear idea in an interesting way, of layout styles etc.

The Pinterest board has become a useful resource for the course; when working with students on creative briefs it is a good knowledge bank of ideas and styles that tutors and students can refer to, which help to frame the student's own creative work. The Pinterest board will hopefully continue to grow thanks to the addition of new 'pins'; if the department promoted it more actively it could increase its audience still further. Tutors could also utilise it more and populate the board with more examples, and students from all years could more actively contribute to the board too.

It has been evident that Pinterest has improved and enhanced students' learning, especially for those in their first year, enabling them rapidly to become more fluent in visual and verbal approaches to advertising. As well as providing a bank of ideas for inspiration, it allows students to see whether an idea can be taken further or be enhanced with a unique and challenging approach. It has definitely helped them to grasp the basics of visual communication and effective formulas of advertising.

This use of Pinterest follows a Constructivist approach, enabling students to build their own knowledge by actively taking part, applying what they have seen to actual practice. Even those who have chosen to remain passive viewers are still learning from the Cognitive aspects of observation and memory.

Instagram

The adoption of Instagram to record student sketchbooks has been very interesting to observe. Students on most of the creative modules have physical sketchbooks/layout pads that they use to capture their ideas for ads, mind maps, and scamps (sketches of ads).

The use of Instagram had a number of benefits. It became an online 'sketchbook' of student work as part of their formal assessment, a practice that was eventually adopted throughout all the year groups. The students could add to their profile and reflect on their work in a digital format, allowing them to include video, links and their own photos of their work, including their physical sketchbooks/layout pads. This followed both a Constructivist and a Connectivist model of learning. Instagram was also used to circulate news material — for example, information about special events and guest lectures — and it acted as a showcase for excellent student work. In this way, it provided a platform for the course to market itself to the wider world.

The Instagram platform also allowed students the opportunity to include other creative work — finished ads, website links, videos, and animations. In essence this experience has been helpful to ensure students are organising their work and therefore their process, which is helpful preparation for building their final portfolios in the second and third year.

Connectivist theory has also been adopted through the use of Instagram, as students are able to share, review and develop their own work in progress as the weeks go by. Siemens (2004) stated that the starting point of Connectivism is the individual. Personal knowledge is comprised of a network, which feeds into organizations and institutions, which in turn feed back into the network, and then continue to provide learning to the individual. This cycle of knowledge development (personal to network to organization) allows learners to remain current in their field through the connections they have formed. Connectivism therefore provides insights into learning skills and tasks for learners to flourish in a digital era.

Nowadays, most portfolios are created on a digital platform so this study has been a useful exercise in learning how to present and share work within a popular and familiar social media platform. Students appear to be very engaged with the platforms that have been introduced and have responded well to using Instagram as a vital part of their final assessments.

Conclusion

The addition of the two social media platforms to the Advertising course has overall been beneficial and they have been adopted quite naturally.

The introduction of Instagram was a completely natural evolution by the Programme team, given the digital nature of the advertising industry. The students have been, and are currently, engaging very well with it and it is a helpful tool to organise their work and show the stories behind the final projects they create. There are some areas in which students could be a little more active — perhaps in commenting on the official LCC Bad Instagram posts or 'liking' them. As far as the tutors are concerned, more frequent and varied posts by the students would be a good way to keep the feed fresh and up to date. The use of Instagram as part of the assessment process has also been very successful — mainly as the students did not have a choice here to use anything else! Since it was mandatory, students used Instagram to organise their work well and learned how to communicate ideas clearly from a familiar platform.

The introduction of a specific advertising Pinterest board has been helpful for giving the students ideas and as a useful backdrop for discussion or data points. It will continue to grow as a visual knowledge bank. In future, students need to be encouraged to add their own contributions and also to follow the board. Tutors should also add more examples to the board so that a wider variety of work is shown. From the experience gained last term, it seems that more would be made of the Pinterest board if students are required to follow it, and to contribute at least a few pins.

In comparison to previous first years who did not use these platforms as part of their studies, the platforms have definitely had an impact on this first-year group, enhancing their rapidly growing knowledge of, and curiosity about the world of advertising. The Pinterest board acts as a guide for good practice and it has been noted by the tutors that subsequent first-year-student output has become fairly sophisticated, relatively quickly, as a result.

Given that students use social media in their social lives and as part of their 'down time' there is some bridging that needs to be addressed to bring these platforms to the fore in an educational environment. Greenhow and Lewin (2016) summarised this in their study of formal and informal learning through the integration of social media:

Others argue that only a small proportion of young people are actually using social media in sophisticated ways that educators might value (Eynon and Malmberg, 2011). Complicating this tension, there is a lack of current models that theorize social media as a space for informal learning. There is also considerable debate about the benefits and challenges of appropriating technologies (e.g., social media) in everyday use for learning and little exploration of the connections between formal, non-formal, and informal learning such technologies might facilitate.

However, one could argue that social media could provide a more rounded and holistic approach to our students' learning experience, if its capabilities are better understood and if we are prepared to make more responsive changes to our courses.

> Technology has the potential to disrupt the boundaries between sites where learning takes place. It can empower learners through greater agency, opportunities to participate in networked communities and access to a wide range of resources to support knowledge building and collaboration. There seems little doubt that engagement with digital cultures offers potential for self-directed or spontaneous learning opportunities of varying degrees. (Greenhow and Lewin, 2016)

On final reflection, the ways in which we can continuously review and respond to the ways in which students are choosing to learn is probably one of the biggest things we have learned from this study. Having experienced how students adopted the new platforms, some valuable insights and learning have been gained. Traditional one-way instructional teaching is not and never will be a part of a creative education, so the adoption of social media platforms has definitely found a place as it helps to address and support many of the learning objectives we aim to fulfil as tutors. As the advertising industry has evolved over the last twenty years to use various digital platforms alongside traditional media, it is also imperative that the course remains completely connected and related to this. When social media platforms in the future morph into another communication format (as they definitely will!) it is critical that the course should reflect the industry symbiotically while also actively engaging with it. There is certainly much more to do, but this has been a really interesting start, with some positive results.

References

Biggs J. and Tang C. (2007). *Teaching for Quality Learning at University*, 3rd edn. Maidenhead: Open University Press.

Eynon R. and Malmberg L.-E. (2011). 'A typology of young people's Internet use: Implications for education', *Computers and Education*, 56:3, pp. 585–95, https://www.academia.edu/1035111/A_typology_of_young_peoples_Internet_use_implications_for_education

Fry H., Ketteridge S., and Marshall S. (2009). *A Handbook for Teaching and Learning in Higher Education, Enhancing Academic Practice*, 3rd edn. London and New York: Routledge.

Greenhow C. and Lewin C. (2016). 'Social media and education: Reconceptualizing the boundaries of formal and informal learning', *Learning, Media and Technology*, 41:1, pp. 6–30, https://doi.org/10.1080/17439884.2015.1064954

Kropf D. C. (2013). 'Connectivism: 21st century's new learning theory', http://www.eurodl.org/materials/contrib/2013/Kropf.pdf

Novotney A. (2010). 'Engaging the millennial learner. New research suggests that offering variety may be the best way to engage today's undergraduates', https://www.apa.org/monitor/2010/03/undergraduates.aspx

McFadzean, E. (2001). 'Supporting virtual learning groups Part 1: A pedagogical perspective', *Team Performance Management: An International Journal*, 7:3/4, pp. 53–62, https://doi.org/10.1108/13527590110395658

Ramsden P. (2003). *Learning To Teach in Higher Education*, London and New York: Routledge.

Siemens G. (2004). 'Connectivism: A learning theory for the digital age', http://www.itdl.org/journal/jan_05/article01.htm

Vygotsky, L. S. (1980). *Mind in Society: The Development of Higher Psychological Processes*, Cambridge, MA: Harvard University Press.

9. Role of Social Media in Learning:
Benefits and Drawbacks — How Social Presence Theory Explains Conflicting Findings

#Intermediate #Facebook

Paul Kawachi

Introduction

Social media can play an important role in education. Its role in creating trust within a group is of particular importance. The face-to-face element in online education may be achieved physically in a classroom, or it can involve a social media platform which features a clear photograph of the student's face. One purpose for the photo is to establish trust among the participants — just as witnesses must appear physically inside a courtroom to take an oath and give evidence. In this sense, where there exists no photograph on a social media website of the participant, or where the face is unclear or hidden in an image, the formation of trust may be impeded. A photograph is usually trusted since it is presumed that the physical person attended the place to get the photograph taken (although photo technology has eroded this somewhat). Likewise, a person may physically present himself at a faraway courtroom and use telephone or video technology to transfer trust to the required courtroom remotely.

Social media provides the mechanics for conveying and constructing Social Presence. The shy introvert student can look through the

https://doi.org/10.11647/OBP.0162.09

webpages of other students, and then tentatively post their own personal information; this or that photograph, these 'likes' and those music favourites. Personal data can be posted gradually on a trial-and-error basis to explore how acceptable the data is to others (and immediately withdrawn if sensed to be outside the social norms of the group). In small safe steps, the introvert can thereby build up a socially-accepted online persona, through which she can interact with others online. In this way, the social media website can offer to the self-conscious outsider a mechanism towards becoming accepted by the community online. Once this has been achieved the group can move on together as a community and engage in collaborative learning tasks.

The Transactional Distance Model — a four-stage Kolb-like cycle — can serve as a practical scaffold onto which Social Presence Theory can be positioned. The resulting model can then be used to explain why some empirical studies show that Facebook is associated with better quality learning, while other studies show the opposite. It is useful to understand Transactional Distance and Social Presence here, and a brief introduction to each is covered in turn in the 'Methods' Section, before looking at how well they explain the findings on social media in the next 'Results' Section.

Social Presence through social media plays a supportive non-academic role in the early stages of the course to reduce anxiety and ease the student into the academic forum of ideas. However, one study has found the social aspects can be detrimental towards future learning (Cunningham, Corprew and Becker, 2009). Moreover, in an online environment using multimedia, Herrington and Oliver (1999) have found much less lower-order discussion and less social chat were correlated with more achieved learning. Additionally in an objective controlled study, Boling and Robinson (1999) found that there was some considerable trade-off (an inverse correlation) between distance students' satisfaction with social aspects of the course and the actual quality of learning achieved.

Tutors as well as the students themselves should be aware of the effectiveness of Social Presence and its implications for the initial stage of the learning process. Social Presence integrates the outsider into the target community, and there serves to reduce anxiety. In an extensive study, the number of forum postings, according to data from 3600 courses over 545 colleges reported by Young (2012), was 25 per term after self-introductions were required and posted, and only 9.5 per term where no self-introductions were made. A lack in student engagement has been attributed by Herrington, Reeves and Oliver (2006) to de-contextualisation. They argue that the student's own perspectives must be brought in and Social Presence should be established early on for the group to take on collaborative learning tasks later as a team. Thus, there is a meaningful role for Facebook and other social media in education, but this is limited to within only the initial early stage.

The correlation between social media and lower achieved learning is not yet determined as causative; in the ensuing confusion, some supporters of social media suggest that those who are weaker academically and who do not put in time and effort into studying tend to spend more of their free time on Facebook and other socialising.

Methods

There are now more than 23 expressions using 'presence' in the published literature related to online distance education. These include social presence (author), institutional presence, teacher or instructor presence (Bouras, 2009), teaching presence, student or learner presence (Bouras, 2009), co-presence (Garau et al., 2005), learning presence (Shea and Bidjerano, 2010), cognitive presence (Garrison et al., 2000), transactional presence (Shin, 2002), virtual presence, online presence, Internet presence, telepresence, web presence, inverse presence (Timmins and Lombard, 2005), physical presence (Lee et al., 2010), mediated presence (Sood and Nevejan, 2012), emotional presence (Campbell and Cleveland-Innes, 2005), witnessed presence (Sood and Nevejan, 2012), natural presence (Sood and Nevejan, 2012), self presence (Lee et al., 2010; Jin, 2011), and absent presence (Gergen, 2002; Rosen, 2004). Many authors do not distinguish among these and refer merely to presence (for example see Waterworth and Waterworth, 2006). More than half of these were explored and discussed previously by Kawachi (2011). Only six of these expressions are discovered to be essential to the learning process: institutional presence, learner presence, social presence, cognitive presence, transactional presence, and teaching presence, are all positioned in a specific sequence on a scaffold framework of the learning process, based on the transactional distance model.

The need for Social Presence is well recognised in online education — even in conventional face-to-face contiguous education, an online presence is considered by students to be an essential part of being an accepted group member. Facebook and other social media — including instant connectivity through Twitter, Instagram, Chat and other software applications — are currently used by almost all students, as well as by teachers and their institutions. The college administration may use Facebook to publicise itself to reach prospective future students, to announce events, awards, and even employment vacancies. Teachers may use it to rally students and to publicise lessons in a media that is familiar to their students, while students themselves may use it to share experiences with each other from both inside and outside the classroom. In all cases, social media acts to establish and foster connectivity in the education world. The problems begin to surface when the cooperative exchanges on social media fail to give way to academic collaboration.

The Transactional Distance Model developed in online distance education, and Social Presence Theory, offer a rational explanation for the conflicting data on the use of Facebook and other social media in education. Both of these are related to and underpinned by Otto Peters' Transactional Distance Theory, Peter Grogono's Conversation Theory and Diane Laurillard's Conversation Model, George Siemens' Connectivism Theory, and Social Presence Theory. Briefly, the Transactional Distance Model (involving imposed Structure S and educative Dialogue D — shown in Fig. 9.1 below) sets out four stages in a learning cycle — first, a cooperative sharing stage; second, a collaborative rationalisation; third, a collaborative disjunctive reasoning stage; all followed by a cooperative experiential testing-out stage.

In Stage 1, learning occurs in a group cooperatively, gathering and sharing information and fostering a learning community. Here synchronous-mode computer-mediated communications are best such as chat and conferencing. This Stage 1 can be characterised by self-introductions, brain-storming new ideas, divergent thinking, and helping each other with projecting content, especially in sharing personal experiences and past literature. The transactional distance initially is at a maximum (S- D-) with no imposed structure and no educative dialogue.

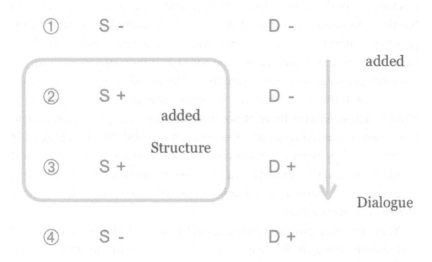

Fig. 9.1 Paul Kawachi, The four stages of the Transactional Distance Model (2018),
CC BY 4.0

In Stage 2, lateral thinking (creative thinking around the problem) is used to generate and develop metaphors (an idea or conception that is basically dissimilar but formed from noting similarities between the initial information and the new concept) or new ideas, and support these by argument. For example, students may discuss their own problem they have found which has brought them to participate in the current course, and then argue to identify possible solutions to each other's problems. Creative thinking here may derive from combining seemingly disparate parts, especially ideas contributed from others in different contexts, into a new synergic whole. The teacher, in their academic capacity, is still keeping at a distance from the content under discussion, while the students are making efforts to achieve some pre-set goal (to present their own problem and their reasons for engaging the current course, for example) which gives structure to their discussions (S+D-). Some time is needed for reflection here, and asynchronous modes such as email and a bulletin board are effective.

In Stage 3, the tutor engages the students with guiding comments in what Holmberg (1983) has described as a guided didactic conversation, helping the students achieve the structural requirements of understanding the general concepts to be learnt (S+ D+). The tutor poses questions and students defend their formulations. This Stage 3 is characterised by hypothesis-testing and logical thinking (termed 'vertical' thinking in contrast to 'lateral' thinking) associated with problem-solving, and is collaborative. The asynchronous mode is ideal here, to allow sufficient time for cognitive connections and the co-construction of new non-foundational knowledge.

In Stage 4, the final stage, the course requirements have largely been already achieved and there is no structure left, except to disseminate the achieved mental ideas and test them out in real-life. This Stage 4 is characterised by experiential learning and is cooperative, and conducted at minimum transactional distance (S- D+), in synchronous mode, with no imposed structure and with educative dialogue to assist the student to reflect on her studies.

These four stages of the Transactional Distance Model are summarised and shown in Figure 9.2 Stage 1 (S- D-) is at maximum transactional distance for the student; Stage 2 (S+ D-) is closer, as the student engages institutionally imposed structure; Stage 3 (S+ D+) is nearer to achieving the learning task, when some educative dialogue is now involved to help the student consider all possible alternatives; and Stage 4 is closest at minimum transactional distance where the student has adopted new knowledge and is testing this out to finally learn.

Findings from a meta-analysis of telepresence for education can be easily visualized using this four-stage model as a framework showing the learning process.

Social Presence Theory draws from a meta-analysis of virtual presence in education that suggests only six forms of presence are essential and occur in turn, purposefully within the educative process — (1) Institutional Presence, (2) Learner Presence, (3) Cognitive Presence, (4) Social Presence, (5) Transactional Presence, and (6) Teaching Presence. The six forms of presence are positioned (shown in Fig. 9.2 below) accordingly within the four-stage Transactional Distance Model process to facilitate learning.

The lines in Figure 9.2 try to show the coverage of each form of Presence occurring throughout the four Stages of learning. Institutional Presence covers the top of the learning process including the Teaching Presence, but not totally enveloping the student who may have extrinsic activities and use non-academic support facilities including family support — so the institutional support along the top of this diagram

Institutional Presence

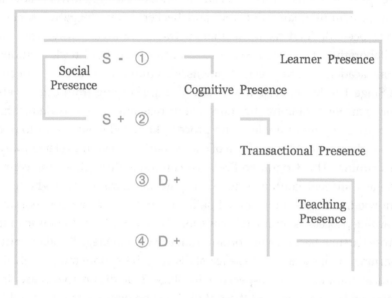

Fig. 9.2 Paul Kawachi, The position of social presence in the educative process (2018), CC BY 4.0

stops short of fully covering the Learner Presence. Learner Presence then envelops everything in the learning process. There are then two distinct forms — Social Presence and Cognitive Presence — exercised by the student, and these two have different functions. Social Presence conveys the party face or human side of the student to others; reducing barriers of physical isolation, communicating shared frustrations with getting the technology to work, working to reduce state anxieties (and in some cases reducing trait anxieties too), helping to bring about initial learning achievements, and develop integrative motivation to learn. Holding hands with group members here can ease the transition into Stage 2 collaborative learning where students must question each other and themselves, which can be stressful. The following Stage 3 collaborative learning is more difficult in that individual ideas are suspended, subjectivity is suspended, and objective disjunctive reasoning is needed — so that Social Presence has no educative role. Any personal distractions or flashbacks to the early social chat is not germane to the task at hand and will be diverted to social support groups off-campus. Indeed, Social Presence can lead to lower academic grades (Cunningham, Corprew and Becker, 2009): 'negative friends' have been defined as those that distract a student away from the collaborative strategies needed for learning, and hold back a student from academic future achievements. Cognitive Presence also begins in Stage 1 to let others know where you are coming from cognitively, your reasons for taking the course, your relevant prior knowledge that you are bringing to the learning process, knowledge you want to pool with others to build some form of shared basis, and your preferred ways of learning. This Cognitive Presence continues throughout the course as each student continues to participate in sharing and co-building knowledge. Some interactional skills are needed in the collaborative learning process as outlined in collaborative scaffolds, and Transactional Presence then becomes important from early on in Stage 2 collaborative learning. Transactional Presence skills may be synonymous with the critical thinking skills especially in Stage 3 of disjunctive reasoning and problem solving, and these skills must be demonstrated for public assessment of learning in cooperative Stage 4 where one also learns oneself through experiential learning. So Transactional Presence begins in Stage 2 and continues through Stages 3 and 4 in this figure. Stages 3 and 4 need guided conversation with a senior student or with a teacher — preferably with many expert teachers, and these stages are characterised by having educative Dialogue (where the earlier Stages 1 and 2 did not).

These six forms are summarised in Table 9.3 below — see Kawachi (2013) for details. Here the important point is that social media serves to facilitate Social Presence within the initial Stage 1 without any Structure imposed by the administration and without any educative dialogue from the teacher or from teaching materials, and carries the student into the Stage 2 academic forum where Structure begins. At this point, social media and Social Presence have no further role to play in achieving learning — except as non-academic support and possibly counselling. In any case the functions of social media are at this time best moved into an online chat-room, to leave the academic forum uncluttered and clear for academic collaborative interactions.

Presence		Definition
1	institutional	The over-arching socio-cultural capital and academic reputation of the institution, its perceived fairness and opportunities, as well as its care and efficacy of contacts with the student.
2	learner	The feelings received by others that suggest the student is at some designated place at some time, conveyed through mediated communications.
3	social	A sense of camaraderie conveyed through mediated communications to others through sharing personal anecdotes, pictures, videos, audio and other media; connections suggesting shared interests, a fashionable lifestyle and friendliness.
4	cognitive	The mental alertness of the student and awareness of others perceived (usually) by others, and carried by ideas and informed comments to the others through mediated communications.
5	transactional	The perceived responsiveness and availability of the student to others, and feelings of connectedness received by others conveyed through mediated communications — not of only one interaction, but of sustained intra-related interactions with others.
6	teaching	Environmental feelings received by students that some desired and effective academic guidance is available and occurring to help them learn, through mediated communications — whether by one or more humans or machines — extending beyond the expected support.

Fig. 9.3 Paul Kawachi, The essential kinds of presence in Online Education (2018), CC BY 4.0

Results

There are no results here in terms of empirical findings for when forms of social media are avoided after the initial stage of constructing a social identity, to show that improved academic learning is achieved. However, the Transactional Distance Model has been extensively validated (Kawachi, 2005) in both online and face-to-face learning, and social presence has also been validated and even measured (Sood and Nevejan, 2012).

The findings of this discussion suggest that the tutor and students involved should limit the role of Social Presence to the initial Stage 1 only in the process of learning. From Stage 2 onwards the collaborative learning forum should be kept uncluttered by social postings which could better be moved away to an online café or other more suitable space online. Social Presence can be measured, and its variations can be followed. Social Presence should be defined as involving the actors rather than the acting, i.e. the 'who' dimension consists of the teacher presence (not teaching presence), learner presence (not learning presence), and other-students presence. Some cognitive presence will then occur in the educative process to move the student from the initial Stage 1 through into the collaborative learning forum and other Stages 2–4 to achieve learning.

The results here are at best a hypothesis for why Facebook and other social media have been associated in some studies with improved engagement and in other studies with weaker learning. While learning requires engagement, it does not follow that simply engaging will achieve learning — there needs to be effective cognitive reorganisation to bring about demonstrable learning. Given that Social Presence Theory can explain the conflicting outcomes using social media, further controlled studies are warranted. What is built is not so much a self-identity but a peer-negotiated acceptance. Any small misstep can be retracted and rebuilt to construct an online persona that paves the way forward for future interactions to foster and enable learning.

Discussion

The general usage of social media by colleges may be related to the increase of older adults enrolling, especially in open distance education. Older adults are well known to exhibit extrinsic social motivation to study (Kawachi, 2003), in other words they are motivated by the desire for socialisation, rather than academic interest.

Teachers and administrators use Facebook and other social media to communicate administrative information to students, such as forthcoming meetings or examinations. Students with mobile technologies can be contacted at any time or place. However, most students already know details of upcoming examinations and these media offer a benefit only when there is an emergency (such as unexpected change in examination venue) and there is a need to reach a large number of students cheaply. Outsider perceptions of social media for augmentative and alternative communication can be high, but in reality they mainly offer cost efficiency; administrators still need to get a response from each student and log this. The efficiency of other technologies such as the iPad for enhancing communication is similarly over-rated by non-users (Allen, Jeans, Ball and Guarino, 2015). Achieving added benefit from using social media technologies requires their use to be well integrated into the learning system.

Suggestions

Social media can ease the student transition into college life. New students can generally be expected to demonstrate academic performance related anxiety. There is therefore a role for social media to support having fun, especially for younger students who may feel isolated and without integrative motivation. The role for fun here is to reduce performative anxiety, which in turn leads to the development of a community of learning. Reduced performative anxiety allows for some achievement in learning. But in order for the student to move on to develop the instrumental motivations for deeper quality of learning as an independent learner or as a collaborative group learner, this social integrative motivation with social media needs to side-lined or otherwise dispelled. Sometimes a teacher could manage this by giving measured personalised advice to the student — even going so far as to give negative comments perhaps by overly correcting slight misunderstandings to prevent the fossilisation of the learning process, and having the student stuck in social media and Facebook.

Colleges — particularly open universities — report stubborn high drop-out rates that recently are tending to increase. The increases over the past five-to-ten years in drop-out may be due to the increase in the numbers of marginal students not so well prepared for college studying. There are data for example from the Open University of Malaysia that tutor interventions can reduce this early drop-out rate. Such data suggests social media can help in the transition process to reduce the early drop-out rate among first-year students, but does not have any significant effect on the non-completion rate. The suggested role of social media is likely related to the socialisation process and the development of Social Presence. Further research is warranted into the correlation between the amount and type of social media usage and student drop-out rates.

References

Allen, A. A., Jeans, C., Ball, C. L., and Guarino, A. J. (2015). 'Caregivers' perception of the iPad's utility for augmentative and alternative communication: A conflict between illusion and reality', *World Journal of Educational Research*, 2:1, pp. 39–43, http://www.scholink.org/ojs/index.php/wjer/article/view/320/291

Boling, N. C., and Robinson, D. H. (1999). 'Individual study, interactive multimedia, or cooperative learning: Which activity best supplements lecture-based distance education?', *Journal of Educational Psychology*, 91:1, pp. 169–74.

Cunningham, M., Corprew, C. S., and Becker, J. E. (2009). 'Associations of future expectations, negative friends, and academic achievement in high-achieving African American adolescents', *Urban Education*, 44:3, pp. 259–79, https://doi.org/10.1177/0042085908318715

Herrington, J., and Oliver, R. (1999). 'Using situated learning and multimedia to investigate higher-order thinking'. *Journal of Educational Multimedia and Hypermedia*, 8:4, pp. 401–22, https://www.learntechlib.org/primary/p/9276/

Holmberg, B. (1983). 'Guided didactic conversation in distance education', in D. Sewart, D. Keegan, and B. Holmberg (eds.), *Distance education: International perspectives*. London: Croom Helm, pp. 114–22.

Kawachi, P. (2013). 'Online social presence and its correlation with learning', *International Journal of Social Media and Interactive Learning Environments*, 1:1, pp. 19–31, http://www.inderscience.com/storage/f122105914113867.pdf

Kawachi, P. (2006). 'The will to learn: Tutor's role', in P. R. Ramanujam (ed.), *Globalisation, Education and Open Distance Learning*. New Delhi: Shipra, http://www.open-ed.net/library/R3107.html, pp. 197–221.

Kawachi, P. (2005). 'Empirical validation of a multimedia construct for learning', in S. Mishra and R. Sharma (eds.), *Interactive Multimedia in Education and Training*. Hershey, PA: IDEA Group, pp. 158–83.

Sood, A. D., and Nevejan, C. (2012). 'Witnessed presence experience', https://eit.europa.eu/kics1/knowledge-and-innovation-communities/overview.html

Young, J. R. (2012). 'What a tech start-up's data say about what works in classroom forums', *Chronicle of Higher Education*, https://www.chronicle.com/blogs/wiredcampus/what-a-tech-start-ups-data-say-about-what-works-in-classroom-forums/38960

10. Bursting Out of the Bubble:
Social Media, Openness and Higher Education

#Beginner #Medium

Jennie Blake, Chris Millson and Sam Aston

Introduction

This chapter will focus on the use of Medium.com to anchor a course's commitment to openness in HE. Its presence online has shaped student engagement with the content and the assessments, driving their work beyond the topics discussed on the day and inspiring them to create lasting content for the wider community. Finally, bursting out of the bubble of the academic community and VLEs has allowed everyone linked to the course to connect with other practitioners and discuss and disseminate the effects of these efforts.

The Context

Open Knowledge in Higher Education (OKHE) is an open module exploring openness in HE, offered through the online writing platform, Medium.com (Medium, 2018). The initial materials were developed by The University of Manchester Library to support an optional module in the University's Postgraduate Certificate in Higher Education (PG Cert HE), a taught programme for staff, comprising a number of optional modules.

   https://doi.org/10.11647/OBP.0162.10

Because of the Library's preference for openness, and the obvious connection with the subject matter of this module, we have taken an approach which is open in a number of ways. It is important that we are honest about how we got here. What we describe in this chapter — a course both exploring and exhibiting many aspects of openness (although of course with much room for improvement) — is not something we can honestly say we could describe in detail from the start. Instead, it is and will continue to be the result of a developmental journey. Our reflections on openness as course developers, many of whom have been prompted by being part of the course ourselves, learning from experts and participants alike — and our building some of this into each iteration of the course. So, if we did not have a detailed plan to take us from conception to the current state of the course, how did we get here? Openness can mean a lot in education (Prunie and Scheller, 2017), but by committing to being as open as we can at the time, to reflecting on this, and improving the course, has led us to where we are.

Where Did We Start, Then?

Initially, we had a couple of aims for the assessment. Firstly, we wanted the process of completing the assessment to contribute to participants' learning, in other words an emphasis on 'assessment for learning' (Brown, 2005) rather than 'assessment of learning'. The course deals with topics such as open practice (and communicating online as one way this can take place) and ownership and licensing (and deciding how to share your work). We wanted participants to have an opportunity to explore and experience these topics for themselves, as they worked on their assessment.

Our first idea was that assessment would provide an opportunity for participants to contribute to a wiki. The wiki would contain discussions of and reflections about openness in higher education; participants would write and/or edit pages in it, thus expanding the resource. As part of our commitment to openness, it would ideally be public and open to all. Ideally it would also be open to contributions by all, i.e. 'our' participants' contributions could be identified for 'assessment' purposes, but that we would also be contributing a resource to the wider sector.

We considered a number of ideas around this — for example, how easy would it be to amalgamate one person's contributions, and 'mark' them? Was this against an open, collaborative ethos anyway ('standing on the shoulders of giants' etc)? Would we ask them to write a blog post or reflective piece exploring what they had achieved through the course, referencing their contributions?

The above ideas seemed to have mileage but didn't quite fit. For example, where would the 'core' course materials be hosted? This might include things like session times/dates, the mark scheme for assessment, and so on. We were following an idea that participants were contributing to the course materials, and trying to avoid the classic separation of assessment and other materials (for example, a 'closed-off' wiki or blog within a VLE course — alongside non-wiki materials). We were also looking for a platform where anyone could contribute. However, putting information such as session dates and times in a public wiki felt problematic in a couple of ways. Firstly, anyone could edit them, and that felt wrong for such fixed, official information with the University's name on it. Fine, a definition of openness will ideally be open to anyone to comment on and edit. But details of when and where sessions take place *should* be fixed. To change it would be unfair to participants.

Separating this information out, e.g. having 'core course materials' locked up in Blackboard, plus 'student contributions' in a public wiki, made the wiki feel synthetic. We wanted all of us to be contributing to the same materials, the course materials, and for this to be of genuine value.

It is clear that our wiki idea exhibited some forms of openness, but wasn't quite what we were looking for. At this point we explored other options, and considered the idea of using a more social platform. Some advantages of this are that authors are more prominent. For example, viewing a Twitter thread on 'Open education', we can read a discussion, and very easily see who contributed which parts to it, without having to look deeper. In comparison, a wiki page may present a more coherent narrative, but superficially, the authors are not acknowledged. The primary concern of a wiki is the content. Behind the scenes we can see an edit history, with associated usernames, but this is more concerned with process and accountability. We wanted something which would: allow participants to write 'as themselves' rather than being a near-invisible contributor; at the same time, to contribute to something bigger, and to be part of a conversation. Twitter or a traditional blogging platform (such as WordPress) might achieve the former. However, bringing the conversation together is difficult in these examples. Perhaps a hashtag could be proposed on Twitter which would bring conversations together. But this could be subject to 'noise' from anyone contributing to it, and Twitter is less successful at surfacing anything but the latest content. It might not feel like a 'home' for the course, more a snapshot of discussion on it. Giving or allowing participants to create a 'traditional blog' is not a new idea in education. Some advantages are that they can write more at length than a network such as Twitter, they create their own space and can consider it as part of their online identity. However, it may also lead to 'single-serving blogs', i.e. those set up for the course, only to go stale afterwards; it is also hard to bring these blogs together — effectively each writer runs their own publication — and we would have the task of unifying all of these publications, along with one or more publications of our own to contains core course information. It felt like we would be running another Library.

Why Medium is Different

In exploring blogging and social networks, we were becoming familiar with one newer platform which seemed capable of achieving our objectives: Medium. The platform was set up as a 'writing platform' or 'ideas platform'. While this may sound like a pretentious refusal to 'just call it a blog', we realised that there is in fact a difference to the way Medium operates. Whereas a system like WordPress gives each writer a publication (and indeed, there is no way to publish a post on WordPress without first setting up a publication, effectively a website), and all that one can do with their account otherwise is comment on others' publications, Medium does not. Creating an account on Medium allows you instantly to publish content. This content does not live on your website/publication/blog, but simply on Medium. Thus, it is a blogging platform but its posts are hosted centrally. This helps us in a number of ways. Firstly, there *is no single-serving blog*. Just as Twitter does not look stale after one person stops tweeting, Medium continues to highlight the community's content after one person stops publishing. Secondly, there is no setting-up of a blog, only a personal profile. On WordPress, your profile allows you to comment. On Medium, it allows you to post. In fact, Medium makes very little distinction between comments and posts — much like Twitter, comments (or responses) *are* posts; posts which reference other posts.

Our open approach has a number of implications. While the Library initially developed and maintains the module, from its first year onwards, most of the materials have been contributed by participants. This learner-contributed approach has continued, and we are continuing to develop it. For example, in the second year of running, we explicitly referenced participant contributions in core course materials. In the third year, we set participant contributions as reading, and featured past participants in every classroom session.

Pedagogy of Open Assessment

From its conception, it was clear that the module had the potential to live and breathe openly through every part its soul. As developers it was vital that within the constraints of organisational policy there was a transparent commitment towards openness in the pedagogical approach, into assessment, throughout the learning resources and in how the unit approached the outcomes of the overall certificate. It was also necessary to consider the cohort of students and their professional experiences connected to the module outcomes. It was with these elements in mind that social media became the vehicle which would allow the module to burst out of its bubble.

Social media has been used to support pedagogical innovation by educators in higher education for a number of years, as it has the flexibility and accessibility to support learning in the HE sector (OU, 2016). In particular, social media has thrived in the arena of openness through its ability to support networks and communities of practice, driving collaboration while allowing for individuals to maintain their individuality and a voice in the conversation. Social media is also recognised as a space where an ongoing dialogue can take place. Therefore, it made sense to align a method by which we could connect with and facilitate the connection to openness as part of the modules assessment. Going beyond the tool the beauty of social media is that it places the voices of the individuals involved at its heart.

Individually, every participant's voice is heard as they submit written assessments to the OKHE publication. Through their online engagements, participants are engaged in open networked participatory scholarship (Veletsianos and Kimmons, 2012). Contributing posts that connect their personal experiences with openness in HE to the publication is an integral feature of the open scholarship that OKHE extols. OKHE publication permits individuals to authentically explore the concept of openness in the context of their professional role, in keeping with the purpose and the philosophy of social media. There is the further added strength of placing the ownership of content into the participants own hands, prompting participants to consider their online identity and creating a backwash of development for each individual's digital literacy skills.

Participants have explored a range of current topics, including how Sci-hub provides access to non-open access research; how openness is considered in relation to academic integrity and academic expectation; as well as MOOCs and their role in openness. It is through the transparency of using a social media platform that participants can connect with current conversations.

In the same way that the publication opens up the voices of the individuals, the publication operates as the mouthpiece for the community that the module draws together. As a community the posts that the publication exposes are the thoughts of professionals at University of Manchester (UoM), those at the 'coal face' that are not only engaging in open education but contributing to and opening up the wider conversation. The publication that is being created by the community is what is used to support the growing community of cohorts: it is a community-built open educational resource.

Framing the participants as co-learners and co-creators on the module was a deliberate objective which social media was able to facilitate. The UoM Library has a reputation for open educational practice and the creation of open educational resources through its My Learning Essentials (UoM, 2018) skills programme and our approach to this module proved no different. As co-creators, the participants' thoughts are collated in one single space that is open for engagement with the wider community.

With the publication acting as a transparent virtual learning environment, Medium has facilitated the opinions and thoughts of the cohort being shared widely, as well as being available to each other and to the learning community at UoM. Dalsgaard and Thestrup (2015) refer to the three dimensions of openness: transparency between students and teachers, communication between educational institutions and partners, and joint engagement with the world. The Medium publication is representative of the first two dimensions, with the aspiration of moving towards working partnerships with others in the wider online community.

The design of the course acknowledging the professional experience of the cohort the developers have used Medium to level the classroom. The cohort are made up of a wide variety of professions from across the University staff: lecturers, researchers, library staff, e-learning technologists and professional support services. It was therefore vital that we provide the right support in the right format. As mentioned previously, there have been a range of topics covered through the cohorts: the online publication of the assessment tasks is a record of the conversations taking place about openness at the UoM. Writing and publishing in this way has enabled the thoughts and reflections of the participants to be a part of the conversations that are taking place in the sector.

Beyond The Ivory Tower

Moving students 'beyond the mark' has been one of the perennial struggles of education. Much work has been done to try and drive students to think of their work as part of a learning journey, as part of a community, and as part of a process of collective thought. Even more rare (though it is becoming more common), is work that deliberately places the assessment into the public sphere, and participates in raucous conversations, from the off. The assessments within the OKHE module, as described earlier in the chapter, take a deliberately, and potentially provocative pedagogical approach and ask that participants join in with the conversations already occurring, and, in the second assessment, make deliberate connections to what they hear in that space.

Higher education, and academia in general, is often dismissed as an ivory tower, a silo, or disparaged as comprising of disconnected and self-indulgent thought exercises. To these critics, it is the very opposite of 'open'; a place where the only sound is the echo of its own voice. The pernicious cycle of a closed system is described by Thomas Pynchon, in his 'Slow Learner' collection, where he states:

> What I mean is something like a closed circuit. Everybody on the same frequency. And after a while you forget about the rest of the spectrum and start believing that this is the only frequency that counts or is real. While outside, all up and down the land, there are these wonderful colors and x-rays and ultraviolets going on. (Pynchon, 1985)

It is as part of our effort to combat the closed circuit that we built social media into our module. After committing to open knowledge as a topic, we felt that putting our discussions, resources and assessments behind the walled-garden of a virtual learning environment would directly contradict the aims of the course. Instead, we pushed everything, and everyone, out into the open. The results: a group of participants that must think about their place in the conversation; pieces that deliberately add to current and 'live' conversations, and, hopefully a more powerful voice when the work 'joins up' in the public sphere, are all down to the use of this open platform. We are, quite deliberately, putting our module where our content lives, in the space where academia and open networks overlap, which, more than ever, has a social component.

Reflecting on the Medium

Using the Medium publication, we have been able to relocate the conversation from what might be a self-contained silo to a wider audience. This has a knock-on effect immediately as the participants must think of their audience beyond the typical groups of others on the course or course convenors to, potentially, include those with an interest in open, an interest in Manchester, or just a liking for Google's 'I'm Lucky' button. This hasn't been without hiccoughs, and though we support the ability for participants to post anonymously to the blog, for some the act of putting their thoughts online (and often reflective and personal thoughts at that) is a truly disconcerting one, prompting them to stop, reflect and possibly self-censor in a way they wouldn't feel necessary in a closed conversation. One participant took this reflection even further, looking at what we, as staff in HE, might need to do when we enter the 'open' world:

What the OKHE course has enabled me to understand is that openness inevitably brings with it challenges, and by being open you will facilitate views that you dislike or challenge your own views. In order to preserve an open environment I think that as staff members [we] have to stop thinking of ourselves as the owners of these online communities and try to engage with them as participants instead.

This type of reflection, one that might not have occurred without the open assessments, materials and resources, highlights a major change when we join in on social media. Often, even with a blue tick-mark in evidence, the hierarchies that we depend on for respect and acknowledgement are absent, forcing us to join in on a level playing field and make our voices heard from the crown instead of at the podium. Indeed, what might seem appropriate (and what might be rewarded) in a closed-system is very different from what resonates and is rewarded online, and for those comfortable with the status-quo, moving to 'open' can be revealing in its discomfort.

Beyond assessment, the OKHE Medium site is meant to drive our participants to think about where their reflection sits in the cohort, in the community and in the wider conversation. Our placement of our assessment, and the entirety of the course, on an open social media platform, allows us to encourage, though not guarantee, that we hear the 'x-rays and ultraviolets' that are happening just outside the bubble we are existing in. Because the posts of previous cohorts are kept online, along with all of the talks and supporting materials, the students are participating in a course that builds links in time as well as between topics. We can see how our thinking has changed, and detail our reactions to those changes, in a way that is predominantly absent in a traditional course.

This change also allows the course to impact the open community beyond the work of one or two stand-outs. Because we are operating as a collective, we are not dependent on the presence of a well-known (or well followed), individual. Instead, the course itself, through the work of the participants, convenors and those giving their talks, makes an impact because of what everyone is doing together. This has meant, in practical terms, that those we reach out to give the talks on the module have often already heard of the course, that the work we do for assessment gets looked at, and imitated in other areas of the University of Manchester, and that we get invited to write book chapters like this one!

References

Brown, Sally (2005). 'Assessment for learning', *Learning and Teaching in Higher Education*, 1, pp. 81–89, http://www.qub.ac.uk/directorates/AcademicStudent Affairs/CentreforEducationalDevelopment/FilestoreDONOTDELETE/ Filetoupload%2C120807%2Cen.pdf

Dalsgaard, C. and Thestrup, T. (2015). 'Dimensions of openness: Beyond the course as an open format in online education', *The International Review of Research in Open and Distributed Learning*, https://doi.org/10.19173/irrodl. v16i6.2146

Medium (2018), 'Open Knowledge in Higher Education', https://medium.com/ open-knowledge-in-he

Open University (2016). 'Innovating pedagogy 2016', https://iet.open.ac.uk/file/ innovating_pedagogy_2016.pdf

Prunie and Scheller (2017). 'Policy Recommendations on Open Education in Europe (OpenEdu Policies)', European Commission, http://publications.jrc. ec.europa.eu/repository/bitstream/JRC107708/jrc107708_jrc_107708_final__ going_open_-_policy_recommendations_on_open_education_in_europe. pdf

Pynchon, T. (1985). *Slow Learner: Early Stories*. London: Random.

University of Manchester (2018). 'My learning essentials', http://www.library. manchester.ac.uk/using-the-library/students/training-and-skills-support/ my-learning-essentials/

Veletsianos, G., and Kimmons, R. (2012). 'Networked participatory scholarship: Emergent techno-cultural pressures toward open and digital scholarship in online networks', *Computers & Education*, 58:2, pp. 766–74.

11. Cambridge Analytica, Facebook, and Understanding Social Media Beyond the Screen

#Beginner #Facebook #WhatsApp #CambridgeAnalytica

Zoetanya Sujon

Introduction

One of the challenges many HE professionals face in classrooms oriented around learning about social media, is that of teaching apparently digitally-savvy students who feel their intense familiarity with social media is the same as critical understanding. While some may of course be critically minded, or even possess a sophisticated understanding of algorithms, privacy, and the complex structures of social media; many do not. As such, guiding learners to move beyond their experience of the newsfeed, stream, or front page can be tremendously challenging as well as tremendously rewarding.

This chapter examines one approach for dealing with this sometimes difficult teaching context, providing a broad overview of the growing importance of critical perspectives on social media. Beginning with an outline of the rich variety of student experiences, this chapter contextualises some of the learning challenges I have encountered in my own classrooms while teaching social media; challenges which require an open classroom and a critical view of the idea of 'digital natives'.

 https://doi.org/10.11647/OBP.0162.11

This chapter also presents Facebook, particularly its interactions with Cambridge Analytica, as an ideal case for tackling the complexities of social media and pushing users beyond the social experience. The aim of this section is to examine the importance of personal data as the core business model of Facebook, and most mainstream or corporate social media.

Finally, this chapter includes three key exercises that can be used in classrooms to help learners to understand how Facebook works, and some of what the Cambridge Analytica case reveals about social media. In sum, the purpose of this chapter is to examine some of the best ways to bring critical thinking into the experience of social media, providing a mix of theory and practical tasks which can help learners understand concepts of personal data collection and 'surveillance capitalism' in relation to their own social media use. The Cambridge Analytica case is particularly important and effective for engaging learners' critical understanding of social media and moving their perspective beyond the screen.

Students, Screens, and Social Media

Many HE professionals regard young adults as 'digital natives' who come into the classroom with an innate understanding of new technologies and digital skills (e.g. Prensky 2001, 2012). Many also draw on ideas from the 'Visitor and Resident' model in order to understand the skills young people develop as a consequence of their engagement with social and digital tools (e.g. White and Le Cornu 2011). Based on what I see in my classrooms, many young people do bring an intense familiarity with social media based on everyday use, yet this is familiarity is uneven across each cohort of students. Many among them have limited experience and understanding, perhaps as a result of a personal or parental rejection of social media in their lives.

This uneven familiarity and understanding is important for two reasons. First, as educators, it is vital to challenge assumptions about young people as 'digital natives', and instead establish a classroom environment that is as open for those with relatively little knowledge as it is for those who are very experienced. In this sense, understanding use based on levels of experience and critical understanding, rather than on levels of expertise, is an important starting point. Growing evidence suggests that the concept of 'digital natives' overstates many young peoples' digital knowledge and skills, so an open classroom can make all the difference for those coming from the more unfamiliar end of the spectrum (e.g. Das and Beckett 2009; Helsper and Eynon 2009). Second, as I will argue throughout this chapter, Facebook, like other social media platforms, does considerable work to keep its users on the newsfeed rather than on the almost infinite options beyond the 'front page' of user experience. In many ways, most peoples' experiences of social media resemble those of automobile drivers — we may know how to drive the car, but that does not mean we know what is under the hood, how roads are built, how traffic is regulated, or anything about the trade fluctuations and power dynamics of the petrol and oil industries.

A broader understanding of the social media landscape does not necessarily require advanced technical skills, and can introduce users to a more critical understanding of what they are interacting with. Given the scope, breadth, and power of social media, this critical approach is urgent, and is the first step towards breaking down common misunderstandings that social media does not constitute anything more than a newsfeed. Facebook's role in reinforcing this common misunderstanding is clearly apparent in the Cambridge Analytica case.

Cambridge Analytica: 'It's a Feature Not a Bug'

In early 2018, revelations were widely published revealing the misuse of 87 million people's personal data, gathered in 2014 by Cambridge academic Aleksander Kogan, through a Facebook app personality quiz called 'thisisyourdigitalife' (Madrigal 2018; Tufekci 2017, 2018). Using the Facebook platform, the app not only collected personal data from approximately 300,000 Amazon Mechanical Turk workers paid $1 or $2 to complete the quiz, but also personal information from each of those worker's friend accounts. Meanwhile, Facebook CEO Mark Zuckerberg maintains that this data was shared with Cambridge Analytica — a political campaigning and marketing company — in breach of Facebook's terms and conditions. Indeed, Facebook did suspend Kogan's app and demanded certification from Cambridge Analytica (CA) that they had deleted all data that had been collected.

While CA apparently did provide certification, the data has since been linked with both Donald Trump's presidential campaign in 2016, and with various Brexit leave campaigns (Chen 2018; Tufecki 2018; Zuckerberg as cited in Thompson 2018; Osborne and Parkinson 2018; Greenfield 2018).

The case involves use of Facebook's open social graph, a service which has allowed app developers and third parties to access certain kinds of user information via the Facebook platform. Drawing from this case, there are two significant implications which are essential for broadly understanding social media, and Facebook in particular. The first is that this case is not a scandal or data breach — instead, it reveals the inner workings and logic of social media platforms. Second, these platforms work very hard to keep users on the 'news feed', obscuring the big business of personal data collection behind the 'social' purpose of these platforms, as explained below.

Leading thinkers on digital media and politics argue that the 'data misuse' of the CA case 'is a feature, not a bug', not just of Facebook, but also social media platforms more broadly (Zuckerman 2018; Tufecki 2017, 2018). Referring to Facebook as a 'surveillance machine' or what Zuboff terms 'surveillance capitalism' (2015), Tufekci (2018) argues:

> Facebook makes money, in other words, by profiling us and then selling our attention to advertisers, political actors and others. These are Facebook's true customers, whom it works hard to please.

The widespread 'misuse' of personal data can also be observed in Facebook's 'shadow profiles' — profiles made up of data gathered from Facebook users' contact lists and web browsing behaviours — which have been long understood to be the basis for the 'people you may know' algorithm. In addition, WhatsApp founder Jan Koum has resigned from WhatsApp and the Facebook board of directors over privacy concerns (White 2018; Solon 2018). Indeed, in the risk assessment section of its 2018 first quarter report, Facebook has warned shareholders that: 'We anticipate that we will discover and announce additional incidents of misuse of user data or other undesirable activity by third parties' (Levy 2018; Facebook Inc. 2018). Many others have pointed to Facebook's problematic data collection procedures, ranging, for example, from the 2014 mood manipulation study (Meyer 2014; Kramer et al. 2014) to targeting 'Jew haters' in advertising and political campaigns, highlighting the profitability of big data (Tufekci 2017; cf. Zuboff 2015; Van Dijck 2013; Morozov 2012).

What is particularly important about this is that Facebook, like other social platforms, presents itself as primarily a social network, giving users 'the power to share and to make the world more open and connected' (Facebook's mission statement, 2004–2018). As such, Facebook claims its primary aim is to connect people and more recently 'to bring the world closer together' (Facebook mission statement 2018), rather than the monetisation of social interactions and personal data collection. For all of these reasons, today's students must work to critically understand social media as more than just social networks and tools for interpersonal communication, regardless of whether they use social media or not.

Personal Data Exercises

Although the CA events clearly illustrate the practice of monetising personal data collection on Facebook, many students may struggle to understand how this applies to them and their data. Drawing from Lave and Wenger's (1990) notion of situated and participatory learning, the following exercises have been developed to illustrate the scope, scale, and applicability not only of personal data collection, but also of the use of the data and the lack of user rights on social media.

Exercise 1: Review Facebook's 'Statement of Rights and Responsibilities' or 'Terms of Service'

Many of today's social media users, including students at many levels, admit to having never read the terms and conditions or end user licence agreements of the sites, platforms, apps, or devices they use. As such, one of the first helpful exercises for introducing users to social media beyond the newsfeed is to ask them to review the terms and conditions which most people click through without reading or considering what their rights may be. Although the CA case has prompted the development of new Facebook terms (introduced as of 19 April 2018), there are still a number of consistencies with prior versions. These can be found by clicking on 'terms' often found on the bottom right of the Facebook.com home page (you can access Facebook's terms if you are logged in and if you are not, see Fig. 11.1 below).

Fig. 11.1 Zoetanya Sujon, Screenshot highlighting Facebook's 'Terms' (2018), CC BY 4.0

The link pathways are different depending on whether you are logged in or not. First, it is important to review the terms which outline your rights and responsibilities as a Facebook user. Many find the terms and conditions off-putting, particularly as the small print and formal language can be difficult to read and understand — these are points which have been addressed in the April 2019 updates. However, despite the challenges of reading the terms, many report that this exercise is eye-opening and worth the effort. While there are many things to focus on during this kind of session, I ask students to review the statement of rights and responsibilities, their privacy settings, and the data policy — identifying what stands out to them and what they think is important — often leading to lively discussion.

One part of the terms and conditions which I draw attention to falls about halfway through Facebook's 'Terms of Service', under section '3.3 The permissions you give us'. In this section, Facebook outlines what kind of permissions they need in order to let you use Facebook (2018, my emphasis):

Permission to use content that you create and share: You own the content that you create and share on Facebook and the other Facebook Products you use, and nothing in these Terms takes away the rights that you have to your own content. You are free to share your content with anyone else, wherever you want. To provide our services though, we need you to give us some legal permissions to use that content. Specifically, when you share, post or upload content that is covered by intellectual property rights (e.g. photos or videos) on or in connection with our Products, you grant us a non-exclusive, transferable, sub-licensable, royalty-free and worldwide licence to host, use, distribute, modify, run, copy, publicly perform or display, translate and create derivative works of your content (consistent with your privacy and application settings).

The highlighted part of the above terms was almost identical in prior version of Facebook's terms and conditions other than moving the placement of this statement from the first section of the 'Statement of Rights and Responsibilities' ('2. Sharing your content and information', 31 January 2018, https://www.facebook.com/legal/terms) to considerably lower on the page, as well as some minor re-ordering of the words within the statement.

Although users and non-users identify community standards, safety, data policy, and privacy settings as important, 'the permissions you give us' are demonstrative of some of the double logic at work, as well as Facebook's total control of personal content and data (i.e. 'You own the content you create and share….[and] you give us non-exclusive, transferable, sub-licensable, royalty-free and worldwide licence to host, use, distribute, modify, run, copy, publicly perform or display, translate and create derivative works of your content'). Participants are also strongly advised to review and reflect on Facebook's 'Data Policy'.

Exercise 2: Activity log

The purpose of this short exercise is to encourage learners with a Facebook account to explore Facebook's record of *all* of their activity on Facebook from the present moment back to the day they signed up for an account. The activity log can be found by clicking on the ▼ icon in the top right-hand corner of any Facebook page (see Fig. 11.2 below).

Once users have found their activity log, they will see a long list of every like, comment, share, video watched, and other kinds of

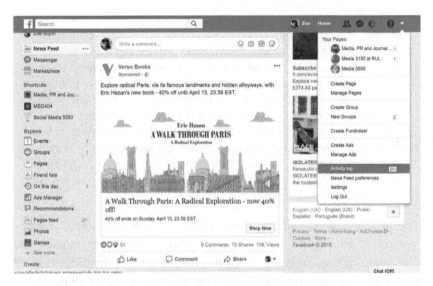

Fig. 11.2 Zoetanya Sujon, Locating the activity log on your Facebook account (2018), CC BY 4.0

behaviour. While it is valuable to ask participants to review their activity log at their leisure, it is worth pointing out that they have a number of filters located on the left of their activity log, which organizes Facebook activity according to particular kinds of behaviour; These categories, found on the left hand side of your activity log, include:

- Posts
- Posts you're tagged in
- Other people's posts to your timeline
- Hidden from your timeline
- Photos and videos
- Likes and reactions
- Comments
- Profile
- Added friends
- Life events
- Songs you've listened to
- Articles you've read

- Films and TV
- Games
- Books
- Products you've wanted
- Notes
- Videos you've watched
- Following
- Groups
- Events
- Polls
- Search history
- Saved
- Your places
- Security and login information
- Apps

Each filter provides a complete list of Facebook activity related to that category. Clicking on 'articles you've read' or 'videos you've watched', for example, reveals a complete list of articles or videos you've clicked on or even hovered over without clicking. While it is possible to clear some of these activity filters (e.g. 'search history' or 'videos you've watched') with a single click, it is more difficult to edit or delete other activities on your timeline (see Fig. 11.3).

On the right side of each event recorded in your activity log, you will see an indication of who your action is visible to, including 'public', 'friends', 'only me', or 'custom' (see icons circled in Fig. 11.3, and a full list of visibility options in box 1).

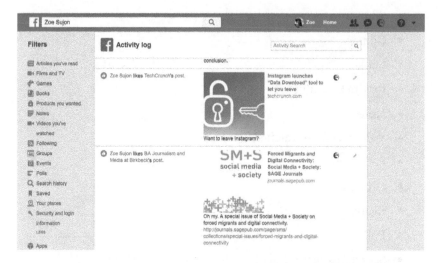

Fig. 11.3 Zoetanya Sujon, One event from a Facebook activity log, highlighting visibility settings (2018), CC BY 4.0

🌐   **Public**: When you share something with Public that means anyone including people off of Facebook can see it.

👥 **Friends (+ friends of anyone tagged)**: This option lets you post stuff to your friends on Facebook. If anyone else is tagged in a post, then the audience expands to also include the tagged person and their friends. If you don't want your photo or post to be visible to the friends of the people you tag, you can adjust this setting. Click the audience selector next to the story, select ⚙ **Custom**, and uncheck the **Friends of those tagged** box.

🔒 **Only Me**: This option allows you to post stuff to your timeline that is visible only to you. Posts with the audience of Only Me will appear in your News Feed but not your friends' feeds. If you tag someone in an Only Me post, they will be able to see the post.

⚙ **Custom**: When you choose Custom, you can selectively share something with specific people, or hide it from specific people. You can also share with specific friend lists if you've set them up, such as Family or Best Friends, or hide posts from your Coworkers list. Custom also provides the option to share with groups or networks you belong to.

Fig. 11.4 Zoetanya Sujon, Screenshot of Facebook's options for who can see your activity on Facebook, from 'What audiences can I choose from when I share?' (2018), CC BY 4.0

Based on the visibility settings, it is possible to identify who can see what activity, although these settings are determined by the original poster, which means they cannot be changed for any content you have not created. The event shown on the activity log in Figure 11.3 is public, meaning it is visible to everyone on the Internet, as indicated by the globe icon. The other editing option shown by the pen icon (shown in the red circle in the figure), allows you to unlike, unfollow, delete or hide a comment or shared post.

Conclusion

In conclusion, this short essay has provided an overview of key challenges many HE professionals face in today's classrooms, including widespread assumptions regarding young people's levels of experience and critical understanding with social technologies. In order to illustrate the importance of a critical understanding, this chapter focuses on recent events between the misuse of 87 million Facebook users personal data by Cambridge Analytica, briefly explaining what happened and what the implications are. Following this, several key exercises intended to demonstrate the wealth of personal data collected and held by Facebook are introduced. The purpose of this chapter is to provide a framework for teachers and HE professionals to use in classrooms, in part or as a whole, to contribute to learners' data literacy, not only of Facebook, but of social media more broadly. #DeleteFacebook may be a temporary solution to personal data infringements, but, as many leading thinkers have argued, Cambridge Analytica is not a breach or scandal, rather, it capitalizes on social media's organizing logic — the monetisation of personal data.

Other Suggested Exercises:

1. Facebook company directory

In order to get a sense of the size and scope of Facebook, review Facebook's key pages and products through its company directory. Note any pages that stand out or are interesting to you. What do these product teams and pages tell you about Facebook as a company? https://newsroom.fb.com/pages-directory/

2. Ad preferences

Based on the information you give Facebook (e.g. name, age, marital status, parental status, where you work, go to school etc.), your browsing behaviour on Facebook (e.g. likes, groups, friends, messages, clicks, etc.), and your online behaviour on other apps and sites shared through the Facebook platform and cookies, Facebook builds an overview of your interests and habits. These interests and habits are organized in categories which advertisers buy access too. These categories are called 'ad preferences'. You can view your own 'ad preferences' here: https://www.facebook.com/ads/preferences (you must be logged in to see this feature and for the link to work).

3. Platform and apps

With the 2007 launch of Facebook log-in (now Facebook Connect) — a service allowing users to log-in to external web-sites using their Facebook username and password — Facebook transformed from a single web site to a MobileFirst platform. Anne Helmond (2015), leading thinker in platform studies, defines the move as 'the extension of social media platforms into the rest of the web and their drive to make external web data "platform ready"'. The Facebook platform enabled personal user data to be collected and shared across services and accounts, just as it was between Aleksander Kogan's personality quiz app, 87 million users, and Cambridge Analytica. Check your own app and platform settings under 'Apps, websites, and games': https://www.facebook.com/settings?tab=applications (you must be logged in to see this feature and for link to work).

References

Chen, Adrian (2018). 'Cambridge analytica and our lives inside the surveillance machine,' *The New Yorker*, March 21, https://www.newyorker.com/tech/elements/cambridge-analytica-and-our-lives-inside-the-surveillance-machine

Das, R., and Beckett, C. (2009). 'Digital natives: A myth?', *A POLIS Paper*. November 24, http://www.lse.ac.uk/media@lse/Polis/Files/digitalnatives.pdf

Facebook Inc. (2018). 'Quarterly report pursuant to section 13 or 15d of the securities exchange act of 1934', United States Securities and Exchange Commission, https://www.sec.gov/Archives/edgar/data/1326801/000132680118000032/fb-03312018x10q.htm

Facebook Inc. (2019). 'Terms of service', https://www.facebook.com/legal/terms/update

Helsper, E., and Eynon, R. (2009). 'Digital natives: Where is the evidence?', *British Educational Research Journal*, pp. 1–18, http://eprints.lse.ac.uk/27739/1/Digital_natives_%28LSERO%29.pdf

Kramer, Adam D. I., Guillory, Jamie E. and Hancock, Jeffrey T. (2014). 'Experimental evidence of massive-scale emotional contagion through social networks', *PNAS*, 111:24, pp. 8788–90, http://www.pnas.org/content/111/24/8788.abstract?tab=author-info

Lave, J., and Wenger, E. (1990). *Situated Learning: Legitimate Peripheral Participation*. Cambridge: Cambridge University Press.

Levy, Ari. (2018). 'Facebook warns investors that more Cambridge Analyticas are likely,' *CNBC*, April 26, https://www.cnbc.com/2018/04/26/facebook-warns-investors-that-more-cambridge-analyticas-are-likely.html

Madrigal, Alexis C. (2018). 'What took Facebook so long?', *The Atlantic*, March 18, https://www.theatlantic.com/technology/archive/2018/03/facebook-cambridge-analytica/555866/

Meyer, Robinson (2014). 'Everything we know about Facebook's mood manipulation study', *The Atlantic*, June 28, http://www.theatlantic.com/technology/archive/2014/06/everything-we-know-about-facebooks-secret-mood-manipulation-experiment/373648/

Morozov, Evgeny (2012). *The Net Delusion: How Not to Liberate the World*. London: Penguin

Osborne, Hilary and Parkinson, Hannah Jane (2018). 'Cambridge Analytica scandal: The biggest revelations so far,' *The Guardian*, March 22, https://www.theguardian.com/uk-news/2018/mar/22/cambridge-analytica-scandal-the-biggest-revelations-so-far

Prensky, M. (2012). *From Digital Natives to Digital Wisdom: Hopeful Essays for 21st Century Learning*. Thousand Oaks, CA: Corwin.

Prensky, M. (2001). 'Digital natives, digital immigrants', *On the Horizon*, 9:5, https://www.marcprensky.com/writing/Prensky%20-%20Digital%20Natives,%20Digital%20Immigrants%20-%20Part1.pdf

Solon, Olivia (2018). 'WhatsApp CEO Jan Koum quits over privacy disagreements with Facebook', *The Guardian*, April 30, https://www.theguardian.com/technology/2018/apr/30/jan-koum-whatsapp-co-founder-quits-facebook

Thompson, Nicholas (2018). 'Mark Zuckerberg speaks to *Wired* about Facebook's privacy problem,' *Wired,* March 21, https://www.wired.com/story/mark-zuckerberg-talks-to-wired-about-facebooks-privacy-problem/

Tufekci, Zeynep (2018). 'Facebook's surveillance machine,' *The New York Times,* March 19, https://www.nytimes.com/2018/03/19/opinion/facebook-cambridge-analytica.html

Tufekci, Zeynep (2017). 'Facebook's ad scandal isn't a "fail2, it's a feature,' *The New York Times,* September 23, https://www.nytimes.com/2017/09/23/opinion/sunday/facebook-ad-scandal.html

Van, Dijck, José (2013). *The Culture of Connectivity: A Critical History of Social Media.* Oxford: Oxford University Press.

White, Jeremy B. (2018). 'WhatsApp co-founder Jan Koum leaving parent company Facebook aid privacy scandal,' *The Independent,* May 1, https://www.independent.co.uk/news/business/jan-koum-whatsapp-leaving-cofounder-facebook-privacy-a8330256.html

White, D. S., and Le Cornu, A. (2011). 'Visitors and residents: A new typology for online engagement'. *First Monday,* 16:9, http://firstmonday.org/article/view/3171/3049

Zuboff, Shoshana (2015). 'Big other: Surveillance capitalism and the prospects of an information civilization', *Journal of Information Technology,* 30, pp. 75–89, https://doi.org/10.1057/jit.2015.5

Zuckerberg, Mark (2018). 'I want to share an update on the Cambridge Analytica situation...', *Facebook,* March 21, https://www.facebook.com/zuck/posts/10104712037900071

Zuckerman, Ethan. (2018). 'This is so much bigger than Facebook,' *The Atlantic,* March 23, https://www.theatlantic.com/technology/archive/2018/03/data-misuse-bigger-than-facebook/556310/

PART FOUR
LEADERSHIP

12. Leadership and Social Media

#Beginner #Leadership #Twitter

Julie Hall

Introduction

Communication is highlighted as an essential leadership skill, yet relatively few senior leaders in UK universities seem to make use of an active social media account. While universities have embraced social media and especially Twitter for marketing purposes, university leaders seem to be more nervous about it than leaders in other spheres. This seems at odds with university missions linked to public engagement, knowledge exchange, and thought leadership. Yet perhaps this reluctance reflects a sense that a social media presence can be tricky. As Bonnie Stewart (2017) says '"the digital" is increasingly a delivery system for surveillance and spectacle and amplified uncertainty.' This chapter outlines some of reasons why university leaders might use social media, despite the challenges, and explores some challenges, especially for women.

Use It to Understand the Time Travellers and Body Shifters with Whom We Are Teaching and Working

Many of our colleagues and our students are with us in the 3D world of offices, seminars, lectures, tables and chairs, while also having a life

  https://doi.org/10.11647/OBP.0162.12

in the 4D of digital space. They are the gamers and the social media residents. Research (Davies S. et al., 2017) indicates that many students are finding it difficult to engage with higher education in the traditional ways which are often taken for granted. 4D identities contrast with their university lives and intersect with race, class, gender and religion. This is potentially a large group in our universities, and I believe we must pay them attention and model some of the practices we are encouraging academics to adopt.

Laurence Scott, in his book *The Four Dimensional Human* (2015), explains how early experiences of the Internet involved the notion of travelling to other worlds through aptly named search engines called Explorer and Safari. This 4th dimension doesn't sit beside real life; it has become a full part of the lives of many students and colleagues. It is no longer a space travelled to via phone lines. People are in our lecture halls, offices and classrooms and simultaneously, often secretly, via powerful mobile phones on their laps, elsewhere in their 4D spaces. The world has taken on extra dimensions and all aspects of our lives are up for digitisation — a building we notice, a meal we eat, a view from a window, a thought, our alternative personas, new adventures, new perspectives. Many of our students exist in multiple places at once, honing skills of communication, leadership, strategy, and dexterity, but then we trap them in lecture halls and tell them things that they could find out themselves. University leaders must recognise the challenges this brings and aid their universities in understanding the multi-dimensional worlds of many students and colleagues.

The digital world is also one of connectedness and gratification with feedback loops that keep a person hooked. This isn't about young students as in Prensky's (2001) 'digital natives', and those in leadership roles as older digital tourists. While students are often confident travellers we can't assume discernment; with unfettered access to everything, it is a challenge to make critical distinctions. Yet familiarity with feedback loops and the associated affirmations of progress or connections mean that work or study can easily feel isolating and alienated when feedback is less forthcoming or less personalised. This can have an effect on motivation and engagement that leaders must take notice of. It is clear that, for many of our students and colleagues, gaming and social media can provide a sense of community, a social experience of cooperation, motivation, problem-based learning and team work, often at an international level. The contrast with the hyper individualism of work in large institutions such as universities is stark. Ironically, it is the digital world that is providing opportunities for communities of learning, metacognition, self-regulation, and for many of the transferable skills universities and employers cite as critical.

Yet while what it means to be physically present has changed, the pressures of 'everywhereness' can produce a sense of absenteeism — despite occupying many places at once and being different people at once, perhaps none of them are fully inhabited. In universities this can take a worrying turn when students or our colleagues are here in the seminar room and there in the digital world at the same time — or more worryingly, they are actually there while only pretending to be here with us in the old confines of 3D. If what Laurence Scott (2015) calls 'intermittent elsewhereness' is their reality, is it not a violent — or at the very least an uncomfortable — act to trap them in 3D? Can we offer something more in the HE classroom, perhaps something that harnesses technology and which is co-produced, building on the motivations of online mastery — something which is worth physically coming to university for? For me, this is a question that university leaders must be engage with.

Use It to Raise the Profile of the University Internally and Externally

Many leaders use Twitter as a simple way to broadcast information to their followers. A number of university leaders have Twitter accounts organised by their PR teams, resulting in tweets congratulating students, highlighting good news such as successful research bids, retweeting university messages, and welcoming people back after the holidays. Often associated with corporate photographs, such tweets are a PR vehicle rather than a personal position or comment. Following such accounts can be dull without a sense of the person behind them or an invitation to engage. Such accounts often ignore trending hashtags and fail to follow others back, relying on a one way production of news rather than the dialogue that social media offers.

Yet such accounts can also be helpful in indicating that someone in a senior position has noticed a conference or a student's achievements. Such posts can become even more powerful with the addition of a personal comment or video clip, communicating a sense of pride or admiration for work conducted. In this sense, the tweets are as much about recognising colleagues as promoting the university. With lack of recognition regularly cited as a reason for leaving an organisation, this can be a good use of social media.

However, for me, too much pre planned material can be a barrier to collaboration, public engagement, and co-creation. Corporate messages rarely invite participation. To make the most of social media, leaders need to embrace openness and the authentic — even the unpolished — traits that may not be normally espoused by university leaders. Getting the balance right can be a challenge, especially with followers connected in the past because of a shared research interest, which a new leadership role might allow little time for. While being wary of the kind of Twitter storms created by the current American president's regular tweets, I would like to see more university leaders going beyond the corporate and engaging with university policy changes and debates through social media. While requiring extreme care, this can be achieved by linking a post to a hashtag and thereby connecting it with something beyond the university, and also by carefully retweeting and replying to others who have tweeted on a similar issue.

Use it to Connect — to Build Relationships and a Personal Profile

For university leaders, an effective social media presence can build networks of external and internal relationships. It can play a critical role in the public engagement or civic mission of the University. When used sensitively it can align a leader with particular campaigns. In 2016, President Dr Santa Ono at the University of British Columbia (UBC) in Vancouver chose to share his own experience of attempted suicide with his 70,000 Twitter followers, garnering much praise for his honesty. This kind of use offers an insight into the ethical stance of a leader and may or may not accord with the stance of the University. Bonnie Stewart (2016) describes such disclosures as 'the political act of putting their face and voice behind an issue — important and strategic forms of awareness-raising.' Like Stewart, I believe this is good for higher education because in sharing our vulnerability we challenge stigma and align ourselves authentically to the things we care about. However, particularly as a woman, it can sometimes be a challenge to provide a glimpse into the causes that inspire, upset, and anger me, my authentic self, while maintaining a responsible leadership profile that represents the university. A leader has a responsibility for the strategic direction, mission, and values of the university; but may also have been appointed because of a commitment to a particular stance on university education or a research background in a particular area. Representing a particular stance in social media can be a way of making leadership values visible, and encouraging commitment and support across a university.

It is not difficult to point to leaders who do not understand their duty to communicate in a way that recognizes the gravity of their words and the positions they take on world events. This isn't an issue linked to the use of new technology, it is about inappropriate communication and, occasionally, the abuse of power. A leader needs to be trusted, and a social media presence, perhaps particularly for a woman who may be in a minority, must demonstrate awareness of power relations and the public nature of the role. Consequently, some kinds of public dialogue may have to be curtailed.

While authenticity is praised as a leadership trait, the inherent risks of engaging so publicly can create reluctance, uncertainty, and unease. Social media fractures the more traditional vertical communication in organizations and opens up channels for spontaneous dialogue across management levels. It can therefore cut across established power dynamics and traditional lines of communication. In contrast with traditional leadership communication, leaders are unable to control a message once it enters the social media system. Yet just because the platform is digital, we can't assume that we are creating a commons — a healthy democratic, decent social space. Twitter, for example, can also accentuate the worst examples of leadership: pronouncements rather than listening, manipulating the visible, garnering acknowledgements in particular spaces. Yet perhaps as a leader we can also model our best intentions — encouraging collaboration, cooperation, creating challenge and engagement, and valuing others.

We must understand how a message might go viral and even how it might be adapted and re-created. This has been described as 'distribution competence' — the ability to influence the way messages move through complex organisations. It is arguably as important as the skill of creating compelling content. When the higher education context changes so rapidly and our students' experiences can be shared, debated, and criticised within a few seconds through media channels, social media literacy can be a critical skill for leadership.

Roland Deiser and Sylvain Newton (2013) argue that 'the dynamics of social media amplify the need for qualities that have long been a staple of effective leadership, such as strategic creativity, authentic communication, and the ability to deal with an organization's social and political dynamics and to design an agile and responsive organization'. The ultimate challenge as a university leader is to balance openness with responsibility: to embrace the opportunity of sharing stories, achievements, and opinions simultaneously with the organization, the public, family, friends, and stakeholders around the world — all while being responsible for the university's standards of integrity. This results in an internal dialogue about the professional and personal. As a female leader, I am keenly aware of the kinds of criticisms we can receive for being outspoken, not so that we temper our presence, but so that we consider any unintended consequences and are prepared, as many female politicians have had to be, for backlash or even attack. Women are particularly vulnerable to attacks from those who imagine we should have a carefully defined role. As Sarah Ahmed (2015) warns, 'When you slip out of what or who you are supposed to be, you slip into trouble'.

For me, social media and Twitter in particular, is a valuable filtered feed of information and news, when the role requires fast decisions and up-to-date news and opinion. Choosing who to follow on Twitter, for example, can result in a complex daily picture of pressing issues, campaigns, opinions, news and good practice which can be shared with others very quickly. In such a responsible role, the provenance of such information is important before retweeting or commenting. In taking a responsible approach we take a proactive role in raising the social media literacy of the organisation.

As a leader I am committed to encouraging academic colleagues to use Twitter and other social media to connect and share their work and ideas. Wider conversations and connections develop and new audiences for research and teaching are located or even created. Interdisciplinarity abounds across social media, and some this can lead to the kind of impact measures universities encourage — requests for collaborative research, invited keynotes, opportunities to bid for grants. What counts online, however, goes beyond research metrics and institutional status; it is the capacity to contribute to the conversation and this is incredibly liberating whether we are university leaders, students, or in the early stages of academic careers.

References

Ahmed, S. (2015). 'Being in trouble — in the company of Judith Butler', https://static1.squarespace.com/static/58ad660603596eec00ce71a3/t/58bec3db3e00be1c14b47723/1488897002949/Being+in+Trouble.pdf

Davies, S., Mullan, J. and Feldman, P. (2017). 'Rebooting learning for the digital age: What next for technology-enhanced higher education?', *HEPI Report 93*, https://www.hepi.ac.uk/wp-content/uploads/2017/02/Hepi_Rebooting-learning-for-the-digital-age-Report-93-20_01_17Web.pdf

Deiser, R. and Newton, S. (2013). 'Six social media skills every leader needs', *McKinsey Quarterly*, https://www.mckinsey.com/industries/high-tech/our-insights/six-social-media-skills-every-leader-needs

Scott, L. (2015). *The Four Dimensional Human — Ways of being in the Digital World*, London: William Heinemann.

Stewart, B. (2016). 'When online disclosures are good for higher ed', Inside Higher Ed blog, 12 October, https://www.insidehighered.com/blogs/university-venus/tactical-twitter

Stewart, B (2017). 'The Crosshairs of the split Hairs: #digciz', The theoryblog, 30 May, http://theory.cribchronicles.com/2017/05/30/the-cross-hairs-of-the-split-hairs-digciz/

Marc Prensky (2001). 'Digital natives, digital immigrants, Part 1', *On the Horizon*, 9:5, pp. 1–6.

13. Leadership and Social Media:
Challenges and Opportunities

#Intermediate #Jisc #Twitter #Identity

Donna M. Lanclos and Lawrie Phipps

Introduction

> The sound of one person talking is not, obviously, a conversation. The
> same applies to organizational conversation, in which leaders talk with
> employees and not just to them. This interactivity makes the conversation
> open and fluid rather than closed and directive. It entails shunning the
> simplicity of monologue and embracing the unpredictable vitality of
> dialogue. (Groysberg and Slind, 2012)

Since 2015, together with a team of colleagues from Jisc, we have been
developing and delivering the Jisc Digital Leadership course. This
course is designed to give institutional leaders the opportunity to
explore how the digital world impacts on their personal practice and
how they can make effective use of digital tools, places, and platforms
in their organisations. Within one particular module of the course, we
facilitate conversations with leaders to explore the implications of social
media practices beyond concerns about platforms and literacies. We
approach social media as a set of practices, and the Internet as a place, to
make room for considering the opportunities presented by social media
and other online places for leaders (Lanclos et al 2016). This chapter
will start with a discussion of the motivations of leaders to come onto
the course, and the major concerns they express during the run of the

    https://doi.org/10.11647/OBP.0162.13

course. Then we discuss what authenticity and credibility mean to the leaders on the course, and explore the ways that personal identity has an impact on their approaches to their work, including digital aspects of their work. Finally, we discuss the methods we use to elicit the necessary conversations within this part of the course, focusing on behaviour mapping rather than trying to define and identify 'types' of individuals.

Motivations to Engage

Before the delegates arrive to the Jisc Digital Leadership course, they submit their motivations for attending, as well as their own definitions of leadership. Over the six iterations of the course thus far, we have had approximately 200 delegates attend, and consistent themes emerge from the stated motivations. Some of the motivations are intrinsic, and some are extrinsic — we have delegates who sign themselves up for the course, because they think it will benefit them personally or their organization, and others who are told to attend by their supervisors because of organisational priorities.

Perhaps most obvious motivations are those of delegates that focus on operational aspects, those who wish to gain more understanding of the potential of the digital, and how and why it can be implemented. They also wish to have opportunities to challenge themselves and push their own practices. Having a chance to gain insights from their peers, and to build a network they can call upon in the course of their leadership challenges, is another primary set of motivations. Delegates are also intent on acquiring strategies for leading or affecting change. There is a significant desire to have chances not just to reflect on practice, but to acquire the confidence to challenge and change what they are doing, and bring those changes to a wider set of people in their organizations.

During the course, it is clear from the conversations that delegates are aware that there are things they should be doing in and around digital and social media, and also things that they do not wish to engage in, because they think it will distract from the work they need to accomplish. In addition, they talk about things they want to do with their personal online practices, in particular to connect with people who they would not otherwise encounter face to face. They wish to find enjoyment in their practices, and in the connections they can make.

These motivations and concerns that delegates bring with them on the course form part of the larger context for the specific conversations we want to elicit. While the Jisc Digital Leadership course is delivered over four days, the module where we have people map, reflect on, and strategise about their individual and organisational practices takes place over only one day. However, the drawing of those maps, and the reflections on them at the outset of the course, are key to understanding and developing the leaders' practice and strategies, and links are drawn from subsequent modules back to those maps (Phipps and Lanclos, 2017).

Being and Leading Online

It is important at the beginning of our discussions of social media during the leadership course to be clear about what we mean by 'social'. Too often this is taken, especially in the UK, to mean 'unprofessional'. Key to our discussions around digital leadership is that when we talk about 'social', we are talking about it in the sense of 'connecting with people'. We are also clear that we are not approaching social media within one particular platform or digital place, but as a collective set of places and practices, which can accommodate a wide range of people and motivations.

In initial iterations of the course, we had delegates map themselves and their digital practices on the Visitors and Residents continuum (White and Le Cornu, 2011). The utility of this framing was several-fold: 1) it moved people away from negative and essentialising narratives around 'digital natives'; 2) it gave people a technique with which to describe their digital practices that allowed for a visual approach, rather than one bound by text; 3) it provided a framework that allowed for the discussion of digital places, rather than just tools, accounts, or platforms. In conceiving of the digital as a place, we gain the ability to talk about where academic work can and does happen, and include the digital in the range of possibilities. Core to these discussions of practice were motivations to engage. There was no one correct way to do this mapping, as individual variation in motivations is a crucial factor in understanding practice.

It is in our discussions of motivations, both to be present and highly visible online and also to be absent or less visible, that we elicited notions of what it means to be 'authentic' and 'credible' while online. We ask the delegates 'where are you online' so that we can also ask the questions, 'What does "Identity" mean?'; 'What are the implications of "being yourself"'; and 'Who are "we?"'

In higher and further education, 'we' does not circumscribe a homogeneous group anymore (even if senior management roles continue to be held largely by white and male people). Frequently 'leadership' acts much like the word 'professional' does, as a means of stripping our individuality away from us (Walker, 2013). Who we are in society follows us online (McMillan Cottom, 2015). Who we are also has implications for what we feel we can or should do when we are online. Concerns about identity are shot through discussions of online practice.

We have a sense from the conversations that delegates have while in this part of the course, that leaders are aware that they perform aspects of themselves, with notions of what is 'appropriate' in mind. 'Being yourself' online can mean a range of things, and during the course we do not propose a monolithic model of online behaviour. People show different parts of themselves in different places, and that is a human phenomenon that we attempt to frame as perfectly acceptable. We also warn them to be mindful about how much or how little of their authentic selves they choose to perform online. While '... we value those moments where we find the antidote to the uncanniness of the disembodied Web in what we perceive to be indisputably human interactions' (Lanclos and White, 2015), there are risks to being online that impact disproportionately on women, people of colour, or any category of person who has less access to the cultural and social privileges that accrue to white men.

Pseudonymous accounts, or separate personal and professional accounts, emerge in the mapping practices as ways to manage some of the perceived risks of being 'too human' (and therefore vulnerable) online. But Stewart (2012) makes the salient point that 'on the Internet everybody knows you're not a dog', that is, it is increasingly difficult to actually hide who you are from the people who want to find out:

> Contrary to much of the digital identity scholarship of the 1990s, which tended to emphasize the fluidity of identity uncoupled from the gendered and signified body — the "on the Internet, nobody knows you're a dog" theme — the concept of networked publics has given rise to a far more enmeshed notion of reality. (Stewart, 2012)

We also facilitate discussion around the fact that whether they choose to be online or not, some aspect of their identity is being put online, either by their institutions or in the 'data exhaust' that their voluntary online activities leave behind, to be harvested by corporations such as Google, Facebook, or Amazon. If we assert that a key part of leadership is a conversation, and accept that online presence is a necessary part of being able to engage in conversations, then who you are (perceived to be) online is a crucial component of successfully engaging with people, not just broadcasting information. If leadership is a conversation, this needs to be considered in both physical and digital places, with a critical understanding of what engagement and conversations looks like, and the role of identity and notions of authenticity within them.

Visualising Practice and Change

We built the individual digital practice elements of that first programme around what delegates gained from doing the Visitor and Resident mapping process (Lanclos et al 2016). At the time, we were intent on getting people away from assumptions that digital capability was defined by their identities, especially their 'generational identity' (Lanclos, 2014), and thought that the V&R model gave them a new place around which to orientate the conversations we wanted people to have about their practices.

For the most part, we were correct. We did have, and were able to facilitate, conversations that went beyond both top-ten tech lists and 'I am X identity,' and brought people together for conversations about what they want and need to do, and what their motivations are. In the setting up of the V&R model we were careful to discuss them as modes of behaviour, not identity types. However, we have continued to see, through three years of iterations of the course, an impulse to pigeonhole, to identify themselves and others as 'visitors' or 'residents'; creating a barrier to freeing themselves up to having new conversations around the digital.

As much as the metaphor freed us from the tyranny of generational stereotypes, it opened up a debate around the nature of what it means to be 'resident' or 'visitor', with participants asking what is 'right', what is best, and how to become more of one or the other. This was never our intention. Substituting the stereotype with a metaphor still, to some extent, obfuscated the real aim — to discuss practice in context. It is difficult to move people away from value judgements around practice, and harder still when they are using language that seems to involve personal identity.

On the programme, we want our leaders and future leaders to have a more nuanced understanding of what it means to practice in a time of ubiquitous digital. We have arrived at the point where we need to go beyond metaphor (White, 2018). Rather than annotating a metaphorical model with allusions to practice and motivation, we will start with the practices, behaviours, and motivations we want people to reflect upon.

The use of tension pairs to uncover behaviours and practices has proven effective as a baseline for change; a visual tool for identifying where both individuals and organisations are in their digital practice and their motivations, and — most importantly for the digital leaders programme — where they want to move their practice on to. The new iteration of this element of the workshop will be more tailored to support delegates in identifying the most appropriate tension pairs for their context.

Rather than using the visitor-resident continuum as one axis, we intend to provide a range of continua composed of actions and behaviours — instead of identities. For example, we might suggest that leaders map themselves against a broadcast — engagement axis. We might even solicit tension pairs from the room. We think this small modification to the leadership course format will make it easier to dig into the important content that has always been a core part of the program: an engagement with practice and current behaviours, developing the delegates' strategic thinking about the ways they want or need to change what they are doing, and what role, if any, digital tools and places can play in those changes. We think it is time in our work in the first place to give people opportunities to visualize and develop their approaches to and within digital environments, in order to focus on what people want to do. Identity is always an important part of why and how people do what they do, but it doesn't have to over-determine their practices. Our intention is to open doors, not close them by making people think that certain paths are closed because of who they are.

In between the running of the last course we facilitated (in late winter 2018) and the writing of this chapter, we have piloted a different practice mapping template, one that tries to centre people's practices as a way of initiating discussions around modes and motivations.

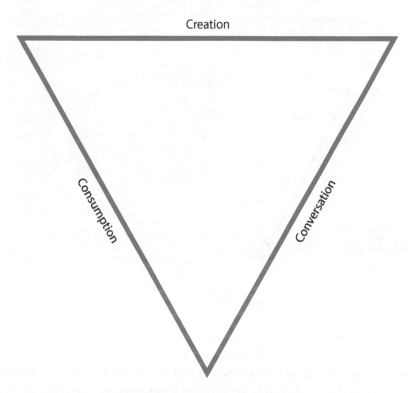

Fig. 13.1 Laurie Phipps and Donna Lanclos, Mapping triangle (2018), CC BY 4.0. The interior of the triangle is where people map the practices that are bounded by their institution and the work they do in institutional digital platforms and places. The exterior of the triangle is where they can map everything else — what they do that is not bounded by the institution. This can be their personal lives, or their work that does not take place in official channels, but rather on the open web, in self-hosted or commercial platforms

As of April 2018 we have run 4 different workshops using this template, and we found that in a swift hour's workshop we did not struggle with conversations trying to figure out 'which thing am I?' and could instead fast-track the discussion to what doing academic work, and otherwise being, in online places meant for them.

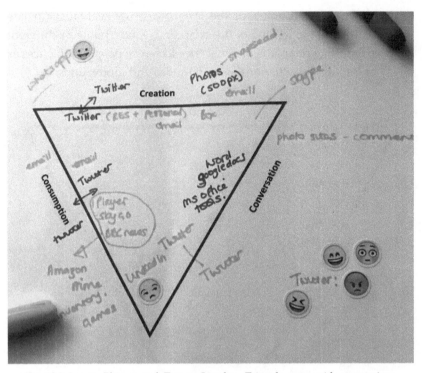

Fig. 13.2 Laurie Phipps and Donna Lanclos, Triangle map with annotations (2018). Image used with permission of participant, CC BY 4.0

As with the earlier mapping techniques, we still have people annotating their maps — we have lately been having success using emoji stickers so that people can signal how particular web spaces and tools make them feel, which then leads to discussions of the difference between the kinds of things within and around the digital that people have to do, and what they want to do. The intrinsic and extrinsic motivations to engage with email, social media, blog posts, and other web places are part and parcel of any individual's digital presence. This kind of annotation process helps create a space in which people can examine what practices do and don't serve them particularly well, and then consider what, if anything, they might be able to do to change things.

Modelling Behaviour — Leading Change

Running the leadership course in a way that focuses on practice, process, culture, and motivations (rather than tools and skills) has yielded a valuable perspective on leadership and the digital in higher education. We see in the feedback about the course that people appreciate the chance to engage in something more than 'how-tos' and 'top-tips' (even if that might have been what they were initially expecting when they signed up for the course). Many of the conversations around digital practices in higher and further education tend to be fairly operational, despite all of the things we do to enable discussions around motivations and meaning behind why they do social media.

There are still not enough places to talk about the ethical implications of human processes happening online, and we struggled even as we ran the course to provide time for such discussions. Being online cannot fix, and often amplifies, the problems of racism, sexism, bullying, and abuse of power among the people who are in those online spaces. It is incumbent on institutions to make sure that conversations about online presence are not simply about concerns such as 'where can I also have conversations with my students'. During the leadership course, we try to also create a space for addressing the continued care we need to take with vulnerable populations who don't necessarily have the same license to 'simply' be themselves and have the same conversations online than a white cishet man would. There is a lot more at stake, and a lot more risk for a black woman on Twitter than a white man, even when they are saying the same things.

As a sector, education has a responsibility to pay attention to the human problems that also exist online, and need to actually do something about it — not just recognise it, but take action to protect structurally vulnerable people. For leaders in higher and further education it is important that they model the behaviours they we want to see, not just within their institutions, but across society. That means we have to develop our leaders, and indeed all staff in higher and further education, not just to be able to use social media in an operational sense, but also understand the deeper ethical and political ramifications of being visible and active online.

References

Groysberg, B. and Slind, M. (2012). 'Leadership is a conversation'. *Harvard Business Review*, https://hbr.org/2012/06/leadership-is-a-conversation

Lanclos, D. (2014). 'How I learned to stop worrying about digital natives and love V&R'. *Donna Lanclos blog*, 7 October, http://www.donnalanclos.com/how-i-learned-to-stop-worrying-about-digital-natives-and-love-vr/

Lanclos, D. (2016, August 16). 'Ta dah: A hitchhiker's guide to doing a visitors and residents workshop'. *Donna Lanclos blog*, 16 August, http://www.donnalanclos.com/ta-dah-the-hitchhikers-guide-to-doing-a-visitors-and-residents-workshop/

Lanclos, D., Phipps, L., and White, D. (2016). 'Visitors and residents: Mapping your digital engagement. A set of mapping activities designed to facilitate reflection and discussion around online engagement', https://docs.google.com/document/d/1Bpmv8CVX_q0rYEG4_zKUQLC12qmw6INWGtwfGaVM9g/edit#

McMillan Cottom, Tressie (2015). 'Who do you think you are?' When marginality meets academic microcelebrity'. *Ada: A Journal of Gender, New Media and Technology*, 7, https://adanewmedia.org/2015/04/issue7-mcmillancottom/

Noble, Safiya Umoja (2018). *Algorithms of Oppression: How Search Engines Reinforce Racism*. New York: New York University Press.

Phipps, Lawrie, and Lanclos, Donna M. (2017). 'Leading with digital in an age of supercomplexity'. *Irish Journal of Technology Enhanced Learning*, 3:1, https://doi.org/10.22554/ijtel.v2i2.22

Stewart, B. (2012). 'Digital identities: Six key selves of networked publics', The theoryblog, 6 May, http://theory.cribchronicles.com/2012/05/06/digital-identities-six-key-selves/

Walker, C (2013). 'On privilege, intersectionality, and the librarian image', Cecily in Libraries blog, 20 December, https://cecily.info/2013/12/20/on-privilege-intersectionality-and-the-librarian-image/

White, D. S., and Le Cornu, A. (2011). 'Visitors and residents. A new typology for online engagement'. *First Monday*, 16:9, http://firstmonday.org/article/view/3171/3049

White, D. (2018). 'Arguing with the Digital Natives guy in four vexations', Digital — Learning — Culture blog, 4 January, http://daveowhite.com/vexed/

PART FIVE
BUILDING NETWORKS

14. Building Cohort Identity through Social Media

#Beginner #Blogs #WordPress #Facebook

David Webster

Introduction

What I want to focus on here is the 'social' aspect of social media, and the way we can, in higher education, leverage human tendencies to network, connect, and interact. I also want to devote a little thought to ensuring that doing so doesn't replicate or further reinforce social inequities, and avoids imperilling students' safety, self-esteem, and focus. I want to suggest that when we bear these concerns in mind, on balance, we are still able to find ways of working with social media that draws positively on our social tendencies. When Aristotle observes in *The Politics* that we are social beings, he sees it as core to normal human functioning:

> Society is something that precedes the individual. Anyone who either cannot lead the common life or is so self-sufficient as not to need to, and therefore does not partake of society, is either a beast or a god. (Aristotle and Saunders, 1992)

The runaway success of social media has shown that very few of us are either beasts or gods. Once smartphones and user-experience design reached a tipping point of socio-economic penetration and ease of use, there was an exponential rate of adoption. The much vaunted, if poorly

    https://doi.org/10.11647/OBP.0162.14

conceptualised, 'digital native' was no longer alone on social media. Grandparents were sufficiently motivated by the connections it could offer to their distributed families to overcome technical barriers, and mainstream commercial organisations began to note its reach to ever wider demographics.

Some in education have always been early adaptors of technology, due to a blend of techno-enthusiasm and a hunger to find more ways of providing effective and transformative educational experiences. Many have seen the 'sticky' nature of social media not as an opportunity, but a threat. Social media can often be a competitor for student attention, and a tireless, monetised, and dangerous competitor as well. Alongside this, the extremist tabloids that dominate the UK newspaper market have decided social media is the latest in its ongoing series of moral panics. In the 1980s parents fretted over the threat posed by ouija boards, *Dungeons and Dragons*, and brainwashing by religious cults. In the 1990s this moved to satanic ritual abuse and the impact of 'video nasties' (Luce, 2013). While the mainstream narrative increasingly portrays social media as a threat to privacy and factual information, research is much more ambivalent in its findings (for instance, see the work of the Australian scholar Catharine Lumby). Nonetheless, it is worth educators being mindful of the way any initiatives involving social media are likely to be received by colleagues, students, broader audiences, and be ready to demonstrate their benefits, and any safeguards they have put in place.

I suggest HE practitioners should consider social media in the development of cohort identity. Cohort identity here refers to the holistic sense of a 'course'. Students sit within broader faculties, departments, and academic schools, and their studies are often broken down in to units or modules; but most consider themselves students of *the course*. After all, this is usually the thing that sits on their degree certificate. While students may say that they are a 'philosophy' student, rather than identify with a broader department of humanities or faculty of arts, that does not mean that their identification is identical with the way their experience is structured. Since the modularisation of higher education in the last quarter of the twentieth century, many students and educators have worried that the course experience has been compromised. The experience can be seen as bitty, disjointed, and a piecemeal collection of modules, whose tutors may or may not have coordinated the content and assessment with each other. It is arguable that such a lack of strong cohort identity, in the area where students feel they are *based*, means that extra and co-curricular events and activities are fewer, or poorly engaged with. Intermittent attendance, and students with jobs, may mean they struggle to see their idea of 'the course' they are studying manifest into reality.

There are many ways a course team might address a sense of an absent identity across a course. Some of these might suffer from the challenges of student availability, commuter students, caring responsibilities and timetable clashes (in terms of staff, students and rooms). In my experience of a particular course, I was able, as a Course Leader, to find ways of, at least to some extent, overcoming these challenges in forging a broader sense of a 'life of the course' through a social media approach.

In the Religion, Philosophy & Ethics (RPE) course here at the University of Gloucestershire, we took both an offline and online approach to the development of cohort identity. This was an ad-hoc, unplanned approach, and required commitment from a number of colleagues, and the school management, as and when resources were required. The off-line activity involved cross-year coach trips and guest speakers as its primary tools. The trips were often to local museums, but also to religious sites in London, or Diwali in Leicester. These are not particularly unusual or innovative ideas in a course, but they were important to our social media approach. Another important aspect of these events was that they were mostly open to all RPE students, on any module, and from any year/level. The on-going calendar of events was then threaded together via the social media side of our approach. I have written elsewhere about the detail of this, but we began where social media was in 2006, with a blog:

> … I started a modest course blog called 'Religion, Philosophy and Ethics at the University of Gloucestershire' with the intended audience being our current undergraduate students.
>
> It took a while to get momentum behind it, but it slowly began to engage both the intended student audience and others with an interest in the subject area. That is, up to a point. While the blog persists today, and actually has a clearer role now than ever before, we found that other forms of new media came to surpass it in popularity.
>
> It took a while to get momentum behind it, but it slowly began to engage both the intended student audience and others with an interest in the subject area.

> During its brief moment in the sun, the blog was a noticeboard, debate hub, event invite, signpost and more. But social media, or more precisely Facebook, killed its wider role. While students still read the blog, by 2009 the comments had dried up: people did their interacting elsewhere. So, as Facebook was where most conversations were happening, we realised that's where we needed to go, too. (Webster, 2015)

The blog can still be found, now with over a decade of content, and I still pop the odd thing on it to keep some sense of currency, and to prevent it from becoming too much of a digital relic. Since then, we have had to match our practice to the shifts in social media usage. Our Facebook group initially became a way to connect current students with each other. It operated better than a 'page', which was something more promotional and didn't have the requisite functionality. While at first we used the group to have students interact across years and modules; we had ambitions beyond interaction and event advertising. This was really intended to develop of a sense of 'us'. The staff were able to adopt a consistent tone, and draw on links, news stories, and articles, in order to give a sense of what we are all about on this course. Hence, we became able to model the way that academics interacted with the world, via the prism of our subject. To some extent, this gave us all a sense of being engaged in some form of common endeavour, using philosophy and religion to try and collectively make sense of the world. What began to happen after a year or so of the Facebook group was that students began, as they do, to leave and new students arrived. What this meant was that the group now had graduates in as well. We also mentioned it at Open Days, and during outreach activities. The group began to have potential students, and Religious Studies teachers in too. It still does, but as time has gone by, the biggest group by far is that of graduates. They are not as active as current students, but the Facebook group has been a key means of keeping a more direct alumni connection with the course. In this same period, of 2006–2009, we made use of a Flickr account to host photo content, and to operate as a course photo album. This worked nicely on Open Days, as it gave a sense of what it was like to be on the course, with lots of shots from coach trips, our visits to Spain, and internal events. This still exists, and is posted to, but we have also begun to use Instagram, due to its dominant position and easy integration with Twitter, and the ability to use hashtags effectively.

For five years or so, the Facebook group was hugely active, and served as somewhere we could bring together our other activity. Guest speakers, including those who had physically visited as well as those we had Skyped into classes, would also join the group and answer questions. It also served as the primary events noticeboard, and way of sharing photos from field trips. There emerged from it a real sense of the course; a sense of something that over-spilled the classroom; of something more than a collection of modules. By 2014 this was clearly not the case in so strong a sense. Facebook was not the dominant market leader in that same way. We had already begun to use Twitter, and had been producing a video-interview resource blog at www.philosvids. wordpress.com since 2012. These began to have a new importance, as we strove to thread all this together to maintain this sense of our course identity. This has been partly effective. The Twitter account seems to resonate most effectively as a means of reaching wider audiences, notably teachers in schools. The video interview blog also has global visitors but we also use it in a conjunction with our internal VLE (Virtual Learning Environment, Moodle in our case) to host video content that is part of our core course delivery — so our students make a lot of use of the wider resource. The Facebook group still has activity, but its dominance has passed.

This fragmentation does mean a certain level of extra labour, and although we have sufficient staff buy-in to largely make it work, and maintain our sense of a collective course identity, it comes at a cost of time. Our response, in part, along with the rest of our wider academic School in the University has been to have a course-level Social Media Intern from the student body, who we give a tablet device to, and who takes a role in tweeting and some posting on the course Instagram account. The hashtags on Instagram also mean that staff and students can share pictures from a trip, without the need for a central course account.

If I was trying to spin out a wider set of recommendations from our experiences, these would open by stating that you shouldn't underestimate the amount of both time and energy that using social media can soak up. Yes, you can use tools to auto-schedule WordPress posts, and tweets, and you can become very efficient, but it requires staff who *really* want to do it. And staff who will be there next year. Dormant social media is like a flag of a stale course to external audiences! It also takes time to keep on top of current trends and norms, and avoid seeming to merely go through the motions. Social media literacy takes time to both develop and maintain, and a reluctant course team will be at a real risk of generating materials that make the students feel less part of the course, rather than supporting and generating a sense of identity.

Another set of considerations relate to privacy, opt-ins, and the nature of online spaces. We never required students to join Facebook, and there are ever-growing reasons to steer clear of doing so. We always sought to post to Moodle a copy of anything important that went to Facebook. We also used a guideline whereby we refrained from being Facebook 'friends' with potential and current students. While the course Instagram and Twitter accounts do follow the accounts of our students, I ensure my personal accounts (which students can follow) do not follow student accounts on those platforms. This avoids me seeing any information that might compromise my role in marking student work, avoids the issue of who I do and don't follow, and allows me to give the students clarity and sense of borders. When we began to make greater use of more public spaces, like Twitter, for students to communicate through — rather than the public-broadcast model of a blog, or the walled-garden of our Facebook group (which requires membership to be approved by a moderator) — another set of issues concerned us. Public Internet spaces are experienced by me (a middle-aged, male, white, straight, professional), quite differently to the way those spaces can feel for, say, young women, BAME students, or openly transgender students. We need to be wary that our enthusiasm for the advantages we might see as accruing from student social media use doesn't blind us to ethical considerations. Should I really nudge my students into spaces where they may experience abuse, or other troubling interactions which I have no control over? It is of course the case that many students may have these experiences anyway, but there is something about them taking place as part of an approved study setting that is problematic and normalising.

In terms of closing, I fear there is no silver bullet, and the target seems to be perpetually moving anyway. However, my sense is that building course identity so that the cohort of students currently studying with you feel something collective, is partly about the off-line activity: the language we use in class, that we 'do things together' (events, trips, and the like) helping them feel included in the wider 'life of the course'. Social media can play a role in broadcasting and showcasing, but also in intensifying and reinforcing the sense of the communal, such that in its best moments it becomes a tool of self-fulfilling prophecy, and that the students really, when they log in and see their course activity, gain a sense of belonging.

References

Aristotle (1992). *The Politics*. London: Penguin.

Luce, A. (2013). Moral Panics: Reconsidering Journalism's Responsibilities', in Fowler-Watt, K. and Allan, S. (eds.) *Journalism: New Challenges*. Poole, England: CJCR: Centre for Journalism & Communication Research, Bournemouth University, pp. 393–409, http://eprints.bournemouth.ac.uk/21051/1/JNC-2013-Chapter-24-Luce.pdf

Webster, D. (2015). 'Lessons learned: How departmental social media use in universities needs to evolve and grow', Jisc Blog, 3 December, https://www.jisc.ac.uk/blog/how-departmental-social-media-use-in-universities-needs-to-evolve-and-grow-03-dec-2015

15. Creating a Sense of Belonging and Connectedness for the Student Arrival Experience in a School of Arts and Humanities

#Beginner #Facebook #FacebookLive

Rachel Challen

Introduction

This chapter outlines the use of Facebook Live in September 2017, to connect with new students prior to their arrival on campus in their first semester. The aim of this approach was to contribute towards creating the conditions in which a community culture could continue to develop within our Arts and Humanities curriculum. Social media formed one initiative within a tripartite strategies (two of which built on existing practices which happen post-arrival) designed to create a nurturing environment, encouraging community, a sense of belonging, and connectedness. Data show that in January 2018, following these initiatives, all first-year student withdrawals were reduced in comparison to the same point in the previous year. The Facebook Live approach attracted 5,600 views and 2,470 comments, likes and shares from September 2017 to December 2017.

    https://doi.org/10.11647/OBP.0162.15

Why Does Belonging Matter?

Belonging and community have long been identified as key areas that can impact on retention and engagement in HE (Foster et al., 2011, Thomas, 2012), especially in the early stages of undergraduate study, where careful consideration must be given to eliminating conditions which may promote alienation (Mann, 2001) and ultimately lead to withdrawal from university. Providing opportunities for students to 'negotiate their new identities' and build initial relationships regardless of their eventual longevity is vital in the early days of the transition into university life: the fear of not being able to build friendships was found by Wilcox, Winn and Fyvie-Gauld (2005) in their empirical study to be the main anxiety for students. To minimise this anxiety in the School of Arts and Humanities, which offers a highly personalised undergraduate degree with both single and joint honours available, the School has developed three new activities — including the Facebook Live event — which were designed to minimise any sense of isolation and encourage students on different courses to get to know one another. The aim was to create an environment in which the successful transition into university life is made easier by engaging students in a supportive social culture. The three activities were designed to align with the following transition success factors, identified by Yorke and Thomas (2003, p. 72):

- an institutional climate supportive in various ways of students' development, that is perceived as 'friendly';

- an emphasis on support leading up to, and during, the critically important first-year of study;

- an emphasis on formative assessment in the early phase of programmes;

- a recognition of the importance of the social dimension in learning activities;

- recognition that the pattern of students' engagement in higher education is changing, and a preparedness to respond positively to this in various ways.

The trio of events included the structured Facebook Live event that took place pre-arrival, a welcome week including a networking party immediately after arrival, and Personal Tutorial Groups embedded throughout the first academic year. The formal induction event was redesigned as a welcome week that focussed more on community-building than information-giving, and placed students at the centre of the experience to promote a sense of belonging and mutual respect, with the hope of reducing instances of social isolation. The structure and content of the Personal Tutor Group were revisited to encourage activities that were more pastoral and less saturated with information to make them more valuable to students. Research by Irwin and Knight (2017) finds that 'welcoming, committed staff and a sense of community with fellow students were factors which were felt to promote belonging'; nurturing and enforcing feelings of mattering which Rosenberg (in Schlossberg, 1989) suggests does determine behaviour.

However, acclimatisation activities in welcome week and first-year pastoral support in Personal Tutor Groups are obviously only available after students have arrived on campus. There are still practical anxieties that can have a negative effect on social engagement in that first week if not addressed before arrival, and this concern was the motivation for the Facebook Live project.

Facebook Live as the Connector

Facebook is a popular social media platform in the UK: 30 million people access Facebook on their mobile devices every day and 70% of 16–22–year–olds report that they use Facebook (McGrory, 2018). In addition to market reach, Facebook was chosen for this project because it links directly to the school's enrolment and marketing strands, and all enrolled students are invited to join the Arts and Humanities Facebook page. Since the audience had chosen to be connected to the School on social media, it was likely that they would be interested in a message transmitted through this channel. The intention of the pre-arrival event was to engage first-year students in a real life, as well as online, community and provide a supported transition bridge into successful university life.

Social media was used to develop students' attachment and the sense of connectedness to the Arts and Humanities School before arriving on campus; this gave us the opportunity to utilize the concept of converging media (Meikle and Young, 2012) where multiple media forms are blended into one platform, with the broadcast element provided by Facebook Live and the personal communication method by Facebook comments. This method allows the presenter of the Facebook Live event to build individual social identities of the members of the group, which contributes heavily to the students sense of self and helps to shape how students start to align with others in the group (Brown, 2000). This in turn builds 'a collective intentionality based on social facts' (Searle, 1996, p. 38) helping to establish the expectations the School has of the students and the expectations the students have of the School regarding study, thus building a practical consciousness (Giddens, 2014) of how to cooperate, cope and get things done. To underpin this, the Facebook Live event was developed to show key facilities on campus, the subject buildings and active learning classrooms, and to introduce academic and support staff that students would encounter and could ask for help if needed. This gave an opportunity to create social bonds, reduce anxiety, and break down barriers for new incoming students.

Planning and Implementing a Facebook Live Event

Storyboarding

Although the whole feel of the Facebook Live event was intentionally informal and relaxed, it took a lot of planning and collaboration between the academic team and marketing department of the School, and the university's video content team. It was important that the message achieved the aims outlined above, and so a series of storyboards were created and refined, one of these was chosen to structure the event. The rejected versions were judged to be too focused on marketing. The intended student audience had already confirmed their place and were due on campus the week after the event was due to take place; any attempt to sell the university was unnecessary and irrelevant to the message. The approach we chose allowed the School to 'address a specific audience — or at least know that there is a generic interest in the message' (Couldry, 2012, p. 64).

The final storyboard focused on reducing anxiety by showing students the spaces they would be inhabiting; introducing them to key administrative staff whom they would see regularly and who could help them with their most pressing enquiries; and interviewing academic staff from different departments to explain what the first week would be like, including their expectations of the students, the first steps the students would take in their studies, and the responsibilities of the School towards the student. Contributing to the aim of breaking down barriers, Dr Karen Randell, Deputy Dean of the School of Arts and Humanities, took on the role of 'guide' throughout the event. Joseph Walther's (1996) model of hyperpersonal computer-mediated communication indicates that online visual interactions form stronger impressions of presenters' personalities, as the visual cues stimulate a more positive response from the receiver. However, since 'the performance of an individual accentuates certain matters and conceals others' (Goffman, 1959, p. 67), it was important that the storyboard and script was collectively written and produced so it accurately reflected the experience that students could expect.

The event was timed to be of twenty minutes' duration, which is the optimum length recommended by Facebook, to give opportunity for followers of the page to see the video in their news feed and view it live if they had forgotten it was happening — the longer run time therefore enhances the probability of more viewers. The storyboard preparation ensured smooth transitions between the key spaces, rooms and staff that were featured. A written representation of the storyboard is given below:

Item	Areas Visited	Purpose
An overview of the campus		To show the layout of the campus and where key items or activities could be found; for example the student union building, the refectory, and the bookshop.
Walking from the centre of campus to the main Arts and Humanities building		To provide visual directions and memorable landmarks that would give confidence to students navigating their first day.

	Administration	On arrival to the Arts and Humanities building, viewers were introduced to the receptionist to reassure students that they could get help finding rooms or buildings. The school administration team were also introduced as the place to get help with any study-related queries. *Staff: Building receptionist, school administration receptionist.*
	Technician support	Media practice is a module option available to students, so the media kit and technician were introduced to give an insight into the support available. *Staff: Media Technician.*
	PC space, Media Labs, DJ room and Language Labs	A tour of the teaching rooms available on the ground floor of the building ended in the Language Labs, highlighting the support and community available for those who wish to study a language as part of their course. *Staff: Principle Lecturer in Spanish / Personalisation Manager.*
Introduction to key staff and areas.	Global Lounge	The Global Lounge Manager is available to all students and leads the 'Languages in Tandem' initiative, highlighting the extracurricular opportunities and community available. *Staff: Global Lounge Manager.*

	Academics	The last section focused on the academic and pastoral support available to students through modules and Personal Tutor groups, with the aim of reassuring students that there was support and guidance available during all aspects of their university experience.
Introduction to key staff and areas.		*Staff: Head of English, Creative and Media, Senior Lecturer in History.*

Fig. 15.1 Rachel Challen, Written representation of the storyboard (2018), CC BY 4.0

Practice Runs

Once the storyboard was in place, the whole team, including academic, marketing and video staff, did one practice run to check that the running order worked smoothly and to test technical aspects like Wi-Fi access and sound. Due to difficulties in Wi-Fi access the storyboard was amended after this practice run. A further practice was held with all the participants involved to give them an opportunity to become familiar with the questions they would be asked and where the camera and host would be placed in relation to them.

The Event

Fig. 15.2 Rachel Challen, Photo of (L-R) Dr Sharon Ouditt, Head of Department, English, Media and Creative Cultures; Dr Karen Randell, Deputy Dean; and Dr Nicholas Morton, Senior Lecturer in History (2018), CC BY 4.0

For the event, there was a cameraman broadcasting to the Arts and Humanities Facebook page, using a smartphone and gimbal (a device that holds the phone steady and allows smooth tracking), with a tie mic attached to the main host, Dr Randell. As the broadcast was happening, there was also a second video technician who was listening live to the broadcast and could indicate if the Wi-Fi or sound had dropped.

Throughout the live broadcast, an extra element of social bonding between host and viewers was encouraged in the style of an ongoing quiz in which viewers were asked a question (e.g. 'the name of the Arts and Humanities building is "Mary Ann Evans" — what was her pen name?') and the first person to add the correct answer to the comment section underneath won a prize to be collected from the Deputy Dean's office when they arrived on campus. This narrative arc provided anchor points during and after the broadcast, helping to cement the personalised approach and provide authenticity to the event.

The broadcast also set out to clarify the School's expectations about teaching and learning and the engagement of students in university life, to help with early transitions and to 'perpetuate a self-fulfilling prophecy that people in the group conform to the level expected of them' (Brown, 2000, p. 75).

This was the first time the Arts and Humanities school had trialled a Facebook Live event, and the reach and engagement of the video went well beyond expectations. The statistics two weeks after the broadcast showed:

- Reach of Art and Humanities Facebook page: **12,650** people

- Views: **5,600** (over 6,000 views when including Twitter, LinkedIn and WordPress).

- Engagement: **2,100** post clicks, and **370** likes, comments and shares.

Reflection on the Approach Taken

Even with the current (April 2018) concern over data mining, we still believe Facebook is an appropriate platform to use for future live video. Followers of the Arts and Humanities group page do not have access to the accounts or data of other followers, and so the information contained in these accounts remains private. This group approach therefore allows students to maintain their privacy before they arrive, so they can adapt to their new circumstances without anyone having preconceived ideas about them. This gives them the ability to make their first transitional steps towards building a community with a sense of freedom. However, it would be remiss to ignore the possibility that the approach taken by using Facebook Live could exacerbate the feeling of exclusion by its social media exclusivity and accessibility. This could happen when students do not have a Facebook account or simply do not want to engage in this type of communication. This was why it was a value-added approach and just one of three new or improved strategies that we employed in 2017–2018, combined with post-arrival activities including the welcome week and Personal Tutor groups. The data collected in January 2018 showed a reduction in withdrawals, indicating that student transitions into higher education have been more successful and the approaches instigated in 2017–2018 helped to nurture a sense of community, belonging and connectedness.

Next Steps

As this was the first Facebook Live event attempted from this specific page, there is no comparable data to ascertain whether the views should be higher, and no correlation can be made between the number of views and the success of the project; success can only be evaluated with a longitudinal study following the new students through to the completion of their course and by qualitative research undertaken with current students about their experiences. Reflections from this year have led to changes in the approach for welcome week and Personal Tutor groups are being further defined, with students playing a big part in creating their own experiences. The Facebook Live video will be reused but in a different way; the recorded video will be chunked into topics and played as forerunner to a live question and answer session on different days, again with a range of staff hosting those sessions through the School Facebook page. These will also be recorded and placed on the group page, to act not only as a frequently-asked-questions section, but to further develop the sense of belonging and an inclusive culture, and to contribute to the reduction of any anxiety in the first weeks of attending university.

References

Brown, R. (2000). *Group Processes: Dynamics Within and Between Groups*. 2nd edn. Oxford: Blackwell Publishing.

Couldry, N. (2012). *Media, Society, World: Social Theory and Digital Media Practice*. Cambridge: Polity Press.

Foster, E., Lawther, S., Keenan, C., Bates, N., Colley, B. and Lefever, R. (2011). 'The HERE project final report', http://www.heacademy.ac.uk/resources/detail/what-works-student-retention/HERE_Project_What_Works_Final_Report

Giddens, A. (2014). *The Constitution of Society, Outline of the Theory of Saturation*. Cambridge: Polity Press.

Goffman, E. (1990). *The Presentation of Self in Everyday Life*. St Ives: Penguin Books.

Irwin, J., and Knight, J. (2017). 'Developing an understanding of why students don't engage'. *Journal of Educational Innovation, Partnership and Change*, 3:1, pp. 198–203, https://doi.org/10.21100/jeipc.v3i1.642

Mann, S. (2001). 'Alternative Perspectives on the Student Experience: Alienation and engagement', *Studies in Higher Education*, 26:1, pp. 7–19, https://doi.org/10.1080/03075070020030689

McGory, R. (2018). 'UK social media statistics for 2018', http://www.rosemcgrory.co.uk/2018/01/01/uk-social-media-statistics-for-2018/

Meikle, G. and Young, S. (2012). *Media Convergence: Networked Digital Media in Everyday Life*. Basingstoke: Palgrave Macmillan.

Searle, J. R. (1999). *The Construction of Social Reality*. St Ives: Penguin Books

Schlossberg, N. (Winter 1989). 'Marginality and mattering: Key issues in building community'. *New Directions for Student Services*, 48, pp. 5–15, https://doi.org/10.1002/ss.37119894803

Thomas, L. (2012). 'Building student engagement and belonging in Higher Education at a time of change: Final report from the What Works? Student Retention & Success programme', https://www.heacademy.ac.uk/node/2932

Walther. J. (1996). 'Computer Mediated Communication, Impersonal, Interpersonal and hyperpersonal interaction', *Communication Research*, 23:1, pp. 3–34.

Wilcox, P, Winn. S, and Fyvie-Gauld. M. (2005). '"It was nothing to do with the university, it was just the people": The role of social support in the first-year experience of higher education', *Studies in Higher Education*, 30:6, pp. 707–22, https://doi.org/10.1080/03075070500340036

Yorke M, and Thomas L. (2003). 'Improving the retention of students from lower socio-economic groups', *Journal of Higher Education Policy and Management*, 25:1, pp. 63–74.

16. Joint Reflection on Twitter, Phenomenography and Learning Friendships

#Intermediate #Phenomenography #Twitter

Margy MacMillan and Chrissi Nerantzi

What Is This All About?

This chapter is about being brave enough to ask, and curious enough to respond to, questions about how a mutually beneficial relationship developed out of social media. One half of the relationship under discussion is Chrissi, an academic developer in the United Kingdom, who was in the midst of completing her PhD when she met Margy, a librarian and researcher in Canada at the time. This chapter presents a reflective conversation between these two individuals, who met via Twitter. Together, they share their experiences of the relationship as well as their feelings, and ask each other questions they didn't (dare to) ask before. Neither the structure nor the themes they explore were pre-defined. As the story unfolds, it illuminates the potential of social media to enable individuals, who would otherwise probably never meet, to connect at a professional and personal level, and to develop honest, trusting, and lasting friendships.

The chapter starts with two stories of prior experiences of seeking and finding help. These serve as an introduction to the story that brought

https://doi.org/10.11647/OBP.0162.16

Margy and Chrissi together in the Twittersphere. These discussions were based around their shared understanding of a research methodology called phenomenography. This is a qualitative research methodology, usually based on interviews that aims to investigate the way people think or experience something. It emphasises the interviewee's refection and description of experiences.

How It Used To Be...

Working in the Dark, by Margy

My first big research project involved examining 300 pieces of writing by students — some aspects of the project were quantifiable, while others were more qualitative and open to a lot of interpretation. Stumbling around in the literature for a way to make sense of what I was reading, I came across a thesis by Christine Bruce (*The 7 Faces of Information Literacy*) that used phenomenography, a method I had never heard of but that she described so clearly it gave me the confidence to use it in working with my data. No-one I worked with knew the methodology, and at the time my institution was teaching-focused with very little support for research in general. Without anyone to talk to about my project or to bounce ideas around with, it felt very lonely. In the end, I gave up. I used Bruce's methods to break down the data and conduct basic qualitative analysis sufficient for the project, but attempting to generate deeper insights by building up categories was like rolling the proverbial rock up a hill, and the 'outcome spaces' (a discussion that enable ideas to be debated in an unfettered manner) that are the hallmark of phenomenography eluded me. Even with the end product of a useful, published article, I felt I had missed the mark and that failure rankled.

Fortunately, I was able re-engage with phenomenography for another project. I went back to its beginnings and read papers that explored how the method developed in sequence. It helped that phenomenography was a more suitable method for the questions I was investigating this time, but even more, it helped that the research culture at my institution had changed and there was far more knowledge and support available. I benefited from a Scholarship of Teaching and Learning (SoLT) research group in the initial study but what really made the difference was a 'critical friend'. Also, Karen Manarin, a Professor of English at Mount Royal University, and I had worked together in teaching and on many projects. While Karen does not use phenomenography in her own work, she understands the method well. The subject of my study, student reading of scholarly materials, is an area of interest and research we share. Being able to talk through my findings with an expert researcher who understood the phenomenon I was looking at helped me to find deeper stories in the data than I ever could have done alone. In countless conversations, she patiently listened as I detailed a set of categories and then asked the questions that prompted me to look again, try again, and categorize again. Throughout it all, she reassured me that the story I was discovering was worth telling, useful, and supported by the data. We know each other well, I trust her implicitly and I am in awe of her knowledge and analytical ability. Having an excellent mentor like Karen so close by was very different from Chrissi's experience.

Phoning a Complete Stranger, by Chrissi

In the days before social media making connections and research breakthroughs often remained an uncertain and time consuming process. I remember in the olden days when I was a translator and I needed help searching for a term or phrase that I couldn't understand with accuracy or find an explanation for anywhere. Usually the author was no longer alive, my reference guides, lexicons and encyclopaedia were letting me down, and nobody I knew, knew.

These were the olden days, before social media. Encyclopaedia and specialist lexicons filled my walls. We had a landline and phone books, with which we reached out to the people we knew or could discover there.

I vividly remember phoning around when I was translating *Der Kurgast* by Hermann Hesse. Herman was referring to some technical casino term. I had no clue what it was. I had no related reference guide, no encyclopaedia that was sufficiently detailed about casino games. I also had no experience of being or playing in a casino, nor did I have a friend who did. I could have just skipped it, but as a translator it was important to me to preserve and transfer what was in the original into the target language. I felt a strong responsibility and obligation towards the author and his work — not because Hesse won a Nobel Prize for Literature; I felt exactly the same when translating the work of any author. I needed help. After asking everybody I knew, I reached for the phone book. A few days and phone calls later, I ended up speaking with somebody who was working in a casino on Siros island in the Aegean. I explained my problem and described my patchy understanding of the specific passage in the book. I was lucky. He understood and our conversation helped me to solve the problem. I could move on, finally.

We all know what the possibilities and the opportunities are now in the time of social media, but the situation was very different when I was working on that book in 1998.

Living in the Recent Now

The story that follows, written as a dialogue, relates to the same two professionals who shared their individual stories above. They were strangers, physically separated by the Atlantic Ocean and their different, if overlapping, professions. They were united via Twitter by their common interests in phenomenography, learning, reading, and helping others. The following is the story of how these two individuals connected, and the human relationship that grew out of that connection.

Margy (M): A question for Chrissy to start — what prompted you to post the request on Twitter?

Chrissi (C): Good question and an easy one to answer. Twitter for me has become a really rich and dynamic human resource for multidirectional help.

However, just buying, as my mum would say, without selling, would not lead to much. Giving with our heart without expecting anything in return can make a huge difference to the connections we form and how others see us. If I can help I will and if I can't, I will try to find somebody who can. A colleague has called me an academic matchmaker. I guess this might be true. So for me, part of who I am personally and professionally is helping others and I regularly do this through social media and particularly Twitter. It came naturally to me to ask for help in this space, and I was hoping, not expecting (there is a big difference there) that somebody would respond in the same way as I offer my help to others.

C: So Margy, you asked me why I reached out via Twitter in my desperation. I am curious to find out, what made you respond. Do you remember?

M: I think our mums may have been kindred spirits! Similar to my work in teaching, if I know something that might help someone else, I can't hold back… vocation? Compulsion? Either way, having had my own struggles with phenomenography and been helped tremendously by someone else, I *had* to respond. I know that even just articulating questions for someone else can help to clarify one's thinking, and I was happy to offer to be a sounding board, idea bouncer, or whatever else might help. I saw the tweet through Penny Bentley (@penpln) and the *Teaching & Learning Inquiry Journal* (@TLI_ISSOTL).

Penny Bentley @penpln 16 Apr 2016

"@chrissinerantzi: Help please! Looking for great examples of phenomenographic outcome spaces. Please RT. Thank you." #phgchat[1]

Once the communication started, the first thing I did was very 'librarianish': I sent a list of resources, most of which you probably already had.

@penpln @TLI_ISSOTL @chrissinerantzi Lots in the information literacy literature — Christine Bruce, Clarence Maybee… Can dm you more[2]

M: I'm wondering now — how much of a response did you get and what prompted you to trust enough to engage with me?

C: It's wonderful to find out what made you respond to my call.

No, I didn't get many responses. I heard from you and Penny Bentley, whom you just mentioned and who was also a PhD student at the time. Penny then set up the Facebook group as she also needed help with phenomenography and felt a community approach would help us both. I think somebody also highlighted the phenomenography

---

1   https://twitter.com/penpln/status/721438168625520640
2   https://twitter.com/margymaclibrary/status/721455459077500928

hashtag on Twitter (#phgchat), which was also useful — I think that might have been a Professor from Sweden called Ake Ingerman; he was very supportive.

You saved me! You saved me from going insane struggling to understand what I needed to do to create that outcome space from the categories of description that emerged through my analysis (Marton, 1981). I found it more productive to discuss and have a collegial exchange with somebody, instead of just reading about the outcome space on my own. Also, seeing and discussing examples was extremely useful. Some might think that this is strange, but I guess it comes from my desire to interact and share, perhaps? And my dialogic approach to learning? It is so easy to get lost in bits of paper, bits of academic writing, and the worst thing is the papers don't speak back when you have a question.

So before the tweet I felt really lonely in my struggles and then after the tweet, I suddenly had a mini network. Just perfect! This instantly made me feel a bit more confident that I would get through this challenge and synthesise my findings in the outcome space to show the logical relationships among the categories of description. Sorry, I am not answering your question. Let me see, what was the question? Oh yes, I have responded to the first part, I think. Why I trusted you? How did I know you were genuine?

I guess, in an open space like Twitter we don't know. Actually in life we never know. But I start with trusting people. I see the good in people. And there are often early signs if somebody is not trustworthy… or when things change…

From the beginning I felt that you were a very warm and giving individual. I actually often felt guilty asking more and more questions of you. I had no idea how this felt to you and I was scared that you felt that I was using you? I hope you didn't get that impression. But it was really tricky for me; I didn't want to over-ask, if you know what I mean, and abuse your kind and generous offer to help me and the time you made to help me.

C: Now that we are writing this, maybe you could tell me how you felt about all my questions?

M: At the start, what I felt most was empathy. Having been in that space fairly recently, I really understood your frustration, anxiety, and 'hitting a brick wall in the dark' feelings, because I had felt them all myself but in a situation with much lower stakes than a PhD. I knew that it had helped me to talk through my work with an interested listener and that I could be that listener for someone else.

It was also wonderful for me to talk to someone immersed in phenomenography… and nice for me to be able to use the knowledge I had gained. Not a lot of people on my campus were interested in it, and no one had gone as deeply into it as you had, Chrissi. It was very gratifying to have my knowledge appreciated, and, actually, strengthened through my having to go into it more deeply with you. I had some misgivings at an early stage about whether my understanding of phenomenography was strong enough to help, but listening was certainly within my skill-set.

Once our conversation took off, I was fascinated by the research, and by your teaching work as seen through the eyes of your participants. It was really clear how important the framework you were developing could be for both research and practice. As a SoTL researcher interested in understanding learning, and as a librarian with a commitment to ensuring good information gets to people who need it, it became important to me that your findings become part of the record.

And yes, there were lots of questions, but they were always interesting questions; often working through them was the most challenging (in a good way) part of my week. And reading through your drafts gave me an amazing, privileged look into your thought processes, as you refined and revised your chapters. I was only sorry that I couldn't always respond as quickly as I would have liked, due to other commitments.

Alongside all of this intellectual stimulation, I felt a real connection, a friendship that grew as we learned more about each other… everything from the weather and politics of the day to families and holidays. I 'heard' your other conversations on Twitter and it felt like hearing you down an office hallway. And also in working with you I've learned a lot about, and felt freer in bringing my whole self to academic work; heart and head, being present as a person, not just an academic, closing up the distance even across oceans.

Long answer to a short question… how did I feel? Engaged, useful, challenged, whole.

M: Chrissi, we conversed through messages asynchronously for a couple of months before we set up a Skype… was there anything different about that mode of communication for you?

C: You are very kind and generous Margy, and I am so pleased it was a useful experience for you too.

I felt that you showed real interest in my work and wanted me to understand phenomenography better, and especially to enhance my understanding of the outcome space. But you also helped me see value in my work. You are very knowledgeable and I really valued our conversations and the papers you shared. You helped me see phenomenography under a different light and actually learn to love it. You had a very soft and gentle way of letting me know what wasn't clear enough and the connections that made sense. This really helped me a lot and boosted my confidence during the construction of the outcome space. I soon realised that step by step, I made a little progress every day until I got there in the end, with your help. You asked me if I felt engaged — I would say, I started feeling immersed into phenomenography thanks to our conversations and exchanges, and I let go of what I didn't understand, if you like. I was clinging on to little bits that made sense and slowly I was knitting my own understanding of phenomenography and particularly the outcome space. In a way, the flexibility and the freedom this methodology brings was torture for me initially, during the analysis stages, and I think this happens with anything we do when we don't feel confident enough. We feel lost. I felt lost initially but when it all started coming together and made sense, I started loving this freedom phenomenography brings and our exchanges contributed massively to this as I could see the outcome space, the final output of the analysis, coming together.

Yes, very interesting that we for some time just communicated asynchronously and via text… however some of our responses to each other were almost done in real time. They were so quick, and almost immediate sometimes. But, I have to say this initial written communication didn't feel strange or wrong for some reason. It worked. It provided focus perhaps? Maybe our experiences in a pre-social-media life played a role in this? I don't know. I would be interested in your thoughts on this too.

My study, as you know, shows that synchronous connections, especially via a video link, can speed up relationships and make them real and increase mutual commitment. But then maybe we were selectively collaborating (see the connection?) and not really immersed fully in the relationship itself and the output, but more absorbed by the task, and we got different things from it? It was more about the process perhaps? And that does link back to my study, actually.

C: What do you think Margy?

M: How fascinating to see it go meta like this. Yes, I think in part because we were selectively collaborating, and benefiting in different ways, it may not have been quite so vital to have early synchronous communication. I think also it may relate to the boundary crossing you describe in your thesis and it may be that some of those boundaries — professional, experience level — may be easier to cross through asynchronous messages, at least initially, than in face-to-face settings (online or in person), with the time that brings for reflection and consideration and the care I think that writing requires, knowing it will be received without body language or expression. In a way, reading what you said made me 'listen' harder, too — and I could 'hear' your confidence in your findings growing with every revision. I also began seeing examples of what you were finding all around me, in my own experiences and in various professional development contexts. Your work gave me another lens to look at my own projects, and since collaborating with you, Lave and Wenger have weirdly cropped up in all kinds of other projects I'm involved in.

Through you, I joined in with so many other interesting conversations, on Twitter, in the literature, through the Facebook group, that have been some of the most rewarding professional experiences of a very long career. Thank you for that! I have also enjoyed pointing others in the direction of you and your work... and look forward to continuing to do so, especially now your thesis is available (Nerantzi, 2017)!

C: Thank you so much Margy. I think what we have articulated together is that answers and questions lie within people and it is the exchanges among them that drive our understanding forward and help us see new and novel connections. Thank you for being you and for your valuable help. I would love to meet you in person one day.

M: One day!

So What Are We Taking Away?

The process of writing this dialogic piece was insightful for both of us, and an adventure at the same time. We didn't have a plan when we started, and we were wandering and wondering while writing it until we reached our destination — or is this a new beginning? We wanted to explore our lived experience and gain insights into how two individuals might come together in the Twitter jungle. The hooks emerged and the connections lit up, similar to what happens in phenomenography that brought us together. This is fascinating. Our experience echoes many of the themes Stewart (2016) found in her study of academic Twitter use. In particular, Twitter helped us overcome geographic and methodological isolation, and further too, as she notes, 'participants also valued the opportunities that hyperpersonal communications offer them to be, in effect, a person who offers care to others' (p. 76). This, we think, was true for both of us as our connections and conversations had a strong current of mutual encouragement. Wenger, White and Smith (2009) would recognize our experience as a 'learning friendship', one of the ways learning in communities is enacted and supported (p. 24). A study by Jordan and Weller (2018) around online networking showed that only 6.3% of academics among 189 study participants were using social media to help others. This came as a big surprise to both of us and we are wondering what the barriers are, since our own experience showed a real potential for peer-to-peer assistance enabled by social media technologies.

Dahlgren (2005, p. 30) characterises the construction of the outcome space as an 'intense examination of empirical data'. We undertook this through our conversations. It really deepened our individual understandings about phenomenography.

C: I can see now how I could have initiated or extended such a conversation much earlier, during the analysis stage. The dialogue with a peer would have been valuable to eliminate fears, uncertainties and dilemmas I was confronted with, but also for scrutinising my personal interpretations (Collier-Reed et al., 2009) during the analysis. It would have been a helpful alternative to exclusively capturing the process in my reflective diary while working on my own through the messy iterative process of constructing the categories of descriptions. Neither Margy nor I think it would have *polluted* the analysis — it could have enriched it.

M: For me, working from that early stage with my own mentor gave a certain sense of validity to the work that encouraged me to look and think more deeply. Working with Chrissi has strengthened my understanding of phenomenography as it has developed, and provided, in the framework Chrissi drew out of her research, a highly useful tool for examining and understanding learning in diverse contexts. Thank YOU, Chrissi!

C: Thank you Margy! I am looking forward to helping you with some of your work.

References

Collier-Reed, B. I., Ingerman, A. and Berglund, A. (2009). 'Reflections on trustworthiness in phenomenographic research: Recognising purpose, context and change in the process of research', *Education as Change*, 132, pp. 339–55, http://www.diva-portal.org/smash/get/diva2:276936/FULLTEXT01.pdf

Dahlgren, L. O. (2005). 'Conceptions and outcomes', in Marton, F., Hounsell, D. and Entwistle, N. (eds.) *The Experience of Learning: Implications for Teaching and Studying in Higher Education*. 3rd edn. Edinburgh: University of Edinburgh, Centre for Teaching, Learning and Assessment, pp. 23–38.

Jordan, K. and Weller, M. (2018). 'Academics and social networking sites: Benefits, problems and tensions in professional engagement with online networking', *Journal of Interactive Media in Education*, 1, p. 1, https://jime.open.ac.uk/articles/10.5334/jime.448/

Marton, F. (1981). 'Phenomenography — describing conceptions of the world around us', *Instructional Science*, 10, pp. 177–200.

Nerantzi, C. (2017). 'Towards a framework for cross-boundary collaborative open learning for cross-institutional academic development'. Doctoral thesis, Edinburgh: Edinburgh Napier University, https://www.napier.ac.uk/research-and-innovation/research-search/outputs/towards-a-framework-for-cross-boundary-collaborative-open-learning-for

Stewart, B. (2016). 'Collapsed publics: Orality, literacy, and vulnerability in academic Twitter', *Journal of Applied Social Theory*, 1:1, https://socialtheoryapplied.com/journal/jast/article/view/33/9

Wenger, E., White, E. and Smith J. D. (2009). *Digital Habitats. Stewarding Technology for Communities*. Portland: CPSquare.

17. PressEd — Where the Conference Is the Hashtag

#Advanced #Twitter #pressedconf18

Pat Lockley

'I've been to conferences that used a hashtag, but this is my first conference that is a hashtag #pressedconf18' (Groom, 2018).

You may ask what a Twitter conference is. There have been five hashtags: #IconTC, #UPMTC, #PressTC, #PATC, and #PressEDconf18 (Lafferty, 2018) that have been billed as Twitter conferences, and of those #PATC has run multiple times. In such fledgling times it would seem dangerous to be prescriptive about what is and what is not a Twitter conference. Can we consider Twitter chats such as #LTHEchat, #digped or #ETCMOOC to be conferences? Innovations such as Virtually Connecting (2018) connected on-site conference presenters with virtual participants in small groups and blurred the distinctions between purely virtual and purely — what? What is the opposite of virtual? Physical, real, absolute? (Webopedia, 2018). We can say the same about some Twitter conferences — they don't happen purely on Twitter. Many use email and WordPress for submission and as a central hub. Does this make it less of a Twitter conference? Could it be seen as a more structured Twitter chat?

While we can see academia and social media intertwining in such ways as the '#icanhazpdf' hashtag (used to request access to academic articles which are behind paywalls), related to the 'I can haz cheeseburger?' meme (Wikipedia, 2018), is this an osmotic process in which one is changing the other, or a didactic co-existence/dependency? Are we seeing a 'sea change', or perhaps something more structural

https://doi.org/10.11647/OBP.0162.17

such as a 'napster moment' (Shirky, 2012)? There are also other Twitter events such as #10DoT developed by Helen Webster, which may well have elements that seem or act conference-like. Perhaps the openness of Twitter makes organising a conference on it a contradiction. Twitter chats often effectively invite in new participants by being open and visible. A Twitter conference with a schedule and fixed speakers is in some way, closed and perhaps 'untwitterlike'. Terras et al.'s (2011) work on Twitter as a backchannel stresses the role Twitter plays at physical conferences, but as per Groom, how does Twitter function when it is not a backchannel but the only channel? Is there a requirement for a hashtag to act as the backchannel? #PressedConf18 had only the main hashtag (with which presenters were encouraged to tag all their tweets). Only once the hashtag became akin to a backchannel was consideration given to potentially having a '#pressedconf18chat' hashtag to act as a backchannel, to reduce the volume of tweets on the #PressedConf18 channel that weren't from the presenters. 'Backchannel' itself though seems a pejorative term, and assumes that the conference has a nature to which a secondary form of backchannel can exist. Is a Twitter conference itself a backchannel to the notion and concept of a conference?

A key question in these opening paragraphs has been the nature, and the character of conferences. Can the role that physical conferences play, and the benefits they offer, become tangible in a Twitter form so that a Twitter conference might act as an alternative? In Vega and Cornell's work (2007) they surveyed nearly 800 librarians and found 'professional rejuvenation' and 'networking' as the top two reasons to attend a conference. Price (1993) lists 'Education, networking, and career path and leadership enhancement' as the key reasons for attendance. There is obvious common ground between the two papers, and there is little reason why a Twitter conference could not perform these functions as well as a physical conference. Networking might even be easier on Twitter, and enhancing careers would be just as possible.

What of the reasons for not attending a conference? Bongkosh and Beck (2000) list perceived risk to one's safety; inconvenience; insecurity or unfamiliarity with overseas destinations; distance; time; money and health problems. Only time, availability of the technology and perhaps government censorship (Twitter is blocked in China) could apply to a Twitter conference. Likewise, Oppermann and Chon (1997) and Sönmez, and Graefe (1998) list reasons including situational constraints of money, time, travel costs, health constraints and family obligation for not attending conferences, and again, only access to devices and time is perhaps true of Twitter conferences.

Do the hashtags of Twitter conferences look differently to the hashtags of physical conferences? Analysis was performed using a tool (Github, 2018) that downloads all of a hashtag's tweets to a file that can be opened in Excel. No effort was taken to remove spam or tweets from hashtag 'crossover' where the tweet didn't appear to be 'from the conference'. On all the following graphs, Twitter conferences are grey, physical conferences black.

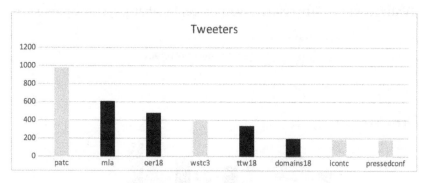

Fig. 17.1 Pat Lockley, Tweeters (2018), CC BY 4.0

Here we see Twitter conferences tend to be smaller in terms of the number of people tweeting on the hashtag.

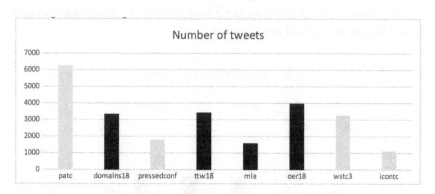

Fig. 17.2 Pat Lockley, Number of tweets (2018), CC BY 4.0

However, Twitter conferences sometimes have more tweets than physical conferences.

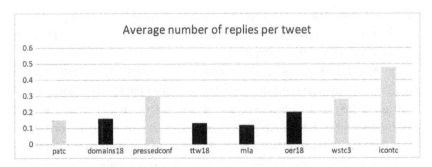

Fig. 17.3 Pat Lockley, Average number of replies per tweet (2018), CC BY 4.0

Twitter conference tweets receive more replies than physical conferences.

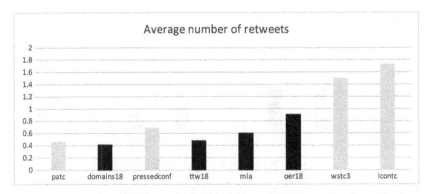

Fig. 17.4 Pat Lockley, Average number of retweets (2018), CC BY 4.0

Twitter conferences tend to attract a higher number of retweets (above) and a higher number of favourites (below).

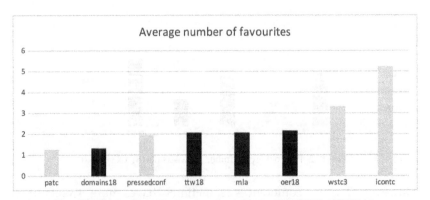

Fig. 17.5 Pat Lockley, Average number of favourites (2018), CC BY 4.0

The following table shows users on the hashtag #pressedcon18 (ordered by number of tweets) and shows a high level of engagement.

Twitter Handle	Status	Tweets	Sum of replies	Sum of retweets	Sum of favourites
LornaMCampbell	Presenter	50	21	61	193
Todd_Conaway	Presenter	46	14	14	57
cogdog	Presenter	35	22	42	125
SFaulknerPandO	Presenter	34	16	14	111
twoodwar	Presenter	32	9	9	49
Derekrobertson	Keynote	32	4	9	23
WarwickLanguage		30	4	7	25
drlouisegrove	Presenter	30	11	22	107
jimgroom	Keynote	29	11	32	183
greeneterry	Presenter	29	9	32	80
cjrw	Presenter	26	20	15	44
Chri5rowell	Presenter	26	8	32	51
HJSears	Presenter	25	12	17	45
edteck	Presenter	22	13	16	38
fearghalobrien	Presenter	21	4	6	24
lisajscott82	Presenter	21	21	30	54
Pgogy	Presenter	21	3	2	8
PgrStudio	Presenter	20	5	28	112
TelPortsmouth	Presenter	20	0	21	52
jar	Presenter	20	4	40	107
urbaneprofessor	Presenter	20	0	1	2
RissaChem	Presenter	19	1	4	13
johnjohnston	Presenter	19	20	22	69
wentale	Presenter	19	6	1	13
clhendricksbc	Presenter	18	2	26	36
econproph		18	2	2	17
TelLibrary	Presenter	17	1	16	47
ThomsonPat	Keynote	17	0	11	44
ryanseslow	Presenter	17	4	5	36
jennihayman	Presenter	16	0	3	29

Twitter Handle	Status	Tweets	Sum of replies	Sum of retweets	Sum of favourites
laura_ritchie	Presenter	16	7	14	45
UoMTELIM	Presenter	15	7	20	86
outwither	Presenter	15	5	10	34
mattlingard	Presenter	14	6	21	48
GKBhambra	Keynote	14	3	41	44
JMUSpeColl	Presenter	13	16	8	48
cinigabellini	Presenter	13	5	8	12
SFarley_Charlie	Presenter	12	5	14	41
villaronrubia	Presenter	12	4	15	18
mkgold	Presenter	11	9	11	48
openetc	Presenter	11	4	20	73
BexFerriday	Presenter	11	5	21	24
ammienoot	Presenter	11	6	15	43
edtechfactotum	Presenter	11	5	30	65
lwaltzer	Presenter	10	11	17	89
Videlais	Presenter	10	13	3	32
esembrat	Presenter	9	3	3	5
frenchdisko	Presenter	8	1	7	29
trixieBooth	Presenter	8	0	0	0
Lucwrite	Presenter	8	3	23	78
LaurenHeywood	Presenter	7	3	5	11
iab_uk		6	0	0	0
debbaff		6	2	2	5
georgeroberts		6	4	0	4
mdvfunes		6	4	2	6
sueinasp		5	4	1	10
philbarker		5	1	0	4
hj_dewaard		5	3	0	10

Fig. 17.6 Pat Lockley, #pressedcon18 user data (2018), CC BY 4.0

We can also consider tweet impressions (Twitter calls the presence of a tweet on a user's timeline an 'impression'). The graph below shows on how many timelines #PressedConf18 tweets were seen, on the day of the conference. Each tweet was seen on an average number of 491 timelines.

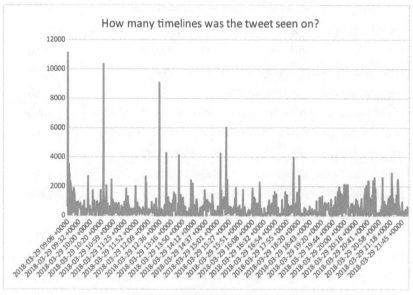

Fig. 17.7 Pat Lockley, Number of times #PressedEd18 tweets were seen (2018), CC BY 4.0

The following table show which tweets received the most impressions and therefore, which users wrote the most read tweets:

Tweet permalink	Impressions
https://twitter.com/GKBhambra/status/979282798195494912	11109
https://twitter.com/drlouisegrove/status/979302732153671680	10335
https://twitter.com/villaronrubia/status/979336097619759104	9067
https://twitter.com/derekrobertson/status/979376506752335874	6011
https://twitter.com/mark_carrigan/status/979342467207254016	4270
https://twitter.com/edtechfactotum/status/979374295682924544	4222
https://twitter.com/johnjohnston/status/979419657009614849	3957
https://twitter.com/jimgroom/status/979468239645245440	2880
https://twitter.com/TelPortsmouth/status/979328316925730817	2672
https://twitter.com/LornaMCampbell/status/979460261236166656	2571

Tweet permalink	Impressions
https://twitter.com/HJSears/status/979309726998638592	2461
https://twitter.com/SFarley_Charlie/status/979377806642688001	2449
https://twitter.com/cinigabellini/status/979358861089017857	2407
https://twitter.com/jar/status/979391986884136961	2278
https://twitter.com/TelLibrary/status/979303912695123968	2060
https://twitter.com/mattlingard/status/979324039318687744	2011
https://twitter.com/lwaltzer/status/979446269490888711	1958
https://twitter.com/urbaneprofessor/status/979287835009265664	1895
https://twitter.com/SFaulknerPandO/status/979358517248196609	1783
https://twitter.com/PgrStudio/status/979301979959721989	1747
https://twitter.com/cogdog/status/979399788075593728	1631
https://twitter.com/Pgogy/status/979402540986101760	1465
https://twitter.com/Videlais/status/979415660093755394	1398
https://twitter.com/edteck/status/979438128908836864	1316
https://twitter.com/mkgold/status/979436054364278786	1220
https://twitter.com/greeneterry/status/979334607945388033	1159
https://twitter.com/BexFerriday/status/979382423359123456	1154
https://twitter.com/cjrw/status/979365871318700032	1143
https://twitter.com/fearghalobrien/status/979451881788502017	1115
https://twitter.com/clhendricksbc/status/979441815731531778	1087
https://twitter.com/lisajscott82/status/979367214502555649	1053

Fig. 17.8 Pat Lockley, Number of impressions (2018), CC BY 4.0

Even the lowest number (1053) is far greater than there would be attendees at most physical conferences, and at over 10000, that is significantly larger than a keynote presentation would garner. It is worth noting these are numbers drawn from data obtained in April and May. The data for these tweets will continue to increase. Each conference presentation is a Twitter moment (Twitter, 2018) and the majority of tweets are still available on Twitter.

So how did the tweets fare for retweets, replies and likes?

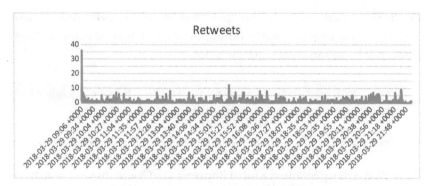

Fig. 17.9 Pat Lockley, Retweets (2018), CC BY 4.0

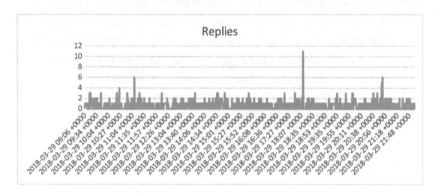

Fig. 17.10 Pat Lockley, Replies (2018), CC BY 4.0

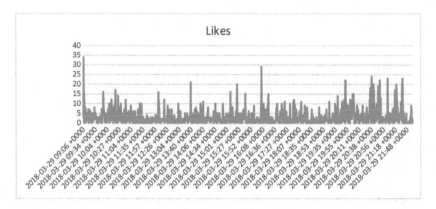

Fig. 17.11 Pat Lockley, Likes (2018), CC BY 4.0

So these varied through the day, and didn't hugely reflect new participants across the world tuning in when it was daytime in their time zone or keynote presentation slots.

impressions	retweets	replies	likes	url clicks	follows
442494	832	402	2611	1171	7

Fig. 17.12 Pat Lockley, Overall #PressedConf18 impressions (2018), CC BY 4.0

Overall, the day generated a lot of impressions. One statistic of note here was that #PressedConf18 tweets didn't generate a lot of direct 'follows' (when someone seeing the tweet opts to follow the tweeter). However, we should consider that any follow-up action might have happened after another tweet or not directly through this route. It would have been useful to have checked for followers before and after the conference to see if there was a distinct change as a result of networking.

So what did the conference offer in terms of promotion and networking for presenters?

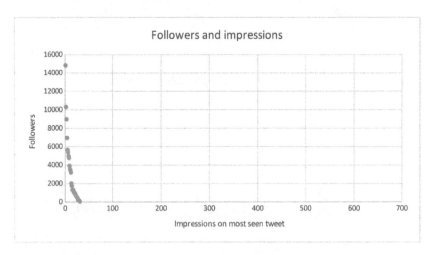

Fig. 17.13 Pat Lockley, Followers and impressions (2018), CC BY 4.0

The chart demonstrates no strong correlation between maximum tweet impression and follower number. This is a correlation coefficient of 0.226343, which shows no relationship between follower numbers and impressions of tweets, which means the conference hashtag helped to amplify the tweets of people with fewer followers to new audiences. In terms of followers to tweet impressions, the average value (for the most seen tweets) was 425%.

Twelve out of thirty-one people (for whom we have data) had more followers than they did tweet impressions — although these numbers are without a control group of how many tweets from that user are usually seen. It would seem, though, that being on the conference hashtag offers greater coverage, which can be tied to the career advancement and networking elements rated highly by attendees of physical conferences. Although this is only holds true if the people who see the tweets are as influential as the people you might interact with at a physical conference.

So we can see the impact in terms of exposure, and differences in how Twitter is used for each conference type. Conference tweeting approaches, such as live tweeting (Nason et al., 2015) when delegates tweet comments while the event is taking place, may well be different when the conference is itself live-tweeted.

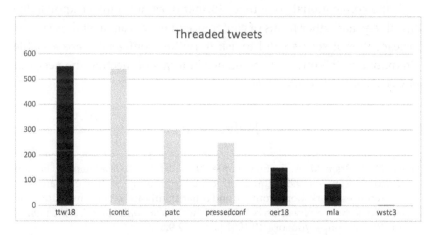

Fig. 17.14 Pat Lockley, Threaded tweets (2018), CC BY 4.0

Twitter conferences (apart from wstc3) appear to be more 'threaded' than physical conferences (apart from ttw18). Perhaps threaded live-tweeting is rarer?

One overlooked aspect of the nature of the conference platform is knowledge transfer. Learning technologists are well versed in how lectures are not the ideal form of teaching. Ross et al. (2011) note that a single speaker has negative repercussions in terms of interactivity and audience engagement: if a Twitter conference lacks a backchannel, consequently leading to a focus on one speaker at a time, does this replicate the problems of the lecture theatre? Or does the reply feature of Twitter mitigate a reluctance to ask questions? Can we therefore consider a Twitter conference to be more open, and to afford a greater equity of participation? Each presenter was asked to leave five minutes for presentations, but perhaps a Twitter conference needs a backchannel as well to encourage further dialogue with the topic and the speaker?

So how efficient could a Twitter conference be at knowledge transfer, even if we consider the replication of some of the negative aspects of lecture-theatre pedagogy in Twitter? We could ask how people versed in educational approaches such as networked learning and Connectivism organise their physical conferences. There is little literature available on the effectiveness of conference presentations (Illic et al., 2013), and conference posters (Davis et al., 1999) remain potentially ineffective as a form of 'knowledge transfer'.

If the conventional conference format does not transfer knowledge effectively, and other forms of conference or event can meet those needs instead, then it seems valid to ask if Twitter conferences are a viable alternative to the physical conference in terms of meeting the needs of physical conference attendees.

References

Davis, D., O'Brien M. A. T., Freemantle, N., Wolf, F. M., Mazmanian, P., and Taylor-Vaisey, A. (1999). 'Impact of formal continuing medical education do conferences, workshops, rounds, and other traditional continuing education activities change physician behavior or health care outcomes?'. *JAMA* 282:9, pp. 867–74, https://doi.org/10.1001/jama.282.9.867

Github (2018), https://github.com/pgogy/ScriptScrape-Twitter

Groom, J. (2018). [Twitter] 29 March, https://twitter.com/jimgroom/status/979464464033394688

Ilic, D., and Rowe, N. (2013). 'What is the evidence that poster presentations are effective in promoting knowledge transfer? A state of the art review', *Health Information & Libraries Journal*, 30:1, pp. 4–12, https://doi.org/doi.org/10.1111/hir.12015

Lafferty, N. (2018). [Twitter] 17 April, https://mobile.twitter.com/nlafferty/status/986279025126633475

Nason, G. J., O'Kelly, F., Bouchier-Hayes, D., Quinlan, D. M., and Manecksha, R. P. (2015). 'Twitter expands the reach and engagement of a national scientific meeting: The Irish Society of Urology', *Irish Journal of Medical Science*, 184:3, pp. 685–89.

Ngamsom, B. and Beck, J. (2000). 'A Pilot Study of Motivations, Inhibitors, and Facilitators of Association Members in Attending International Conferences', *Journal of Convention & Exhibition Management*, 2:2–3, pp. 97–111, https://doi.org/doi.org/10.1300/J143v02n02_09

Oppermann, M., and Chon, K. S. (1997). 'Convention participation decision-making process', *Annals of Tourism Research*, 24:1, pp. 178–91.

Price, C. (1993). 'An empirical study of the value of professional association meetings from the perspective of attendees'. Unpublished doctoral dissertation. Virginia Polytechnic and State University, Blacksburg.

Ross, C., Terras, M., Warwick, C., and Welsh, A. (2011). 'Enabled backchannel: Conference Twitter use by digital humanists', *Journal of Documentation*, 67:2, 214–37.

Shirky, C. (2012). 'Napster, Udacity and the academy', *Clay Shirky*, 12 November, http://www.shirky.com/weblog/2012/11/napster-udacity-and-the-academy/

Sönmez, S. F., and Graefe, A. R. (1998). 'Determining future travel behavior from past travel experience and perceptions of risk and safety', *Journal of Travel Research*, 37:2, pp. 171–77.

Twitter (2018). PressEd Conference Moments, 6 April, https://twitter.com/pressedconf/moments

Vega, R., and Connell, R. (2007). 'Librarians' attitudes toward conferences: A study', *College & Research Libraries*, 68:6, pp. 503–16, https://doi.org/10.5860/crl.68.6.503

Virtually Connecting (2018), http://virtuallyconnecting.org/ Webopedia (2018), https://www.webopedia.com/TERM/V/virtual.html

Wikipedia (2018). *I Can Haz Cheezburger*, https://en.wikipedia.org/wiki/I_Can_Has_Cheezburger%3F

PART SIX
INNOVATION

18. Expertise in Your Ears; Why You Should Jump on the Podcasting Bandwagon

#Beginner #Podcast #Podcasting

Dave Musson

Small speakers inside your head
About as intimate as it can get
I'm privileged to be in this position and
We haven't really got thumping yet.

Jamie Lenman, *Hardbeat*, 2017

Introduction

It doesn't take much effort to find marketing strategists and social media experts extolling the virtues of video. Moreover — when you consider that online videos are likely to account for more than 80% of all Internet traffic by 2020 (CISCO, 2016) and that companies using video in their marketing grow revenue 49% faster year-on-year than those that don't (Aberdeen Group, 2015) — it is perhaps not difficult to see the cause for their excitement.

Yet, there's another content vehicle that has its claws firmly locked into today's online media consumers: podcasting. Not only that, the medium continues to flourish. More Americans listen to podcasts on a

 https://doi.org/10.11647/OBP.0162.18

weekly basis than go to the movies; the average listener subscribes to six shows; and 85% of listeners take in the whole show (Baer, 2017) — the kind of low drop-off rate you'll never get with video.

But, when it comes to higher education, the sector still seems somewhat hesitant to get involved, despite being blessed with some of the best stories to tell, and the most informed storytellers to tell them. Higher education podcasting has the potential to vastly improve research dissemination, public engagement, career support and even student recruitment, yet there aren't that many examples to hold up as good practice. This chapter will explain why podcasting should be on your agenda. It will make the business case for the medium and will offer ideas for the sort of show you could make, using case studies of existing podcasts from the sector.

The First Decade of the Podcast

The word 'podcast' was first coined by the *Guardian* journalist Ben Hammersley in 2004, at the height of the iPod era. He was writing about a boom in amateur online radio that was driven by the combination of blogging being well-established, audio editing software being freely available, and devices such as Apple's iPod being in the pockets of millions of people around the world. Hammersley's only struggle was what to call this fledgling scene, so he offered a few options:

'But what to call it? Audioblogging? Podcasting? GuerillaMedia?' (Hammersley, 2004).

Podcasting — a portmanteau of references to broadcasting and the iPod — soon stuck and quickly became a buzzword, even if its creator now reflects on it as merely part of a 'bullshit sentence' (Ulanoff, 2015). Google searches for this new word jumped from 6,000 in the year of its birth to more than 61 million by the end of the following year (Berry, 2006, p. 144).

This rise in popularity is unsurprising really; as a species we've been telling stories — creating our own audio — for centuries and have embraced any technology that helps us continue to do that. Just as President Roosevelt's fireside chats in the 1930s were a 'revolutionary experiment with a [then] nascent media platform' (LaFrance, 2017), we can arguably also credit those early podcasts with being a similar catalyst for today's booming audio industry. But podcasting in those early years was, at best, a clunky experience that required consumers to track down an RSS feed, paste it into iTunes, download a file and synch it to a iPod or similar device — all before being able to listen to their show.

It didn't get much easier until 2008, when 3G-enabled smartphones such as the iPhone from Apple and the Android G1 let users download audio on the go (Quah, 2017). Even then, it took another six years for the medium to really break through. This was due in part, to Apple's podcasting app becoming part of the furniture of iOS 8 and, to a much larger extent, to the show *Serial* (Quah, 2017). Sarah Koenig's real crime series was an unprecedented success; awards, media coverage, and academic articles (for example, Berry, 2015) set a new benchmark for podcast quality, and it garnered a lot of listeners — 6.5 million per episode for its first series in fact (Daniel 2015). Not only that, *Serial* changed the way people thought about the medium of podcasting; almost a quarter of *Serial*'s listeners were podcast virgins, and 89% of those first-timers were inspired to try other shows off the back of it. What's more, around half of them went on to listen to podcasts on a weekly basis (PR News Wire, 2015). It was the perfect blend of captivating content and technology that made it incredibly easy to consume.

The Business Case for Podcasting

It is safe to say the medium has continued to flourish post *Serial*. 67 million Americans listen to podcasts every month (Baer, 2017) — a huge jump from 32 million in 2013 (the year before the iOS update and *Serial*, Quah, 2018), while in the UK 4.7 million adults have listened to some sort of podcast (Russell, 2017). Sticking with the UK, listenership continues to edge upwards. eMarketer reported in 2017 that 42% of podcast listeners were queuing up more shows than they had done a year earlier, while only 13% had decreased their consumption (eMarketer, 2017).

With ever-improving mobile Internet connections, along with in-car Bluetooth technology becoming commonplace, it has never been easier to listen to a podcast. This will only continue to be the norm as more new cars are 'connected' as standard, such as the latest generation of General Motors vehicles (della Cava, 2017). Moreover, podcasts have a distinct quality that gives them an edge over video: the ability for passive consumption in people's busy lives. As marketing influencer Gary Vaynerchuk said: 'You can listen to the podcast while doing something else. You can listen to the podcast in a shower, while you're driving, while you're working out. It's time arbitrage.' (Vaynerchuk, 2017). Eric Zorn put it as: 'The medium of podcasting is ideal for our busy, mobile, on-demand lives.' (Zorn, 2014)

And that's not just it; podcasting continues to improve and innovate. Casey Newton wrote in 2017 that 'podcasts are getting better faster than audiobooks are getting cheaper' (Newton, 2017), while Jaguar Land Rover's innovative use of a human-head shaped microphone to record their Discovery Adventure series — an immersive, family adventure show designed to sound best when listened to in a car — just hints at some the creative options available (McCarthy, 2017).

This is all without acknowledging the fact that the podcast is 'an intimate medium and one that spurs creativity, akin to reading' (Mollett et al., 2017, p. 165) and that no topic is too niche. You can work up an idea and ride out the long tail (Mollett et al., 2017) because you don't have to grab a listener's attention in a matter of seconds like you do with video; you have room to breathe and explore ideas (Musson, 2018). Not only that, podcasting has a remarkably low barrier for entry, particularly when compared to video. It is absolutely possible to create something and post it online using only your smartphone — indeed, this is the premise of the app anchor.fm. Good quality microphones are easy to find and won't break the bank — for example, the Blue Snowball USB mic — while free editing software such as Audacity is ideal. In fact, this is the exact setup of some huge shows, such as *Welcome to Night Vale* ('I Only Listen to the Mountain Goats', Episode 7, 2017). For some excellent advice on effective podcasting setups for different budgets, see The Podcast Host's 'Ultimate Resource List' and Alexander and Barrows (2016).

Podcasting and Higher Education

So, what of the relationship between podcasting and the HE sector? The sector was on board early on in podcasting's existence; as Berry (2006) pointed out, Duke University in the USA were particularly forward-thinking, giving out 16,250 free iPods to new students in 2004, preloaded with lectures and academic content, as well as giving the students the chance to record themselves as part of their work. Duke was also the setting for the first academic symposium on the medium in 2005. There was also the launch of iTunesU in 2007, a free repository of academic content from universities across the globe, which became part of the general Apple Podcasts app in 2017 (Hardwick, 2017).

But it still feels like there is huge opportunity to be had by the sector in this space — in particular when you realise that 26% of people in the UK who listen to podcasts do so to learn something (eMarketer, 2017). If anyone can lay claim to being skilled at delivering learning, it has to be the HE sector.

For the rest of this chapter, you'll find a range of ideas for how a HE institution might want to approach podcasting — ideas that will be explored using existing shows from the sector. There is also an excellent and comprehensive chapter about podcasting in Mollett et al. (2017) that will be of particular use to anyone looking to use podcasting to help communicate academic research.

Podcasting to Show off Your Expertise:
The University of Liverpool Podcast

The most obvious way for a HE institution to use podcasting is to get under the skin of its research. After all, your research is likely to be one of the pillars on which your organization is based and judged. However, the difficulty for many universities is likely to be deciding where to focus your efforts. Which stories should you tell? What will people be interested in?

There is nothing to stop you using a podcast as a way of cutting across all of your research strengths, which is exactly what *The University of Liverpool Podcast* does. Launched in 2017, the fortnightly show does not have a set subject. Well, that's not true; its subject is right there in its name — The University of Liverpool. Each episode focuses on something different and features one or more of the university's academics discussing research in their field. A brief look at their episode back catalogue underlines the variety of content on offer, with episodes on the future of farming, obese dogs and mental health.

The show is hosted by Canadian journalist and producer Neil Morrison, who combines an interview format with a narrative top and tail to produce something that is eminently listenable, interesting, and entertaining. Liverpool's podcast has production values that sounds impressive, but is actually fairly pain-free to achieve once you have some familiarity with audio-editing software. The podcast is great listening for anyone with a curious mind — episodes often feel like broadsheet magazine articles being read straight into your ears. However, the University of Liverpool clearly has a specific audience in mind with this show, which becomes apparent a couple of times each episode.

Instead of a paying sponsor, this podcast is delivered in partnership with the University of Liverpool's online learning programme. The university is clearly pitching the show at people who might be interested in turning a half-hour listen into something deeper. The result is a really clever marketing tool. Aside from the fact that it is difficult not to be impressed with the scope of research happening in Liverpool, within a couple of episodes you are also fully aware that Liverpool offers online and distance learning on a range of subjects. And, when they're presented as well as they are in this podcast, the idea of applying for a course is certainly tempting.

Podcasting for a Deep-Dive on Topical Subjects: *Talking Politics*

Getting across the scope of what your institution does is one thing, but what about if you want to go deeper and devote a podcast to a particular subject? As we've already seen, the ability to go niche and ride the long tail is a huge boon of podcasting, so a university throwing its weight at a subject should make for a great show. A fine example of this approach is the show *Talking Politics*, one of the more positive things to come out a political year in which Trump and Brexit were the big headlines.

Talking Politics is, in effect, a departmental podcast — in this case, the University of Cambridge's politics department. It is hosted by Professor David Runciman — Cambridge's Head of Politics and International Studies — and is recorded every week in his office. The format is less of a formal interview and more of a chance to be a fly on the wall eavesdropping on informed and interesting individuals talking politics. Each episode features Runciman and his regular panel of fellow Cambridge academics discussing key issues. As the show says on its website, 'it's the political conversation everyone is having.'

While offering far less value as an obvious marketing tool — unlike *The University of Liverpool Podcast* — the *Talking Politics* model offers plenty of benefits. First is the insight and learning to be had for the listener. Each episode allows you to hear experts in their field having informed conversations and discussions. It speaks to that 26% of podcast listeners who want to learn something. Second is how topical this sort of show can be. The podcast was born in a time when politics was a discussion topic on many a tongue, and by releasing a new episode each week they are able to remain relevant and timely. And, for the listener, there is always a reason to check out the newest episode. A final advantage of this podcast model is that it is fairly self-sufficient. Being presented and managed by academics, they can be left to focus on the show's content, while the university can chip in with marketing and technical assistance if needs be.

Podcasting as a Window onto Campus Life: UNH Podcats, Rhymes with Orange, This Is Skidmore

Your university podcast doesn't have to appeal to audiences outside of your campus boundaries; you could simply make a show for your campus community. A number of universities have taken this approach and are producing content that is aimed at and celebrates its internal community. These kinds of shows have plenty of flexibility; no need to explain campus jargon or in-jokes, no need to sell the university and no real barrier on who could be a guest.

Take as an example *The UNH Podcats* from the University of New Hampshire. If you don't know that the UNH community refers to themselves as the Wildcats, then you'd have assumed their show's title was a typo, rather than an immediate marker of which tribe this is for. There's a similar strategy being adopted with Campbell University's *Rhymes with Orange* — this time the show's title gives a knowing nod to the university's colour scheme. As with *The UNH Podcats*, *Rhymes with Orange* features the voices of staff, students, faculties and alumni, all talking about life at that institution. Lastly, and perhaps the stand-out example of this type of podcast, is Skidmore College's *This is Skidmore*. This show celebrates the college's close-knit community, from the theme of its episodes right down to its logo and theme music being designed and composed by different Skidmore alumni.

What is particularly interesting with these types of podcast is that, even though they might not necessarily have been created with marketing purposes in mind, they are still an invaluable tool in selling their institutions. These shows offer the outside world a window onto their campus — not to look into, but to listen through. They give you a sense of life at that institution, they let you have a taste of what being part of their community is like, and could help persuade a prospective student that it is the place for them.

Podcasting to Highlight Your Alumni:
The Low Down

Finally, how about a podcast to celebrate your alumni? There are hundreds, if not thousands, of them across the world, they're a huge part of your story and they're likely to be some of your biggest fans. One fine example of an alumni-focussed podcast is *The Low Down*, by Columbia University's Alumni Association. As the show says itself, Columbia's alumni are 'leaders in every field imaginable' and so make for worthy and interesting podcast guests. *The Low Down*'s format has similarities with all of the examples listed above. It is interview based, with informed, excellent guests, all of whom share Columbia University as a common link.

As such, the show serves many purposes. Aside from the obvious interest for other Columbia alumni wanting to stay connecting to their alma mater, it offers learning and thought for the general public and can be used as an effective marketing tool for the university. After all, what is more captivating — another case study posted deep within your alumni pages, or a well-produced podcast where you can hear those alumni tell their story in their own words, using their own voice? And, similar to the University of Liverpool model, having a podcast about your alumni allows your scope to be fairly broad — you don't have to devote it to one subject, but use it as an opportunity to showcase all of your strengths.

Conclusion

Podcasting is a medium to which we, as humans, really react well. That's because we're tuned into the human voice and the stories and information it has to tell. From tales told round a campfire centuries ago, through Presidents using then-modern technology to do exactly the same and into today's post-*Serial* podcast industry of immersive and captivating content, podcasts are here to stay.

The window for HE institutions to get involved in the podcasting space is far from shut; in many ways it is wide open, beckoning the sector to climb through. For those willing to do just that, there are plenty of rewards to be had. Podcasting might not have the same glamour as the overly-crowded video space, but it offers deeper, more meaningful relationships with your audience and a chance to ride the long tail, take your time and let ideas breathe.

Whether you create a show that explores your research, tells your institution's story, or helps recruit new students — the opportunity is begging to be taken. It is time to put your institution's expertise, lifestyle and culture right into the ears of people. It is time to jump on the podcasting bandwagon.

References

Aberdeen Group (2015). 'The impact of video marketing' *Vidyard*, http://awesome.vidyard.com/rs/273-EQL-130/images/Vidyard_Aberdeen_Impact_of_Video_Marketing.pdf

Alexander, C. and Barrows, C. (2016). *Podcasting in Higher Education*, http://www.whyisocial.com/wp-content/uploads/2016/11/Podcasting-in-Higher-Education-Guide.pdf

Baer, Jay (2017). 'The 11 critical podcast statistics of 2017', *Convince and Convert*, http://www.convinceandconvert.com/podcast-research/the-11-critical-podcast-statistics-of-2017/

Berry, Richard (2006). 'Will iPod kill the radio star? Profiling podcasting as radio.' *Convergence*, 12:2, pp. 143–62.

Berry, Richard (2015). 'A golden age of podcasting? Evaluating Serial in the context of podcast histories.' *Journal of Radio and Audio Media*, 22:2, pp. 170–78.

CISCO (2016). 'Cisco visual networking index: Forecast and methodology, 2016–2021', *CISCO*, https://www.cisco.com/c/en/us/solutions/collateral/service-provider/visual-networking-index-vni/complete-white-paper-c11-481360.html

della Cava (2017). 'GM turns 1 million cars into rolling podcast destinations', *USA Today*, https://www.usatoday.com/story/tech/2017/12/21/gm-turns-1-million-cars-into-rolling-podcast-destinations/962612001/

eMarketer (2017). 'The number of podcast listeners in the UK keeps inching up', *eMarketer*, https://www.emarketer.com/Article/Number-of-Podcast-Listeners-UK-Keeps-Inching-Up/1016292

Hammersley, Ben (2004). 'Audible revolution', *The Guardian*, https://www.theguardian.com/media/2004/feb/12/broadcasting.digitalmedia

Hardwick, Tim (2017). 'iTunes U Collections will move to Apple Podcasts from September', *MacRumors*, https://www.macrumors.com/2017/08/21/itunes-u-collections-to-apple-podcasts-september/

'I Only Listen to the Mountain Goats' podcast (2017). Episode 7: 'Pink and Blue', http://ionlylistentothemountaingoats.libsyn.com/episode-7-pink-and-blue

LaFrance, A. (2017). 'Donald Trump is testing Twitter's harassment policy', *The Atlantic*, https://www.theatlantic.com/politics/archive/2017/07/the-president-of-the-united-states-is-testing-twitters-harassment-policy/532497/

Lenman, J. (2017). 'Hardbeat' from the album *Devolver*. Big Scary Monsters record company.

McCarthy, J. (2017). 'Jaguar Land Rover tests immersive, adventure podcasts to drive a Discovery brand narrative into other cars', *The Drum*, http://www.thedrum.com/news/2017/09/21/jaguar-land-rover-tests-immersive-adventure-podcasts-drive-discovery-brand-narrative

Mollett, A., Bromley, C., Gilson, C. and Williams, S. (2017). *Communicating Your Research with Social Media: A Practical Guide to Using Blogs, Podcasts, Data Visualisations and Video*. London: Sage.

Musson, Dave (2018). 'This year I will be better at…podcasting', *The Native*, https://thenative.com/2018/01/year-i-will-better-at-podcasting/

Newton, Casey (2017). 'Podcasts are getting better faster than audiobooks are getting cheaper', *The Verge*, https://www.theverge.com/2017/8/8/16109968/audiobooks-versus-podcasts-audible-amazon

PR Newswire (2015). 'First survey of Serial's listeners sheds light on the Serial Effect', *PR Newswire*, https://www.prnewswire.com/news-releases/first-survey-of-serials-listeners-sheds-light-on-the-serial-effect-300104734.html

Quah, Nicholas (2017). 'The three fundamental moments of podcasts' rise', *Wired*, October 4, https://www.wired.com/story/podcast-three-watershed-moments/

Quah, Nicholas (2018). 'Hot pod: Setting up twenty eighteen', *Hot Pod Newsletter*, Issue 145. *Nieman Lab*, http://www.niemanlab.org/2018/01/apple-podcast-analytics-is-finally-live-and-with-it-the-ability-to-see-how-many-people-are-skipping-ads/

Russell, Mike (2017). 'UK podcast statistics: 4 actionable stats for British podcast hosts', *New Media Europe*, https://newmediaeurope.com/uk-podcast-statistics/

Ulanoff, Lance (2015). 'Podcasting embraces a new era of cool (thanks, Serial)', *Mashable*, https://mashable.com/2015/08/29/podcasting-mainstream/#oOGI7hSMtZqy

Vaynerchuk, Gary (2017). 'Marketing in 2018, Brand Minds Keynote, Singapore 2017, Dailyvee 337', https://www.youtube.com/watch?v=WdTscOvoBnY&feature=youtu.be

Zorn, Eric (2014). 'Smartphones usher in golden age for podcasting', *Chicago Tribune*, http://www.chicagotribune.com/news/opinion/zorn/ct-smartphones-usher-in-golden-age-podcasts-perspe-20140930-column.html

Further Reading

Podcast Host (2018). *The Ultimate Podcasting Resource List*, www.thepodcasthost.com/ultimate-podcasting-resource-list [What it says on the tin — an incredibly useful list for any aspiring podcaster!]

Vetrano, J. (2017). 'What I learned by producing a podcast for a college'. *Medium*, https://medium.com/@jackie/podcasting-for-a-college-57ba009ea7bd [Useful tips from the host of *This is Skidmore*.]

Further listening

Aside from the examples used in this chapter, below are a selection of the author's favourite podcasts — just search for them wherever you get your podcasts.

Conversations With People Who Hate Me — online social justice activist Dylan Marron tracks down people who have directed hateful and hurtful comments at him online and calls them for a chat.

Football Fives — discussion about football for grown-ups.

Heavyweight — simply wonderful storytelling.

Reply All — a show about the Internet that explores online culture and features some of the best storytelling you'll hear.

That's Not Metal — the show that will give you your new favourite band, assuming you like rock and metal of course.

The Native Podcast — inspiring resources for education and youth marketers, presented by the author of this chapter.

The Science of Social Media — weekly social media learning from Buffer, a social media management platform company.

The Turnaround — an interviewer interviews other interviewers about interviewing.

Welcome to Night Vale — imagine if Stephen King and David Lynch created a fictional town together. Night Vale is that town and *Welcome to Night Vale* is that town's local radio station.

19. Etiquette for the Anthropocene

#Intermediate #Instagram #Optimismasresistance
#Snapchat #Twitter

Jane Norris

'Toto, I have a feeling we're not in Kansas anymore…'

Spoken by Dorothy in *The Wizard of Oz*

The introduction of Web 2.0 in late 2004 tilted our perceptions, opened up new vistas of communication, and it enabled the creation of global online communities structured around content made largely by users. Like Dorothy, we found ourselves in a different world, one that we are still exploring and seeking to understand. Perhaps initially, it seems as if not much has changed; I still say hello to the neighbours as I shut the front door in the morning and walk around the corner to catch the bus to work. But it is when I am at work teaching students that I am most aware that the landscape has shifted, and that all is not as it has been. Things have tilted and I am not completely sure in what ways.

The video artist Hito Steyerl captures this in a striking piece of writing in e-flux (2011) where she describes society as being in 'freefall', suggesting that because everything is falling at the same rate, no one notices. This captures perfectly the strange sense of cultural vertigo that I keep feeling and describes the out-of-place-ness that occasionally occurs in interactions in the class. Not so much misunderstandings, but rather misalignments in my approach and students' responses.

https://doi.org/10.11647/OBP.0162.19

Asynchronous communities have always co-existed at universities; faculties are often considerably older than the students. But there seems to be an increasing gap in translation with academic communication when teaching contemporary HE students.

I have been challenged by a couple of experiences: one in my 'Creativity and Sustainability' class discussing global warming, and one whilst trying to discuss effective goal-setting for both academic studies and life in general with a class of freshman students (Richmond University is an American University in London and home to a wide mix of American, international and home students, all of whom carry high family expectations when studying abroad). How do we find ways of discussing global warming, rising sea levels, the Anthropocene and future-goal-setting in classes without increasing the anxiety levels of already stressed and depressed students? A number of my class come from Miami which of course would be wiped out with a 3% sea level rise. I became convinced of the need to reconsider at a structural level how shifts in the students' online environments might require changes in my behavioural and educational frameworks. Perhaps more importantly, I would need to consider how these 'misunderstandings' point to the need for a new 'etiquette' in this digitally soaked age. What is an appropriate way of planning in a physical world that my generation has trashed and has now labelled as Anthropocene? How can we communicate with others in a world of 'wicked' problems? What is an appropriate way of meeting or being in a digital environment with students which is ubiquitous but largely ignored by the larger academic institution?

Reflecting on my student interaction has led me to initiate an experimental project I am at present calling 'Etiquette for the Anthropocene'. I hope to look over the wall of my own educational experience and map some of the digital landscape that exists outside the 'academy' that is undoubtedly seeping in but is currently either being resisted or politely ignored, as if a bit of digital dampness here and there is just unfortunate. Professors mostly ask students to put their phones away during class — mostly unsuccessfully.

One starting point seemed to be the mismatch between institutional (and sometime my own) perceptions of student pessimism, lack of engagement, and little desire to problem solve, with student concern for the preservation of their mental health through a heightened cynical fatalism, and a refusal to engage more widely in the often misguided institutional structures. This binary opposition is interestingly shot through and disrupted with moments of intense engagement when students speak truth to power. Members of my goal setting class, who insisted that the established goal approaches caused more damage that they helped, being one example.

These windows onto different behavioural landscapes led me to consider applying ideas from my research on Design Para-fiction to trial a communication activity. Design para-fiction describes the insertion of fictional objects into the everyday at the point of crisis, to affect change. This model uses the approach of the para-medic that is first to the scene and acts 'in-situ' rather than removing the patient to another space (usually a hospital). In the same way, Para-fictional objects might act as a form of cultural currency in the everyday, in a way they would not be able to in a gallery or a design museum. The movement of objects between the physical realm and digital social media spaces also reveals something of cultural transaction patterns and exchange rates often invisible between the two environments. So, I designed an 'optimism as resistance' enamel badge to be handed out as a gift. The card that the badge was pinned to had the following text on one side:

> This work explores the relationship between physical and digital memes. It questions how and why objects might crossover to the digital realm and what happens if they do. How online versions of objects provide a digital shadow that can become much larger than the original object.
>
> The badge forms a physical 'seed' that is carried by you, attached to your clothing like burrs in the countryside, to then travel worldwide. The photo that you take and send back is a form of harvest, and the Instagram account takes the role of a garden where you can then view these images-as-blooms.
>
> This word resonates in society today, and has become something that has become quite difficult to do. Because of this it reveals itself as an essential form of mental health performance therefore of resistance.

And on the other:

> Please accept this badge as a gift.
>
> In return, take a photo of yourself wearing it. Then email the image with the location where it was taken, to me at:

optimism.janenorris@gmail.com

This digital image will then be added to the optimism.janenorris Instagram page.

#optimismasresistance became the hashtag for the project.

Fig. 19.1 Jane Norris, Cards and badges and Instagram page, https://www. instagram.com/optimism.janenorris/ (2018), CC BY 4.0

I handed out the badges to fellow faculty staff, and students in my classes at the end of the Autumn semester. Several of my colleagues were travelling over the break and most of the students were flying back to their families, so there was the potential for these badges to migrate globally.

As often happens when you release design into the real world, the unplanned for happens. Of the 100 badges given to my students — who all expressed delight in them, none sent a digital image back for Instagram. Of the 15 badges, I handed out to colleagues I received responses from 6 in the form of 12 images in total. This is an ongoing project and part of the process of seeding ideas in the form of objects into the real world is like plants — some travel a long way before they find fertile soil and I receive a return image, and some just fall down the back of cupboards and never do... it is a waiting game, and I am still getting images coming in from afar. What I found particularly interesting though was the fact that several the students took photos of themselves at the end of the class very enthusiastically, unprompted by me, but did not send me the image. Also, a number of the students followed the Instagram account but did not send me an image. The only person of equivalent age to my student cohort who sent an image was my niece, who used a Snapchat filter to disguise her face.

I have used this pattern of response as a point of discussion with a subsequent group of 20 students. I handed out a set of badges again and inquired if the wording or sentiment was not appropriate, or was not something they could relate to. Their response was that they really liked the text and the badge as an object, one asked for an extra one for a friend. In the discussion, it was suggested that students would not send images to post unless there were thousands of images on the account — i.e. that it had become a 'public space'. One student related how her 13-year-old sister and her friends constantly 'remade' their Instagram accounts, rearranging and refurnishing their public account and through this continually decontextualising their place in the digital world. Several students said that social media was not 'fun' anymore as everyone was on it, and that they barely used it now. One referred to Facebook as his CV as that was where potential employers looked first. Some said that they now only used closed groups such as Snapchat or Instant Messenger / WhatsApp software to communicate with friends. The shift of social media platforms such as Facebook, from what were perceived as safe spaces for small groups of friends and family to public archives mined for company profit, requires a parallel readjustment in on-line etiquette. When I leave the house in the morning I do not peer through the neighbours' window to say 'good morning' and I am careful to shut my own front door. It feels as if an equivalent understanding of personal privacy needs to be recognised for digital social media spaces. Suggesting that groups of students join a course Facebook group or build a collaborative Instagram site may not be met with enthusiasm — even though they might be using these platforms in their personal life.

This ties in with Daniel Trottier's observation in his book *Media as Surveillance: Rethinking Visibility in a Converging World*, that we often think about social media as if it is a kind of anonymous digital space in the cloud. But by analysing our use of it and its functionality, we need to reconceptualise our understanding of social media as a kind of 'dwelling'. We communicate through social media, but we also live (to different degrees) on social media. The more we invest time and attention in 'furnishing' our Instagram account or Pinterest boards with our curated content, the more we 'move in' and spend more time tending to our personalised spaces. My fast-flowing Twitter habitat requires maintenance in the form of regular tweeting, otherwise *I disappear* in the global context I have built. This maintenance of 'self' naturally forms part of the addiction in using these sites.

More importantly, these environments are characterised by 'social convergence' and this has an additional effect on visibility. Trottier refers to social convergence as 'the increased social proximity of different life spheres' (2016). This trend naturally provokes a sense of discomfort because we often maintain different representations of ourselves in different contexts which may clash or directly contradict one another when viewed together. This discomfort also suggests that while in an analogue world, we have learnt to live compartmentalised lives which has allowed us to perform differently in each context, enabling us to 'try out' different ways of being. Whereas post-Web 2.0, online spaces are increasingly blurring these borders. Facebook in particular seems eager to demolish them, having the effect of making different facets of our lives more visible than all the other facets. Foucault's writing in *Discipline and Punish* on control by viewing in Panopticon prisons (Foucault, 1985), is perhaps relevant here.

This bleeding of private information from one sphere to the next, and beyond to other unknown public domains, leaves users feeling vulnerable and open to abuse. Extending Trottier's idea of social media as a dwelling, is useful to consider the etiquette of our use of social media with students or others that we may have professional relations with. As we usually would not consider inviting an entire class to our home on a daily basis, it is perhaps also not appropriate to demand that we visit their dwellings or demand that they set up a cul-de-sac where they have to live together in sight of each other. The walls between Instagram, Facebook, Snapchat, Twitter etc. have not just the thinness of a new build flat: they can often be transparent without us realising.

Our social media profiles act as a repository for personal information; a body of information that stands in for our actual bodies, our profile marks our presence. But as danah boyd writes in a paper titled 'Nobody Sees It Nobody Gets Mad', 'the visibility provided by social media offers a conundrum: it can deliver social support, attention, and even celebrity, but simultaneously leaves one open to criticism, drama, and conflicts' (Marwick et al., 2017). Students in class describe their online privacy practice and those of their peers in terms of individual responsibility. This frame of personal responsibility is common across social classes and generations. It is the primary way that people understand privacy and agency both online and off. However, this emphasis on 'personal responsibility' over social obligation and as a remedy for institutional failures not only blames victimized individuals for privacy violations but also implies that privacy is only necessary if one has 'nothing to hide' See Daniel Solove's piece 'I've Got Nothing to Hide, and Other Misunderstandings of Privacy'(Solove, 2007).

It is this relationship of our digital profiles or virtual bodies to our social media 'dwellings' that forms a key part of the Etiquette for the Anthropocene project. The architecture of dwellings is a focus of interest for both designers and sociologists. Their construction and use makes the terrain for our social life. They are also the structures where cultural meaning is built and negotiated. Their increasing migration to online environments raises concern over how permeable their walls are and what sort of surveillance and exposure can seep through to these spaces. In educational settings, it has been accepted practice to consider Pierre Bourdieu's theories (1997) on different 'habitus' as structuring structures. Our engagement in diverse social fields through our understanding of their particular behavioural rules (Doxa), highlights our ability to operate in different social groups and behave accordingly. We instinctively adjust our posture or accent or the music we like, in order to fit in. However, we are now inhabiting a digital landscape, swimming in a different medium from our separate physical social groupings of home, neighbours, sports club, university. In a physical world, we go from one place to another and I have yet to find a way to be in two places at once. By contrast, the digital medium is much more fluid and flows sideways across all these social grouping, connecting them continuously. We are truly in many places at once, all the time, requiring that we stretch ourselves to accommodate an expanded consciousness.

Part of the stress and anxiety-inducing nature of this expanded environment, is our growing awareness of digital nakedness and how this vulnerability might be used against us. To return to the work of Hito Steyerl, an artist speaking truth to power in our age, her video 'How Not to Be Seen: A Fucking Didactic Educational' (Steyerl, 2001), is a witty and acerbic take on how to avoid government and military surveillance. Her bleakly humorous tactics are to be employed to resist the ubiquitous tracking of our lives by authorities for unknown purposes, without us even volunteering information on social media. Another artist, Zach Blas, addresses the increasing threat to the personal safety of members of minority groups through instances of overt prejudice in facial recognition algorithms. His work *'Fag Face Mask — Facial Weaponization Suite'* (Blas, 2013), compiles supposed gay visual traits into one mask to act, in a counterintuitive way, as a disguise; a baroque visual excessiveness acting as tactic to 'hide in plain sight'. These responses mark new forms of creative resistance to the pressures and dangers in this new digital medium.

So, how do we need to 'be' in the shifting digital landscape we now find ourselves in? How ethical is it to expect students to join institutional social media spaces, when those spaces expose them and then harvest their likes, and the likes or dislikes their own social subgroups? How ethical is it to lead students back to the spaces deliberately designed to be 'sticky' and attentively addictive to enable such harvesting to take place?

During this project, I have started 'hearing' other phrases that point to other ways of being. Which may lead to other badges in the series:

China Mieville

Timothy Morton

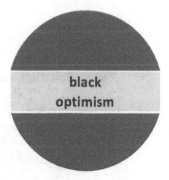

Fred Moten

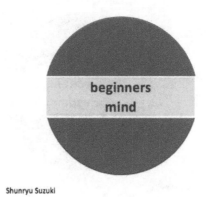

Shunryu Suzuki

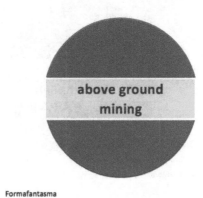

Formafantasma

Shanzhai lyric

Fig. 19.2 Jane Norris, Other badges (2018), CC BY 4.0

But for these badges, I will not be suggesting a formalised response to an established social media site like Instagram. This was my previous approach, and could be misunderstood as furnishing my digital dwelling and asking students to do digital labour for my harvesting. Rather, perhaps a longer period is needed for the badges-as-seeds to germinate in the students off digital world life. Perhaps it is important to allow emergent new behaviours to surface in this more fluid medium of digital communication. Perhaps that is the point — it is important not to plan or make 'goals' for these little pieces of design para-fiction. Perhaps it is important to stop saying, and to start listening to what 'other than human' objects in their social ecologies can tell us. As Alice discovered, in her *Adventures in Wonderland*, the world she found when falling down a rabbit hole was not all roses. The virtual Cheshire Cat, who fades until it disappears entirely, leaving only its wide unnerving grin suspended in the air, offers an apt visual warning of unconsidered approaches to the digital environment.

References

Blas, Z. (2013). 'Facial Weaponization Suite', Zach Blas blog, http://www.zachblas.info/works/facial-weaponization-suite/

Bourdieu, P. (1977). *Outline of a Theory of Practice*. Cambridge: Cambridge University Press.

Foucault, M. (1985). *Discipline and Punish: The Birth of the Prison*. Harmondsworth: Penguin.

Marwick A., Fontaine C., and Boyd D. (2017). '"Nobody sees it, nobody gets mad": Social media, privacy, and personal responsibility among low-SES youth', *Social Media + Society*, https://doi.org/10.1177/2056305117710455

McCurry, J. Phillips, D. and Michaelson, R. (2017). 'From Miami to Shanghai: 3C of warming will leave world cities below sea level', *The Guardian*, https://www.theguardian.com/cities/2017/nov/03/miami-shanghai-3c-warming-cities-underwater

Norris J. (2017). 'Narrative materials / material narratives — a provocation', *UNPLUGGED LINES: Narratives in Practice*, University of Edinburgh, http://www.porty.net/sublime/lines.pdf

O'Reilly Network (2005). 'What is Web 2.0', https://www.oreilly.com/pub/a/web2/archive/what-is-web-20.html

Solove D. J. (2007). '"I've got nothing to hide" and other misunderstandings of privacy', *San Diego Law Review*, 44, pp. 745–72.

Steyerl, H. (2001). 'In free fall: A thought experiment on vertical perspective', *e-flux*, http://www.e-flux.com/journal/24/67860/in-free-fall-a-thought-experiment-on-vertical-perspective/

Trottier D. (2016). *Social Media as Surveillance: Rethinking Visibility in a Converging World*. London: Routledge.

20. Learning to Twalk: An Analysis of a New Learning Environment

#Intermediate #Twitter #BYOD4L #MELSIG #Twalk

Andrew Middleton

Introduction

A Twalk is a learning walk in which a Twitter chat is used to capture and share key ideas amongst dispersed but connected walking groups. The Twalk concept represents a range of disruptive learning approaches in which social media, personal smart technologies and reconfigured learning spaces can be used to produce engaging student-centred and experiential learning. This chapter explains more about Twalks and how they can be designed to support learning in a range of disciplinary contexts.

The Twalk as a Learning Space

A Twalk involves walking as a member of a learning group to discuss a given topic, typically using a simple structure involving posing a new idea, question, or problem every ten minutes over the course of an hour. Groups in different locations follow a similar walking plan structured around the same discussion stimuli. Twitter, or potentially other social media such as Instagram, are used to augment the walk so that participants receive information through the social media channel and

   https://doi.org/10.11647/OBP.0162.20

communicate their discussion outcomes this way too. Therefore, Twalk participants act as co-producers of knowledge by addressing ideas and questions together.

Several disruptive factors establish a Twalk's pedagogic rationale including understanding both walking and tweeting as valuable learning activities in which the learner enacts a high degree of autonomy as part of an active networked learning group.

The use of personal smart technologies underpins these essential pedagogic ideas, empowering the learner and the facilitator by disrupting their dependence on traditional learning space. Smart technologies support the synchronous passing of digital and social media amongst networked participants. These ideas are found in the concepts of Social Media for Learning (#SM4L), Bring Your Own Device for Learning (#BYOD4L), and smart learning (Middleton, 2013). The Twalk concept emerges from this discourse on academic innovation as an example of a disrupted learning space.

An important context for the conceptualisation of Twalks is the investigation of learning space in the digital age, and specifically the agency of the learner as placemaker. Indeed, the first Twalk was initiated as part of a Media-Enhanced Learning Special Interest Group (MELSIG) event in May 2017 which involved walking groups located in multiple locations in the UK, North America and Australasia walking in concert to address a set of ideas about non-formal learning spaces.

Learning and Walking

A learning walk is a peripatetic space, a space defined primarily by the act of walking and talking. The intention for learning to occur is one of several factors that make the idea of learning walk both versatile and hard to define. Intentionality is key to understanding learning space in general and leads us to think about the formal, non-formal and informal nature of learning, participant agency, and control of the learning space, as well as the suitability of the educational spaces we already use (Middleton, 2018).

The relationship between learning and the quality of the spaces can be conceptualised as 'built pedagogy' (Monahan, 2002). This suggests that a peripatetic space might cause a different kind of learning.

Learning walks have been run at Sheffield Hallam University since 2014 as a convivial space for engaging academic staff in their continuing professional development (CPD) (Middleton, 2015). Here, the idea of a peripatetic CPD was intended to spotlight the significance of physical co-presence in learning design with the act of conversational walking challenging binary notions of formality, while raising questions about member and networked-based social constructivist learning. The walks demonstrated how the characteristic conversational fluidity of walking groups accommodates not only the sharing of practice, but the sharing of thinking. This creates an experience that is markedly different to that accommodated by a traditional classroom where participant agency and autonomy are usually subdued, with learners being anchored by their seating and where previous experiences of learning cause learner acquiescence.

More than anything, the peripatetic learning space is non-hierarchical and, as such, demands a dynamic, fluid and networked form of interaction. Its essential fluidity stems from our natural desire to be sociable in a walking group; to seed, listen to, pick up on and expand, share, and compare ideas. Wickson et al. (2015) highlight how building trust amongst strangers is an important outcome of their 'walkshops' because they are conducive to conversations.

Solnit (2014), in her history of walking as a form of activism, describes learning and walking in terms of the mind working at three miles an hour. In this, she is mostly reflecting on the individual thinker. Whatever its purpose, walking is steady, stimulating, and essentially therapeutic. This slow, individual pattern of thinking and walking is developed by introducing conversation to the walk.

The act of walking in partnership as a form of peripatetic learning space is not new, being Aristotelean in origin (Solnit, 2000). Aristotle's habit of walking the perimeter of the Lyceum defines the idea of ancient Greek teaching, where the walk provided an intellectual scaffolding. The walking act itself is stimulating and removes the thinker from mundane worldly distractions while opening their mind to wider horizons.

Ruitenberg (2012) identified non-formality as being significant in her study of school children learning through urban walking. Non-formality as a concept of experiential learning space sits between the systemic functionality of the formal space and the personalised experience of self-directed informal learning space. The non-formal learning space accommodates individual and collective intentionality and the adoption of a loose structure that will serve a group's mutual learning purpose. In her case study, Ruitenberg reports on *Walking Home Carrall Street*, a series of experiential school walks curated through an area of Vancouver. Her students learned about their district using the alternative lenses provided by different invited walk leaders. She observes that school walks establish a novel learning space in which different factors affect the nature of the educational experience: the topic, the expertise, and style of the walk leader, and the extent to which the participant's voice is heard. Our investigation into the Twalk as an emergent learning space is similarly hard to generalise due to the multiple design factors involved. The addition of a social media layer to augment the physical walk multiplies these experiential factors and the educational possibilities that this new form of non-formal learning space affords.

Learning and Tweeting

Typically, tweetchats and learning walks have much in common and this led to the idea of combining the two to explore how each could enhance the other.

A tweetchat, as a learning space, is characterised by its networked design. It is made up of individual learners who, of their own volition, come together to learn in a non-formal space through joint enterprise and for mutual benefit around a common interest. In this respect, the tweetchat has much in common with a Community of Practice (Wenger, 1998). However, the extensive literature on networked learning (see Ryberg and Larsen, 2008; Jones and Esnault, 2004) identifies problems with the concept of community as an adequate representation of the actual social behaviours evident in networked spaces. Community models suggest the importance of coherent, tightly knit, strong social ties. In reality, communal socially networked relationships are hard to circumscribe and are innately fluid, reflecting weak tie structures that are more dynamic and socially agile. Furthermore, the concept of networked individualism (Castells, 2001) embodies the intensified personalisation and individualisation evident in online spaces while recognising the growth of interdependence amongst participants in online groups (Ryberg and Larsen, 2008).

Learning networks thrive through a co-operative ethos in which mutual interest, joint enterprise, and collaboration remain evident, and where cultural identities and values offer richer, more sustained conditions.

The tweetchat hashtag is a common identifier that allows associated tweets to be aggregated into a shared stream alongside other tweets that incorporate the same hashtag. Knowing and using the hashtag gives anybody access to the Twitter chat as a reader, author, or curator. Curation refers to the manipulation of media and, in the case of Twitter, is found in the favouriting and saving of messages, the replying to messages, retweeting and quoting messages, and the copying of others into messages by incorporating their Twitter handles. The power of these actions is multiplied by the number of participant curators. This creates an unusually equitable and student-centred learning environment and even those with a nominal leadership role have no more rights than other participants.

While the hashtag creates a way to assemble participants, the formation of a question set gives the tweetchat its focus and structure. Approximately five questions are designed on a given topic to be delivered, in most cases, over the period of an hour. Following a brief welcome tweet, the nominal session leader will post the first question in a single tweet. It will take the form 'Q1 question text #ourhashtag' where the question text and hashtag are replaced by the respective details. On receipt of the question tweet anyone can post a reply incorporating their answer by using the syntax 'A1 answer text #ourhashtag'.

A further development of the tweetchat in recent years has been the capacity for participants to incorporate images and video. Smart devices enable this because the integrated camera, web connectivity, and digital media apps support the finding, taking and modification of photographs, graphics and videos. Such media can be used to draw attention to topic matter, flag question tweets, create a sense of participant presence, and can provide non-written information pertinent to the discussion. All of these enhance the mobile Twalking environment giving the physical space new significance.

Multilogue

Perhaps the most significant characteristic of the tweetchat is what Megele (2014) refers to as the multilogue; a term originally coined by Shank (1993). The simplest way of defining this is as 'everyone talking at once in a constructive way'. On the face of it the idea of multilogue suggests an unhelpful cacophony, but in the user-centred networked space of the tweetchat it produces a discourse-rich space in which each participant constructs their own route through the semi-structured conversation. Participants are able to control their own pace, weaving in and out of the trajectories of other participants. Further, it is argued that the tweetchat participant acts in neither a synchronous nor asynchronous space, with individual conversations and routes traversing, forwards and backwards, through time at a user-defined pace. This can create the effect of eddying in the Twitter stream as some conversations linger longer than others at the discretion of those participants keen to explore or resolve a particular point. This has been referred to as 'multichronous space' (Middleton, 2018).

Common Structures and Connected Spaces

The Twalk method was designed to incorporate the respective strengths of the tweetchat and learning walks.

The most obvious similarity between the two is their semi-structured conversational design. Both are designed to address an over-arching topic typically organised around about five open-ended discussion points spaced evenly over an hour.

Learning walks are characterised by the number of small group conversations that happen amongst walkers as each question, activity, landmark, or topic is encountered. Ruitenberg (2012) noted her walks were less effective when the invited walk leader was too prescriptive and did not allow enough space for the walk participants to contribute and talk intuitively. Nature walkers do not shout at each other, but converse in two's or three's; in a walking group of eight people, for example, it is probable that three or four conversations take place concurrently. These are guided by the outline structure and purpose, so that conversations find connections without being overly determined by the walk leader. Similarly, tweetchat participants tend to self and co-direct their navigation of the topic. Megele's ENABLE framework (2014) refers to leaderful participation as a feature of a well-designed social media-enhanced learning environment. As people walk and talk at difference paces, eddies occur. As sub-groups catch up with other sub-groups there is the potential for ideas to be shared naturally. Therefore, whether walk, tweetchat or Twalk, the networked environment allows space for leaderful learning and participant voice.

A third similarity relates to the use of knowledge, experience, and content. Both spaces epitomise student-centred active learning environments. Knowledge is brought into the respective environment by the participants themselves, although introductory knowledge may be shared beforehand by the facilitator. Once the walk or the tweetchat is underway there is no didactic teaching. Instead, participants develop their knowledge and their learning together by working with the facilitator's prompts. Using conversation, participants share and challenge opinions, knowledge, experience and ideas in an act of co-production. Learning, in both cases, is an outcome of this collective act.

These three factors demonstrate some of the similarities evident in learning walks and tweetchats that led to the development of the Twalk concept and its potential as a media-rich blended learning environment.

By bringing the idea of walk and tweetchat together, connecting one walk to another in real time becomes possible. Potentially, this allows a walking group in London to walk alongside a walking group in Liverpool, Sheffield, or Ireland, Canada or Australia, as we have experienced. The idea of common map emerges in which the same walk can be followed by groups wherever they are located (if time zones permit) by using the same structure. In May 2017, and then in subsequent Twalks, the author and other colleagues have designed multi-location Twalks. The intended benefits of this global approach depends on the actual learning context (e.g. the Twalk topic, level, and generalisability), however this level of connectivity situates Twalk participants in a connected context that helps them to challenge their parochial outlook while valuing their knowledge and experience in relation to that of others.

Practically, then, the idea of a 'map' is problematic. While the use of the nomenclature emphasises the geospatial aspect of the Twalk, the term 'plan' or 'schedule' explains what is needed to ensure geographically dispersed Twalks keep in step with each other. To achieve this, the map design needs to include generalisable landmarks. For example, on our campus Twalks we have included landmarks such as cafes, PC Labs, an atrium, a lecture theatre, and so forth; features typical of any campus.

How to Plan a Twalk

Beyond the pedagogic rationale of the Twalk there are several design factors that need to be considered to ensure the Twalk integrates properly with the disciplinary context.

Theme

A Twalk, as with any learning event, needs an over-arching theme. This will relate to learning outcomes or a weekly topic. The topic creates the basis for the question design and the selection of physical landmarks that give the Twalk its character, structure, and route.

Common sites

The Twalk's landmark stages create a sense of purpose and structure so that walkers are challenged periodically to summarise and share their discussion before moving to the next phase.

In our work so far, Twalks have largely been used to develop awareness about learning spaces amongst academic staff so the connection between the topic and the material space has been quite literal involving groups located on different sites comparing the designs of their respective campuses; but we have also used metaphor and challenge-based approaches.

Discipline and place-specific challenges reflecting the learning context can be devised. Participants can be asked to respond to the space in a number of ways. For example, 'describe the equipment you find here and offer tips for its use', 'look for the clue', 'discuss what the place means to you', 'ask someone you meet what they think about…', etc. The essential challenge for groups is to compare what they think with others.

Imagery

Landmarks can be selected to prompt the taking of photographs. Participants should be free to use photographs as they see fit, but questions can be set to create an explicit photographic challenge. Twalk participants can be asked to capture their thoughts visually accompanied by tweets used as captions. Visual challenges allow participants to creatively elicit new meaning from a situation, reinforcing the stimulating and permissive nature of the Twalk learning space. Even when the use of imagery is apparently superficial (e.g. a photograph of blue sky to represent creative thinking), the response can convey something of the tone of the Twalk and the readiness to play with ideas. Such playfulness can foster a collective spirit and creative bond that transmits well through the social media, establishing 'the urge to return, recreate, and recapture the experience' (McArthur and Farley White, 2016, p. 39). In a recent short Twalk we incorporated selfie challenges along with more serious discussion points which helped to establish a playful tone, even while keeping the Twalk groups on task.

Roles and Teams

Keeping up with the Twalk schedule can be demanding as teams navigate the topic. Assigning roles within Twalk teams has been helpful. In some cases we have established triads in which participants have been given the roles of Leader, Timekeeper, and Scribe to ensure that each team focuses on the question, keeps to time, and posts, reads and replies to the Twitter stream.

The Hashtag

Creating a suitable hashtag is straightforward but important nonetheless. A hashtag gives the event its identity. It holds the myriad components together.

You can choose any string of characters and numerals preceded by '#'. Your hashtag should be unique as participants use it to search for and aggregate any postings that incorporate the tag. It needs to be short and easy to read as it will be typed in numerous times by those responsible for tweeting and typing will often happen on the move due to the pace of the Twalk. It will probably not include whole words as these are likely to use up characters, so meaningful abbreviations are usually chosen as the basis of good Twalk hashtags.

The Map

The 'map' is an instruction sheet that includes everything a Twalk participant needs during the Twalk. There is a template to follow in MELSIG's online Twalk Toolkit (MELSIG, 2017).

The map is site-specific. While co-Twalkers will follow the same schedule and question set, the map needs to show details of the actual route being walked in each location. Therefore, Twalk organisers need to co-ordinate the production of their respective handouts across sites.

Ideally, each person should have a printed copy of the map and if there is a chance of rain, it is advisable to laminate the maps or provide them in protective sleeves. It can be distributed online as a PDF, but this is not ideal where small screens are used, where connectivity may fall out, and where screen collateral is best dedicated to the Twitter stream. Further, we have found that rain and shine can make screen reading impractical.

The Twalk hashtag needs to be presented clearly and in large bold type, some visual annotated representation of the route including landmark viewpoints should be given; as should a tabulated schedule that includes a small photograph of each destination, its question, and the syntax required for tweeting responses.

Inside, Outside and Incorporation with Special Events

Twalks can take place anywhere. There is no reason for them to be inside or out; instead, Twalk designers should focus on what will work in their context. Walking outside introduces management issues to do with the weather, safety, and keeping local walking groups within sight of each other to ensure coherence and cross-fertilisation of conversations. On a practical basis, walks outside are likely to go beyond the range of Wi-Fi networks and this then introduces issues relating to connectivity and the cost of tweeting, especially where large media are incorporated.

We have successfully incorporated Twalks within special events such as conferences. They can enhance such events by promoting networking and changing the dynamics of the day. This can help to enliven delegates in an early afternoon, for example, where energy levels tend to dwindle. We recently conducted a half hour Twalk as part of a one-hour workshop at a national event. Having sight of the conference building during the planning phase was helpful. The short Twalk format we used was stimulating and allowed us to engage participants beyond what is normally possible in room-based workshops (Middleton et al., 2017).

Similarly, Twalk methods can be adopted to facilitate events such as poster assessments, field trips and placements to enhance interactivity.

Safety

Finally, it is recommended that participants involved in Twalks are briefed about keeping safe. Successful Twalks will deeply engage walking groups, though there are numerous dangers not normally present in a static classroom, for example walking along and crossing roads, or climbing and descending stairs. We have produced a Twalk Toolkit that explains more about this and provides other materials to help with the planning of a Twalk (MELSIG, 2017).

The Twalk as a Hybrid Learning Space

To conclude, we consider what kind of education a Twalk can offer.

Twalks can be configured to engage students in ways that challenge them by re-situating learning away from familiar and predictable spaces. They can be used to,

- foster a sense of belonging;
- develop learning and knowledge through an ethos of co-production;
- develop co-operative learning and working strategies, team building, communication skills and networking skills;
- develop interdisciplinary and cross-institutional activities.

The Twalk is an intrinsically stimulating, versatile, and novel learning space that can be adapted to context.

The Twalk concept was created to demonstrate the potential for future experiential and blended learning environments. In particular, development of the concept has intentionally set out to play with the possibilities of social media for learning (#SM4L) and bring your own device for learning (#BYOD4L) and to explore these phenomena within the context of the hybrid learning space in which the learner is networked across the physical and digital space (Middleton, 2018). A hybrid learning space allows the learner to find their own pathway through authentic problems on their own or amongst clusters of co-located and remotely located people. This takes ideas often perceived as essentially digital phenomena such as Personal Learning Networks (Cronin et al., 2016) and social networking, and allows the academic to consider them as integral dimensions of future blended learning spaces. The Twalk demonstrates the feasibility of this spatial conception and so it is hoped that the pedagogic basis of the Twalk not only leads to further adoption of the method, but to a wider appreciation of hybrid learning spaces.

References

Castells, M. (2001). *The Internet Galaxy: Reflect on the Internet, Business, and Society*. Oxford: Oxford University Press.

Cronin, C., Cochrane, T., and Gordon, A. (2016). 'Nurturing global collaboration and networked learning in higher education', *Research in Learning Technology*, 24, https://doi.org/10.3402/rlt.v24.26497

Jones C. and Esnault L. (2004). 'The metaphor of networks in learning: Communities, collaboration and practice', in S. Banks, P. Goodyear, V. Hodgson, C. Jones, V. Lally, D. McConnell and C. Steeples (eds.),*Proceedings of the Fourth International Conference on Networked Learning*. Lancaster: Lancaster University and The University of Sheffield, pp. 317–23.

McArthur, J. A. and Farley White, A. (2016). 'Twitter chats as third places: Conceptualizing a digital gathering site', *Social Media and Society*, July-September, pp. 1–9.

Megele, C. (2014). 'Theorising Twitter chat', *Journal of Perspectives in Applied Academic Practice*, 2:2, pp. 46–51.

MELSIG (2017). 'The Twalk Toolkit', https://melsig.shu.ac.uk/melsig/resources/twalk-toolkit/

Middleton, A. (ed.) (2013). 'Smart Learning: Teaching and learning with smartphones and tablets in post compulsory education'. MELSIG/Sheffield Hallam University, https://melsig.shu.ac.uk/melsig/smart-learning-new-book-project

Middleton, A. (2015). 'Spacewalking: A mobile ethnography, principles and typography to learn about learning spaces', Liverpool John Moores University Teaching & Learning Conference, 17 June 2015.

Middleton, A. (2018). *Reimagining Spaces for Learning in Higher Education*. London and New York: Palgrave Macmillan.

Middleton, A., Rowell, C., Spiers, A., Vasant, S., Moscrop, C., and Waldock, J. (2017). 'Walk this way: Reflections on a #Twalk'. SocMedHE17, Sheffield Hallam University #SocMed17 conference, 19 December 2017.

Ruitenberg, C. W. (2012). 'Learning by walking: Non-formal education as curatorial practice and intervention in public space', *International Journal of Lifelong Education*, 31:3, pp. 261–75, https://doi.org/10.1080/02601370.2012.6 83604

Ryberg, T. and Larsen, M. (2008). 'Networked identities: Understanding relationships between strong and weak ties in networked environments', *Journal of Computer Assisted Learning*, 24, pp. 103–15.

Shank, G. (1993). 'Abductive multiloguing: The semiotic dynamics of navigating the Net', *Arachnet Electronic Journal on Virtual Culture*, 1:1, http://www.ibiblio.org/pub/academic/communications/papers/ejvc/SHANK.V1N1

Solnit, R. (2000). *Wanderlust: A History of Walking*. New York: Penguin.

Wenger, E. (1998). *Communities of Practice: Learning, Meaning and Identity*. New York: Cambridge University Press.

Wickson, F., Strand, R., and Kjolberg, K. L. (2015). 'The walkshop approach to science and technology ethics', *Science and Engineering Ethics*, 21:1, pp. 241–64.

21. Academics' Understanding of Learning Spaces:
Attitudes, Practices and Outcomes Explored through the Use of Social Media

#Beginner #Twitter #Twalk

Santanu Vasant

Introduction

It means little to have 'thick' technology in our classrooms if our faculty and students do not have the skills and the gear to utilise those classrooms.

Brown and Lippincott, 1993, p. 16

Twenty-five years after this quote from the *Educause Quarterly* magazine was written, this chapter explores how academics understand Learning Spaces, specifically their attitudes, practices, and outcomes through the use of Twitter, via the contemporary continuing professional development activity commonly referenced to as a tweetchat. During the course of this chapter, a series of specific tweetchats and Twitter walks will be referred to anonymously to illustrate the main themes. Before we continue, for the purposes of understanding, let us define

    https://doi.org/10.11647/OBP.0162.21

social media as 'websites and applications that enable users to create and share content or to participate in social networking' (Oxford English Dictionary Online, 2018)

Next, let us turn our attention to the definition of a tweetchat. Whilst there isn't a widely agreed definition of a tweetchat, for our purposes a tweetchat is a live Twitter event, where people from across the world join by searching for a hashtag (a set of characters with a hashtag (#) symbol preceding it). The tweetchat is usually moderated and focused around a general topic, where specific questions are asked by the moderator or host at regular intervals. A set time is also established so that the moderator, guest, or host is available to engage and steer the conversation.

In contrast to a tweetchat, the Twitter walk, also referred to a Twalk, is 'to walk while sending a tweet on Twitter' (Urban Dictionary, n.d.). Twalks have been organised that explore the topics of blended learning, where questions are asked at regular intervals, just as with a tweetchat.

Social media platforms such as Twitter have only been around since the mid-2000s; however, in this short period of time, we have seen it being used in many contexts from journalism to marketing, and increasingly in politics. Before we begin to look at some of the possible themes and its purpose in relation to academics' understanding of learning space, there needs to be an understanding of what a learning space is.

The following is a popular quoted definition of a 'Learning Space':

> Learning is the central activity of colleges and universities. Sometimes that learning occurs in classrooms (formal learning); other times it results from serendipitous interactions among individuals (informal learning). Space — whether physical or virtual — can have an impact on learning. It can bring people together; it can encourage exploration, collaboration, and discussion. Or, space can carry an unspoken message of silence and disconnectedness. More and more we see the power of built pedagogy (the ability of space to define how one teaches) in colleges and universities. (Oblinger, 2005)

In the early days of the Internet, information was created by a handful of people and posted on the Internet for people to read. The interactions that people had were through chat rooms such as MSN chat, ICQ and online forums, which were all text-based communication and did not bleed into the web pages. It was not until the mid-2000s that platforms such as Facebook, YouTube and then Twitter saw the rise of what was defined as social media. These platforms allow users to create and share content — text, images and videos and comment on each other's creations to create this notion of user-generated content. As a result, the amount of content on the web has increased enormously. These interactions often occur publicly online.

During the course of the chapter, we will be examining a series of ideas around the tweetchat and Twalk and how they relate to the development of an academic understanding of learning spaces. Through greater access, many people can be connected on these social media platforms at different physical and virtual locations and devices at the same time. This connectedness provides an opportunity for academic staff developers and academics to engage in a discourse via the tweetchat or Twalk on a given topic, in a way that was not possible even a decade ago.

We will look at how these interactions often allow for richer communication than a face to face classroom, as they are not only captured on the Twitter platform, but can be revisited after the tweetchat has finished — a concept that many social media platforms allow participants to do (Mason and Rennie, 2008). Ideas discussed on these platforms in different contexts have informed changes in policy, created communities of practice, and have seen collaborations between people who would not have met otherwise. Finally, we will look at the idea of educational democracy, the identity of the university teacher and the ways their beliefs interact with this democracy.

As the higher education sector searches for a new identity, it will be argued that using platforms such as Twitter for tweetchat and Twitter walks, strengthens these communities of practice — only if we see the value in them for developing staff and if we know how to use them sparingly at the right stage of teacher education and development.

Main Issues

For centuries, teaching spaces have been structured around didactic teaching from the front of the classroom and students sitting in rows listening to the lecturer drone on about one concept or another. With the widening participation and natural changes in the traditional and non-traditional student body (i.e. those with A-Levels and those transitioning through other routes, for example BTEC etc.), and as universities move from lecturing to teaching, this model of curriculum delivery is no longer effective. There has been a postgraduate certificate in higher education for new staff for a number of years, but due to time constraints the topic of physical learning spaces has not featured in many postgraduate certificates.

As a result, the academics' learning space literacy (i.e. their awareness and application of learning space to planning and delivery) has not been explored to its full potential (Temple, 2007, 2008). It was not until May 2017 that Andrew Middleton at Sheffield Hallam University (Middleton, 2017), introduced participants to the concept of a Twalk to explore issues of staff understanding what they could do in a physical space and how this relates to the pedagogy and the technology. The Twalk has followed almost ten years after seminal work on the concept of pedagogy, space, and technology (Radcliffe et al, 2008), which is one of the key frameworks in understand the interplay between these key areas that any teacher must navigate, whether new or experienced. The illustration of pedagogy, space and technology below, visually represents this connection.

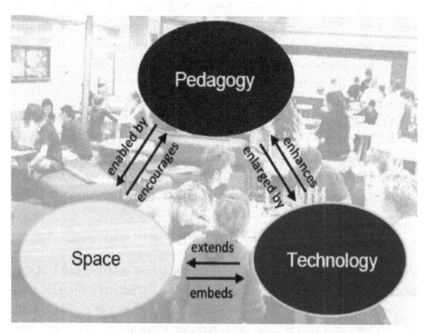

Fig. 21.1 Radcliffe, A Pedagogy-Space-Technology framework for designing and evaluating learning spaces (2008), http://openarc.co.za/sites/default/files/Attachments/UQ%20Next%20Generation%20Book.pdf

This lack of discussion and awareness about learning spaces as a tool, during the planning of a module or programme and during a taught session, was explored during a Twalk in May 2017 through a series of topics and locations. The main points that arose were the sense of connectedness across different institutions from as far away as Toronto, as well as UK cities such as London and Sheffield. Also, answers to the topics from different contexts enriched understanding by presenting ideas of different learning spaces through the use of photographs and short video clips of physical spaces, which in a traditional classroom setting would not be possible. Furthermore, this type of interaction 'overlaps formal, non-formal and informal education' Megele (2014) as participants weave their various learning experience into tweets.

The learning space is an important topic within educational development, not least because a lot of teaching in universities is still face to face and in a physical environment. By understanding learning spaces, the higher education teacher is better able to prepare the learner for life outside academia through better interactions in the physical learning space (setting up spaces for debates; the 'jigsaw classroom' where tasks are split into groups and only by coming together do the students solve the bigger problem; group work and discussions etc.). By understanding the physical learning space, the university teacher is able to set up a safe environment to try out ideas, concepts, and ways of thinking that will ultimately be useful to a student in employment.

In the changing higher education landscape, where variables including the key metrics of Teaching Excellence Framework (TEF) and a desire of many universities to look at blended and distance learning, academics and academic developers are re-examining the role of learning space in the delivery of instruction or teaching in the physical space. Questions regarding how, when, and where we teach are being debated. What is asked less frequently is how academics are to be developed to meet these new challenges. It is with this in mind that a growing number of academic developers are seeking alternative, flexible, and innovative approaches to staff development and embracing social media in optional sessions. The most recognised of these is the Learning and Teaching in Higher Education chat (LTHEchat) in the United Kingdom, which began in 2014 (LTHEchat, 2014).

Walk the Walk, Tweet the Twalk

In many PGCert in higher education courses, there is little or no time devoted to understanding physical learning spaces, although A-Z Creative Teaching in HE (Ashton and Stone 2018) has a chapter for on how to facilitate spaces for learning in a classroom. Indeed, during the several tweetchats I ran on the topic, I found the understanding to be patchy at best and absent at worst. This is in part due to the ways in which these courses are structured, but also to the importance placed on theories of education (i.e. Bruner, Vygotsky, Piaget, etc.), over practical examples of effective higher education practice.

With the advent of a myriad of technologies at the academic developer's disposal, now discussions need not solely be in the physical learning space. They can be asynchronous or synchronous with tools such as forums and webinar platforms, or increasingly with a social media platform such as Twitter. This is where the idea of a tweetchat or Twalk can be unique. It not only brings together people synchronously, but also allows people from outside the institution to join in to the discussion, which is very powerful to widening perspectives and the experiences of teachers who are undergoing initial teacher training in higher education. It can provide a true networked learning approach and a possible solution to the problem of understanding learning spaces and the complex issues that this encompasses.

The use of tweetchats and Twalks give staff the opportunity not only to learn digital skills in context, especially with the use of images and short video clips which is so important to motivation, adopted and conversion to practice (Blackwell and Blackmore, 2003), and to experience the issues that their students could encounter if they decide to embed the platforms in their teaching. With social media platforms, text and images (including images of drawing and the use of vector drawing applications, where participants can draw the layout of learning spaces to explain their points), can be posted at the same time, aiding informal learning (Mayer, 2002). This can include visiting classrooms that you could not visit before social media, while vector drawing tools allow staff to visually represent their ideas and exchange feedback in real time.

Organising your own tweetchat or Twalk in your institution or beyond is easier than you might think, but there are some things to consider. Let us first look at the tweetchat. The central idea of a tweetchat, as discussed earlier, is a topic, followed by five to six questions at regular intervals during an hour. Once these have been agreed, you can either tweet these via Twitter or use a scheduling application such as TweetDeck or Hootsuite, which frees you up to respond and facilitate the tweetchat if you don't have another person helping you. Remember to include a hashtag in your tweets and ask those who join to use the same hashtag, so the tweets can be followed during the chat and displayed after the chat. You should ideally have a minimum of two facilitators of the tweetchat, so they can steer the debate and ask follow-up questions etc. The facilitators can choose to use the direct message private chat as a discussion space before and during the tweetchat. In established tweetchats, it is not uncommon to generate 500 tweets within the tweetchat, so participation is cognitively demanding but allows for freer discourse, though sometimes shorter due to the character limit. Participants answer with A1, A2 at the start of their reply.

In contrast to a tweetchat, the Twalk adds the extra dimension of space (i.e. a lecture theatre), including more informal spaces (a seminar room etc.), and has topics (T1, T2 etc). A map is provided, with room location for participants to walk to. Participants also answer with A1, A2 at the start of the reply at the relevant location. Middleton (2017), aided by others, has devised a Twalk toolkit to summarise some of the key points to remember when running a Twalk. As this is done in teams, you can ask the group to assign a couple of roles similar to the concept of team roles proposed by Belbin (2003). In this case, you would need a coordinator to guide the walk, to keep everyone on the right route and a scribe or tweeter to summarise responses from the group along the way and post on Twitter. You would pause at regular intervals to allow for reflection in a learning space, which is the central idea of the Twalk, to reflect in the physical space where you might be teaching or where your students might be. Lecturers may not consider how their learners will learn a concept and where they will learn it. By positioning the academic in a room and asking them questions to elicit their behaviour and that of their students in a given space, this changes their point of view and is a partial demonstration of Kolb's Learning Cycle, as shown below.

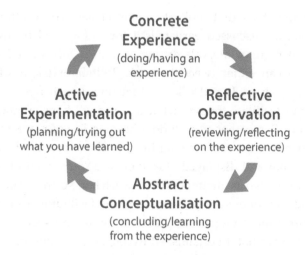

Fig. 21.2 Kolb, *Learning Cycle* (1984)

Two things these tweetchats and Twalks don't currently do is allow the participants to conclude and learn from the experiences they have with social media in a blended context.

After the tweetchat, there is the potential to have a shared online document to curate all the responses and have a 'virtual development buddy' to continue the reflection. There is great value in reflecting on practice, to see what worked well and what did not. As the Kolb diagram shows, this reflection concludes the experience and initiates the active experimentation or a tweak of practice, which is experienced again, and so on.

Conclusions

More time needs to be spent on exploring the issues around physical learning spaces, as we discuss, debate and decide the future direction of higher education teaching in the 21st century. The days of ignoring the physical space are gone, especially as external pressures such as TEF continue to impact the sector.

Seminal pieces of work focused on higher education, including Learning Spaces (Oblinger, 2005 and Radcliffe et al., 2008), have shown us the benefits of bringing an understanding of physical learning spaces understanding into the higher education curriculum. However, in the UK higher education sector, there is a barrier to changing academic practice, which has been commented on (Blackwell and Blackmore, 2003; Pates and Sumner, 2016; and Walker et al., 2016), yet Walker et al. cite Edinburgh Napier University who reward and recognise academic innovation explicitly and link it to promotion, motivating educators to review their practice. A more open culture like this, would benefit the academic community and the sector as a whole.

It is clear that further work needs to be done to help staff to utilise these new or existing physical spaces in different ways, either with the incorporation of technology in the classroom or arranging the furniture to match the teaching activities, reminding academics of constructive alignment (Biggs and Tang, 2011). It would seem natural to use opportunities such as tweetchats as tools to facilitate this development. However, this practice is taking place in the shadows of educational development and if we are to see a shift in the quality of teaching, which has occurred in the school sector in the past 10 years, we need to bring the best of these practices into the educational development classroom, consisting of practical showcases of good practices, challenging academics' understanding of physical learning spaces and beginning with their beliefs and motivations for adopting practices. Educational developers have to bring context into the practice they discuss; as Blackmore and Blackwell (2003) say, 'most obvious is context, whether disciplinary or institutional ... this shapes individuals' motivations (affecting their willingness to engage) and also the influences the acceptability of any of these above models'. (They refer to models to develop practice i.e. formally accredited courses, institutional workshops, staff secondments and using technologist and informal learning at work). Furthermore, they add 'that teaching basic technology skills (how to use something) particularly in isolation, is insufficient".

One area of development for tweetchats and Twalks is a follow up after a given period of time, to see if the practice has changed, which is a problem in more traditional continuing professional development (CPD) activities, 'most teaching related CPD is evaluated through post event questionnaires, sometimes called "happy sheets"' (Spowart et al., 2017). Spowart et al. advocate pre-post surveys, which involves revisiting a sample of those trained to ascertain whether practice has changed, including students, as the goal of much of academics' understanding of learning spaces is intended to improve their teaching practice, and ultimately make an impact on student outcomes. As Spowart et al. (2017) conclude:

> student awareness of staff CPD is implicit. Therefore, in order to determine an impact on student learning, even at a basic level, we need to raise student awareness of the CPD that academics engage with and the impacts it can have on their teaching and learning.

In order for practice to change, several things need to happen. Firstly, academics need to engage in meaningful reflective practice, which in order to be taken seriously, needs to have some assessment attached to it. Secondly, there needs to be an evaluation of their practice in relation to others, which is where practices such as tweetchats via social media channels come into play in making it easier to engage in bite size CPD. Thirdly, there needs to be recognition from institutional management and a nationally recognised progression route on a teaching-only contract, that promotes staff to professorship based on their teaching and scholarship in teaching research. If this were to be nationally implemented, then teaching would be on a par with research. Finally, there needs to be more openness about what works and doesn't in higher education practice, which again, tweetchats can aid, so that practitioners can learn from one another.

References

Ashton, S. and Stone, R. (2018). *An A-Z of Creative Teaching in Higher Education.* London: Sage Publishing.

Belbin, R. M. (2003), *Management Teams: Why they Succeed or Fail,* 2nd edn, Oxford: Butterworth-Heinemann.

Biggs, J. B. and C. Tang (2011).*Teaching for Quality Learning at University,* 4th edn, Maidenhead: Open University Press.

Blackwell, R. and Blackmore, P. (eds.) (2003).*Towards Strategic Staff Development in Higher Education.* Maidenhead, UK: SRHE and Open University Press.

Brown, M. B, and Joan K. Lippincott, J. K. (2003). 'Learning spaces: More than meets the eye', http://www.personal.kent.edu/~tk/ocde/learning_spaces.pdf

Ellis, R. A. and Goodyear, P. (June 2016). 'Models of learning space: Integrating research on space, place and learning in higher education'. *Review of Education,* 4:2, pp. 149–91.

Gibbs, G. (2013). 'Reflections on the changing nature of educational development', *International Journal for Academic Development*, 18:1, pp. 4–14.

Kolb, D. A. (1984). *Experiential Learning: Experience as the Source of Learning and Development*. Upper Saddle River, NJ: Prentice Hall.

Mayer, R. E. (2002). 'Multimedia learning', *Psychology of Learning and Motivation*, 41, pp. 85–139, https://doi.org/10.1016/S0079-7421(02)80005-6

Megele, C. (2014). 'Theorising Twitter chat', *Journal of Perspectives in Applied Academic Practice*, 2:2, pp. 46–51.

Middleton, A (2017). 'How to plan a Twalk', https://melsig.shu.ac.uk/melsig/resources/twalk-toolkit/how-to-plan-a-twalk/

Mulcahy, D. (2015). 'Re/Assembling spaces of learning in Victorian government schools: policy enactments, pedagogic encounters and micropolitics', *Discourse: Studies in the Cultural Politics of Education*, 36:4, pp. 500–14.

Long, P. D. (2005). 'Learning space design in action'. *EDUCAUSE Review*, 4:4, p. 60.

Oblinger, D. (2005). 'Learning spaces', Educause, https://www.educause.edu/research-and-publications/books/learning-spaces

Oxford English Dictionary (2018). 'Social media', http://www.oed.com

Pates. D. and Sumner, N. (2016). 'E-learning spaces and the digital university', *The International Journal of Information and Learning Technology*, 33:3, pp. 159–71.

Radcliffe, D. et al. (2008), 'Learning spaces in Higher Education: Positive outcomes by design', http://openarc.co.za/sites/default/files/Attachments/UQ%20Next%20Generation%20Book.pdf

Spowart, L., et al. (2017). 'Evidencing the impact of teaching-related CPD: beyond the 'Happy Sheets', *International Journal for Academic Development*, 22:4, pp. 360–72.

Temple, P. (2007). *Learning spaces for the 21st century: A review of the literature*. York: Higher Education Academy.

Temple, P. (2008). 'Learning spaces in higher education: An under-researched topic', *Review of Education*, 6:3, pp. 229–41.

Urban Dictionary (2018), 'Twalk', https://www.urbandictionary.com/define.php?term=Twalk

Walker, R., Voce, J., Jenkins, M. (2016), 'Charting the development of technology-enhanced learning developments across the UK higher education sector: A longitudinal perspective (2001–2012)', *Interactive Learning Environments*, 24, pp. 438–55.

Wenger, E. (1998). *Communities of Practice: Learning, Meaning, and Identity*. New York: Cambridge University Press.

PART SEVEN
THE PERSONAL JOURNEY

22. Somewhere in Between:
My Experience of Twitter as a Tool for Continuous Personal Development

Andy Horton

> *Somewhere in between*
> *The waxing and the waning wave*
> *Somewhere in between*
> *What the song and the silence say*
>
> Kate Bush (2005), 'Somewhere in Between'

Of all the social media platforms, Twitter has taken up a space that crosses boundaries between the private and public, and the personal and the professional. Over the years, my own use of Twitter as a librarian in the HE sector has moved increasingly into my professional life, while retaining a personal focus and voice.

Networking and the sharing of best practice among educators are key benefits of conferences and events for continuing professional development (CPD). Social media — Twitter in particular — has made it possible for a live 'backchannel' of communication to emerge around a presentation or workshop, enabling commentary, critique and contribution by audience members. In this sense, it allows online

https://doi.org/10.11647/OBP.0162.22

communication among those physically present, while also starting conversations with interested colleagues elsewhere.

This use of Twitter also sparks a blend of online and physical learning and networking, as participants discover common ground with colleagues at other institutions through shared social media discussions which can lead to real-world collaboration.

Outside of conferences and associated events, Twitter — through the hashtag, the Twitter chat, and through dialogues around courses and developments in HE — has for me been a staple of communication, CPD, networking and personal brand-building.

My use of Twitter began in 2008, and has increased — in my home and work life — over the last ten years. My use of the platform in my personal life has influenced and enhanced how I use it for professional purposes, and vice-versa. Perhaps its value lies in its ability to move between spaces — the personal and the professional, the physical and the digital. Perhaps it has now become necessary for us each to decide how we will use this in our careers, and what we choose to share of our private and public selves.

In July 2007, I attended a conference session presented by librarians from the University of Illinois at Urbana Champaign, about their various means of outreach to students. One of the things they mentioned in passing was their use of Twitter, described as a 'micro-blogging' site. I think I had heard of Twitter, but this was the first example I had encountered of it being put to a purpose in libraries or HE.

It was some months later — March 2008, my Twitter profile confirms — when I created my own account. I had a journal on the Livejournal blogging site, and when prompted for a user name for Twitter I chose the same one I used there and became @fechtbuch. It was distinctive — and untaken — and I was able to use my own name alongside it. I have never changed it — over time, as my follower count has grown, it has become my Twitter identity. What I did not do — or think to do — was choose a professional username, a library-related one, even though I was originally inspired to sign up by a library Twitter account. It was an experiment; to investigate, use and explore Twitter, with a view to perhaps using it in some way in my professional life. Discussions of Twitter by academics and information professionals often assume its adoption as a tool for professional development or scholastic communication (Stranack 2012, Filgo 2011, Fenwick 2016), and may discuss the intersection of the personal and professional (Ollier-Malaterre et al., 2013, Fox and Bird 2017); but they rarely examine the professional use of an originally personal account.

At first, I was unsure what to post, and how to act, on this new stage. I barely even knew who to follow. A few friends and colleagues had adopted Twitter, and they were quickly added. I followed a few celebrities too, as it seemed to be expected of me. And then the numbers began to grow. Slowly, steadily, @fechtbuch made connections with others, and built a network of followers. This was without design or strategy. Friends of friends, people with shared interests, people I had conversed with. And some colleagues, acquaintances at other libraries or other people I had met online and discussed work with. My Twitter account remained personal at first — it certainly wasn't work-focused or linked to my role. I was tweeting as myself, in a personal capacity, largely about my personal interests. In doing so, I was starting to learn the medium — the mechanics of replies and retweets, the etiquette of conversations with strangers. I also learned about the hashtag, that simple, effective mechanism for drawing conversation and posts on a topic together.

Hashtags marked my developing use of Twitter in a professional context. Initially, this was at another conference. A few years later, in 2012, I had changed jobs and institutions. I was at a library conference in Newcastle. The conference had a hashtag and I had been including it in my tweets. I was still tweeting as myself, not on behalf of my institution — though this time as myself at work, in my professional life. As it happens, I was in a workshop on composing content for library Twitter accounts, and I was hoping to pick up tips for a nascent institutional account we had created where I worked. I was tweeting about the session, using the conference's hashtag, and someone replied — the person sitting next to me in the room. A conversation was taking place online between people in the same physical space, about the event we were both participating in. This for me was a memorable moment, but there were many other interactions through Twitter at that event. For the first time, I was aware of social media as a 'backchannel' at conferences.

Through the hashtag, the delegates were able to participate in the event as it unfolded. This has become increasingly common and has arguably changed delegates' conference experiences. Some tweet key points from presentations, a behaviour which is both a form of note-taking and of broadcasting content to a wider audience outside the venue. It is not uncommon for people to virtually follow a conference via the hashtag conversation on Twitter. Others will comment on presentations, perhaps adding their own perspective or with examples from their own professional experience. It is not uncommon for a presenter to make a reference in passing to a piece of research, online resource, or other digital object and for someone in the audience to quickly tweet a link to it for their peers. Most useful, perhaps, is the use of the Twitter backchannel to share practice and experience. This kind of sharing was always one of the most useful aspects of attending a conference; this was originally limited to conversations outside the scheduled sessions. Twitter allows conversations to start and interested parties to find each other much more quickly, putting them in contact and often sparking face-to-face conversations. The communication may move on from the hashtag-focused Twitter discussion. Kimmons and Veletsianos (2016) in their research into use of Twitter at conferences found that 'it seems that the backchannel may serve as an initial connector to begin conversation but that as discussions become disjointed and divergent authors may naturally leave the backchannels'. In this, participants' Twitter online conversations can be seen as corresponding to the way a face-to-face conversation unfolds.

In tweeting from a conference, a conversation is created which includes those present, but also colleagues and contacts outside the event following the hashtag or the timelines of participants. It creates a space for participation that encompasses those physically present, but also those online.

This further makes it more likely for people expanding their professional network to expand their social media network too. People will follow each other during conferences, sometimes only for the conference duration but often afterwards. It is at this point that different users' approaches to their Twitter accounts become apparent, as some are wholly subject- or profession-focused, while others' cross over between their personal and their professional lives. My account, having started as a personal one, has always had that aspect. I have taken to posting a tweet (often on my way home) to let new followers know that my account is not solely library-related content. While this has lost followers, at least one person has commented that this is why they follow me.

Connections initially established through conference conversations, hashtag discussions, and interaction with mutual friends in libraries have steadily increased the professional network aspect of my Twitter experience. However, as I increased my follower count — now at over 1500, or 3 'milliwheatons' (Kovalic, 2009) — I was connecting with as many people from non-work friendships, or through mutual interests such as games, as I was with librarians or learning technologists. Conversations on Twitter can cross over between groups — a friend from outside HE might comment on an issue raised in a post from a conference, or a colleague at another institution might chat online about a television programme we are both watching.

Just as traditional communication crosses boundaries between groups, so can social media practices. The tweetchat is a regular online conversation, using a hashtag and moderated by one or more people around a common interest or area of practice. Tweetchats often take place weekly, and usually with a selected theme for discussion each time. I have participated in the Learning Technology in Higher Education tweetchat, with the hashtag #LTHEchat (Nerantzi et al., 2014). My first experience with tweetchats though was with the #RPGChat and #RPGlifeuk games chats. In both cases there is a community of regular attendees, with newcomers welcomed and accepted for their contribution to the discussion. In participating in the game chats, I learned how to negotiate these chats, keeping track in real time of online conversations with multiple threads and new questions being posted while discussions for older ones were still live. This made my forays into #LTHEchat easier to navigate. In terms of benefits, both the games and HE tweetchats were an effective way to share practice and hold conversations around shared interests, and helped make connections and build a network.

My presence on Twitter, blending personal and professional content, became noticed by colleagues at my institution. Specifically Chris Rowell, at the time deputy head of Learning Technology at Regent's University London where I was deputy library manager, found in me a kindred social media spirit. He and I had collaborated on delivering a range of training to colleagues. We worked together to present a workshop for the annual staff conference which we used as a springboard for facilitating an iteration of Helen Webster's Ten Days of Twitter course (Webster, 2018), an introduction to the platform for novices. Whilst being worthwhile in itself, this also helped outreach for our Learning Resources department to academic colleagues within our institution. It also helped foster an effective working partnership, which led to Chris inviting me in 2014 to work with him on his 12 Apps of Christmas course (Rowell, 2015).

The 12 Apps of Christmas was an online course, intended initially to support teaching staff at Regent's, which showcased a range of free mobile apps with applicability to teaching. It was an open course, and numbers participating rose massively in the days before it started. The course was meant to be discursive, and we were aware that it was important to maintain the online community around MOOCs for them to work; the management and engagement of a community of over 500 learners became a priority in order to make a success of the course. To this end, I spent a lot of time monitoring and responding to posts on the course forums, but I was also actively using Twitter — checking the hashtag, engaging with learners on the course, and commenting on each day's activities.

The course was a success, winning the Credo Digital Literacy award which Chris and I received at the 2015 LILAC conference — during which event I was tweeting. It also established itself as an annual fixture, and Chris and I have presented on it at conferences and symposiums in learning technology and librarianship. This has brought with it a new perspective in my use of Twitter. While I was still participating in Twitter conversations as a conference backchannel, now I was aware that I was tweeting as a speaker myself. Conversations among the audience on Twitter were sometimes supplemented by virtual questions from the floor, and I was seeing my own references augmented by tweeted links.

I also became involved with the Business Librarians Association as their training officer, and my tweets from their annual conference, while still in my own voice and from a personal perspective, had to take into account the organization which I was representing. In some ways, this had always been true — tweeting about work from a personal account always requires an awareness of appropriate behaviour. Now, though,

I was aware that my public profile on Twitter was part of what could be considered as my social media brand. It was almost a surprise to see that I had a brand. The connections I had built, and the activities I had tweeted about, meant that I was not anonymous. The @fechtbuch Twitter account was a significant part of my online profile, and it crossed over between the personal and the professional.

Connections made on Twitter can remain in the virtual world, but still be no less solid for that. They can also cross over into the physical, as we meet colleagues with whom we have conversed online. People often comment, on meeting online friends for the first time, on how their online presence reflects their real personality. Some research suggests that a strong online presence can influence, and become part of, a person's identity (Ward and Coates, 2016). Or, as a friend of mine likes to say on meeting a social media contact for the first time: 'an imaginary friend just became real'.

Twitter contacts crossing personal and professional spheres have led to involvement in other projects. In 2015, Matt Finch invited me to participate in Lambeth public libraries' contribution to the Fun Palaces community engagement project (Doctorow, 2015). This was based on my Twitter presence as a professional academic librarian, a supporter of public libraries, and a gamer. The work I did on this community project was in turn cited as evidence of community engagement by library staff for a Customer Service Excellence initiative where I worked. It also led to my continuing involvement with events at Upper Norwood Library. This involved my personal and professional life, as well as my leisure interests and career, all linked by my Twitter profile.

My Twitter account is not my only presence on social media. Facebook remains a personal space, although even here there is a crossover as I am an admin of the university library's account. There are also the library Twitter accounts for my current and previous posts — here, I have sought to include a sense of the personal where appropriate. Even an institutional social media account needs an authentic voice, and genuine contact with its audience. I have an account on LinkedIn, that most professional of platforms. A service which has taken a certain amount of time to find its place, LinkedIn is now strongly established as a professionally-focused social media platform. It works for sharing appropriate and relevant content, for communicating with professional contacts. It certainly works as a place to establish one's professional profile — it could host a ready-made conference speaker biography, for example. Still, the point at which I felt it had established itself was when a conversation with a friend on work matters turned seamlessly into a personal chat.

Increasing follower numbers on Twitter have meant that my feed of posts is full and diverse. This can be a good thing, but it also diffuses the posts of a range of contacts — professional connections, friends, those with shared hobbies or interests. This also applies to my own timeline. Though at different times I may have a narrower focus — if I was at a work event, or a games convention, for example — my posts inevitably range from professional conversations to leisure interests. This is true of many Twitter users, and there is sometimes a process of filtering out posts on topics in which we have little interest. Doubtless many people scroll past my tweets from library conferences, or from Sunday morning games chats. Relevant content for a particular person may well be swamped by irrelevant posts. Although the discursive nature of Twitter encourages engagement and interaction, it can lack focus. The ratio of meaningful signal to meaningless noise online can be challenging (Stranack, 2012), and requires coping strategies (Gleick, 2011).

The @fechtbuch account certainly does not have an exclusive focus on my professional role. In 2017, I enrolled on a postgraduate certificate in professional higher education, a teaching qualification. This is a course with a high level of reflection on my teaching activities. While I believe Twitter can be a good platform for this, I felt that my account would not be suited to the purpose. For this reason I have created a second account, focused on my professional role and development. Sharing less of my private self, and centred on my professional identity, @apjhlib is centred on my role as a librarian and in particular my teaching and professional development. My first account remains, though, as my primary presence on Twitter. In a space which mixes the personal with the professional, apart from — yet sometimes interacting with — the physical, connecting with others met or unmet in real life; somewhere in between.

References

Bush, K. (2005). 'Somewhere in Between', *Aerial* [CD]. London: EMI.

Doctorow, C. (2015). 'Fun palaces: Locally made art, science and play, for participants, not audiences', boingboing, https://boingboing.net/2015/10/01/fun-palaces-locally-made-art.html

Fenwick, T. (2016). 'Social media, professionalism and higher education: A sociomaterial consideration', *Studies in Higher Education*, 41:4, pp. 664–77.

Filgo, E. H. (2011). '#Hashtag librarian: Embedding myself into a class via Twitter and blogs', *Computers in Libraries*, 31:6, pp. 78–80.

Fox, A. and Bird, T. (2017). 'The challenge to professionals of using social media: Teachers in England negotiating personal-professional identities', *Education and Information Technologies*, 22:2, pp. 647–75.

Gleick, J. (2011). *The Information: A History, a Theory, a Flood*. London: Fourth Estate.

Kimmons, R., and Veletsianos, G. (2016). 'Education scholars' evolving uses of Twitter as a conference backchannel and social commentary platform', *British Journal of Educational Technology*, 47:3, pp. 445–64.

Kovalic, J. (2009). *The Milliwheaton*, https://web.archive.org/web/20110927025143/http://www.dorktower.com/2009/05/21/dork-tower-may-21-2009-the-milliwheaton/

Nerantzi, C., Beckingham, S., Reed, P., and Walker, D. (2014). *About #LTHEChat*, https://lthechat.com/about/

Ollier-Malaterre, A., Rothbard, N. P., and Berg, J. M. (2013). 'When worlds collide in cyberspace: How boundary work in online social networks impacts professional relationships', *Academy of Management Review*, 38:4, pp. 645–69.

Rowell, C. (2015). *Reflections on the 12 Apps of Christmas*, https://altc.alt.ac.uk/blog/2015/11/reflections-on-the-12-apps-of-christmas

Stranack, K. (2012). 'The connected librarian: Using social media for "do it yourself" professional development', *Partnership: The Canadian Journal of Library & Information Practice & Research*, 7:1, p. 1.

Ward, J. and Coates, N. (2016). 'Developing a Methodology to Research the Avatar/User Relationship'. Paper presented at American Marketing Association — Winter Conference, 2 January 2016.

Webster, H. (2018). '#10DoT Ten Days of Twitter', https://10daysoftwitter.wordpress.com/

23. The 'Healthy Academic', Social Media, and a Personal and Professional Journey

#Beginner #Twitter #Facebook

Neil Withnell

Introduction

Embracing social media as a potent tool in nurse education has become a large part of my working life. I fully embrace, and see the value of, social media and try to engage positively with Twitter, LinkedIn, YouTube etc.

I am aware of many potential pitfalls in the use of social media and I endeavour to avoid these and assist others in avoiding them, where possible. Whilst avoiding the pitfalls is important, an overemphasis on this aspect might be having a counterproductive effect, resulting in practitioners and educators feeling wary of social media and failing to harness the connectivity that it allows. The purpose of this chapter is to look at the pitfalls and the relative ease of avoiding them, whilst juxtaposing this with the great creativity that social media affords for those who are confident enough to use it professionally. In order to use social media in a creative but safe manner (safe for you and others), individuals have to be able to look objectively at their own use of social media on a professional and personal level. Developing the ability to question your personal use of social media against the wider

    https://doi.org/10.11647/OBP.0162.23

background of your online professional identity, and recognising the need to ensure that one does not compromise the other, is essential in promoting that safety whilst learning just how powerful a tool social media can be. Ollier-Malaterre and Rothbard (2015) found that some professionals are avoiding social media altogether but that this limits opportunities to connect people and collect information.

Social Media in Healthcare

Within the healthcare professions, professional bodies have produced guidelines for the use of social media. The regulatory body for nursing and midwifery in the UK, the Nursing and Midwifery Council (NMC), provides guidance for professionals in avoiding the misuse of social media whilst encouraging familiarity with social media tools (NMC, 2017). The NMC remind professionals to 'think before you post', indicating that what might feel private may not be.

The Health and Care Professions Council (HCPC) regulates 16 professions including social workers, occupational therapists, dieticians, paramedics and many others. The guidance also provides the same message, 'think before you post', and similarly encourages professionals to keep on posting, seeing social media as a worthwhile communication tool (HCPC, 2017). These guidelines promote public and corporate safety by adhering to a code of conduct with online presence whether it be for personal or professional use.

The British Medical Association (BMA) guidance for doctors and medical students refers to its guidance as 'common sense' (BMA, 2017). This is a vague term that inadequately guides members in recognising where they may be acting inappropriately within their online presence. The BMA guidelines take a similar stance to those adopted by other professional bodies advocating awareness of the potential to compromise professional status if personal use is not managed appropriately, and reinforcing the importance of other professional guidelines published by the BMA and General Medical Council (GMC, 2013). There appears to be a unifying message within the aforementioned professional guidelines: do not do anything online — even in a seemingly private domain — that would breach the Code that you adhere to in your professional life. As nurses we are made aware of our duty to the public at all times within the Code of Practice (NMC, 2015). This clearly states a nurse's duty to act in the best interests of people at all times. In reference to supporting colleagues, the Code states that this should never compromise or be at the expense of patient or public safety. The statement about respecting and upholding people's human rights does not have a caveat of 'only when on duty' and it can be assumed that the Code extends to our use of social media. Journalists increasingly find old online social media posts for celebrities, politicians and public figures which can have a devastating impact on their careers. Take the example of Labour MP Jared O'Mara, who resigned from the Women and Equalities Committee after it was revealed that he had posted a series of homophobic and sexist comments 15 years previously (The Guardian, 2017).

Ollier-Malaterre and Rothbard (2015) comment that social media is risky and explain that a single unfortunate post can throw a career off track. Whilst it may seem common sense not to post highly personal or controversial material in a work web chat, you may not be so guarded in a Facebook comment on a personal online chat. You may feel that your personal comments in such arenas are only for people of your choice to view and therefore are more private. However, unless a site is encrypted, such as WhatsApp, the material can be found and may affect how you are perceived professionally and/or publicly. The BMA guidance (2017) mirrors that of the NMC in terms of wider accountability; 'you are still a doctor or medical student on social media, even if you don't identify yourself as such or post about medical matters'. The ethical and legal standards expected of you by the GMC and the broader, less well-defined professional expectations of our peers can still apply online as in any other part of everyday life. Respect patients and colleagues and take a cautious approach to anything that you think could affect your professional standing. The BMA guidelines offer advice about risks such as taking caution if taking pictures of your workplace which could inadvertently capture anything or anyone that breaches confidentiality.

Shapira (2008) provides examples of teachers in America making what they perceive as personal posts on sites such as Facebook which have subsequently been viewed by employers and parents of children at the school. One young woman defends her pictures of herself drinking, stating that her work and social lives are completely separate. Indeed, the article goes on to mention that such individuals could claim the right to free speech under the First Amendment. However, it also points out that the Supreme Court in America has ruled that Governments could fire employees if their speech harmed the workplace's mission and function.

Lagu, et al. (2008) identifies the potential to compromise professionalism through a conflict of interest. Any online presence with a large number of followers has the potential to attract public relations professionals asking for endorsement of specific products. The study found blogs that promoted health care products within their entries but they were not able to determine if these were paid endorsements because they could not find any disclosures indicating the authors' conflict of interest. The NMC Code of Conduct states 'never use your professional status to promote causes that are not related to health' (2015).

Ollier-Malaterre and Rothbard (2015) details preferred social media strategies that individuals can adopt after diagnosing their own most natural online behaviour. Ask yourself the following to determine your own online behaviour:

- Do you value transparency and authenticity, and if so, do you post whatever comes to mind on social media? If so, this is an *open strategy* that can be viewed as risky.

- Do you prefer to keep personal and professional networks separate? This is regarded as less risky and referred to as an *audience strategy*. Examples include the Facebook users who learn to deflect friend requests from professional contacts by directing them to a LinkedIn account. A downside to this is managing the 'fluid' nature of networks as people who begin as friends can later become co-workers, or even bosses, in which case, an audience strategy can be compromised.

- Do you feel compelled to accept friend requests from professional contacts? If so this is referred to as *content strategy*, whereby accepting these requests but going on to post content that has been carefully considered.

The above strategies are very different, with the content strategy being almost a polar opposite of the open strategy. The content strategy is very controlled and does not allow for unfettered posting and impulsive responses.

BMA (2017) guidelines advise that even ostensibly private spaces could be shared more widely than you intended and uses the example of a Twitter feed being screen captured and shared out of context.

There is a developing theme here in regard to so-called 'private' postings that have the potential to land you in hot water. I find when using social media professionally I am more aware of my professional accountability. This is less at the forefront of my mind when making private posts but I do hold the view that anything I post can be viewed against the professional requirements of my position as a registered nurse. Whilst I do have a private online presence, anything I do post on social media I regard as open and as such acknowledge that it can be seen by anybody. I particularly enjoy Twitter chats as the discussion is controlled, shared and enjoyed by other professionals, and this helps to keep the discussion focussed. I am however aware that many people prefer a more delineated separation of their personal and professional online presences.

Ollier-Malaterre and Rothbard (2015) concur with this stating that the more posts are tailored to a specific circle the less risky they are. To this end they suggest a further strategy, in which users control both their audience and their content. An example of this is Facebook users creating two lists, one personal and one professional and posting content accordingly. This can allow the safeguarding of professional reputations whilst still maintaining an honest and authentic Facebook identity. This they refer to as a *custom strategy*.

When considering posting online it is worth remembering the notion of a digital footprint (Madden, et al. 2007), in that anything posted leaves a mark. This is worth having at the back of your mind before pressing the 'send/post/submit' button, as it may have undesired negative consequences in the future, leaving a mark that you cannot remove.

Suler (2004) wrote about the online 'disinhibition effect' acknowledging that people behave differently in cyberspace and will say things they may not in face to face contact. When using social media on a professional level people should be wary of the pitfalls of the disinhibition effect. Anonymity online can contribute to this disinhibition, as Suler points out, with a list of 'ingredients' which include;

- You don't know me
- You can't see me

Suler further describes 'toxic disinhibition' where users may express anger, hatred and threats. He further describes 'benign disinhibition' where users may share personal things about themselves and show unusual acts of kindness or generosity. Both are viewed within psychodynamic theory as possible processes of 'working through', or even pathways towards 'self-actualisation'. Whilst this can be a developmental process for an individual both personally and professionally, it may not be a journey that we want in the public domain no matter how enhancing it transpires to be for our own development.

A useful quote to keep in mind when using social media is from Haig as it encourages integrity in how you portray yourself (Guardian, 2017). Haig wrote about the damage of anonymity, quoting Kurt Vonnegut 'We are what we pretend to be, so we must be careful who we pretend to be'

Conclusion

Social media is a valuable tool in my professional life. In many ways it has become more aligned to professional use and I tend to use it less for personal reasons. The reasons behind this are partly due to the potential pitfalls I have discussed, but more importantly due to the benefits I have found in using it professionally. If using social media as a professional tool, I advise careful adherence to your own professional code of conduct. Whereas I tend to use it less for personal use, I would advocate maintaining the same standards in personal use to avoid compromising professional status. Assumed anonymity can create a false sense of security and lead to posts that reveal more than you intended to audiences you did not intend to reach, or even result in breaching your own professional standards.

References

British Medical Association (2017). 'Social media, ethics and professionalism', file:///C:/Users/nus676/Downloads/Ethics%20guidance%20on%20social%20media%20FINAL.pdf

General Medical Council (2013). 'Doctor's use of Social media', https://www.gmc-uk.org/guidance/ethical_guidance/21186.asp

Haig (2017). 'I used to think social media was a force for good. Now the evidence says I was wrong', *The Guardian*, https://www.theguardian.com/commentisfree/2017/sep/06/social-media-good-evidence-platforms-insecurities-health

Health and Care Professions Council (2017). 'Use of social networking sites', http://www.hpc-uk.org/registrants/standards/socialnetworking/

Lagu, T., Kaufman, E. J., Asch, D. A., and Armstrong, K. (2008). 'Content of Weblogs written by health professionals', *Journal of General Internal Medicine*, 23:10, pp. 1642–46.

Madden, M., Fox, S., Smith, A., and Vitak, J. (2007). 'Digital footprints', http://www.pewinternet.org/2007/12/16/digital-footprints/

Nursing and Midwifery Council (2017). 'Social media guidance', https://www.nmc.org.uk/standards/guidance/social-media-guidance/

Nursing and Midwifery Council (2015). 'The code: Professional standards of practice and behaviour for nurses and midwives', https://www.nmc.org.uk/standards/code/read-the-code-online/

Ollier-Malaterre, A., and Rothbard, N. (2015). 'How to separate the personal and professional on social media, https://hbr.org/2015/03/how-to-separate-the-personal-and-professional-on-social-media

Shapira, I. (2008). 'When young teachers go wild on the Web', http://www.washingtonpost.com/wp-dyn/content/article/2008/04/27/AR2008042702213.html

Suler, J. (2004). 'The online disinhibition effect', *Cyberpsychology & Behaviour*, 7:3, pp. 321–26.

(2017). 'Labour MP quits Equality Committee over homophobic posts', *The Guardian*, https://www.theguardian.com/politics/2017/oct/23/labour-mp-jared-omara-sheffield-hallam-sorry-girls-aloud-orgy

Glossary

Backchannel is an online conversation that happens at the same time as a specific event, such as a conference. The backchannel will often happen through Twitter where participants will share comments about the live event. They may also ask or answer specific questions and share related resources or links.

Blog is a website that displays content or posts in a chronological order.

Connectivism is a relatively new theory of how learning takes place in a digital environment. It proposes that learning does not just happen at an individual level but that learning and knowledge can develop outside of the individual through connections between organisations, the Internet, or even data.

Digital badges are indicators of a skill, accomplishment, quality or achievement earned in a learning environment. Badges earned can then be displayed on a social media site or app.

Facebook is the most well know of the social media sites, which enables users to share comments, links (on news or other content) and photos/videos across the Internet. This shared content can be with just close 'friends' or groups or made publicly available to everyone at a global level.

Facebook Live is a feature of Facebook that enables users to live-stream video recordings. After the live broadcast has been made, a recording will be posted and made permanently available.

GIF is an acronym for Graphics Interchange Format. They are a file type that can support static and animated images and are often used on Twitter and Facebook.

Github is a website that allows IT developers or groups of programmers to share and manage their code or projects and collaborate with others across the world.

Handle is a person's online identity and is often used as someone's user name of their social media account.

Hashtags are used in social media to identify messages on a specific topic, for example:

#iacanhazpdf — used on Twitter to request access to academic journal articles which are behind paywalls.

#LTHEchat — Learning and Teaching in Higher Education Twitter chat.

#DigPed — Digital pedagogy

#BYOD4L — 'Bring Your Own Device 4 Learning' course.

#12AoC — '12 Apps of Christmas' course.

Instagram is a photo and video sharing social media app. Users can share photos and videos which can then be edited using different filters and additional information can be added, such as tags or location information.

LinkedIn is mainly used as a professional networking website and app where employees advertise their vacancies and employees can post their CVs. It allows users to create profiles, post content and make connections with others using the service.

Lurking is being present in an online environment such a chatroom or Twitter chat but not participating in any interactions.

Meme refers to an image or video with a short piece of text, often with a humorous content, that is copied and distributed on social media platforms.

Medium is a website that publishes a wide variety of content, from personal blog posts to professional publications.

Moodle is an open-source virtual learning environment (VLE) used by education institutions to host content, deliver courses and facilitate blended and distance education.

MOOC is a Massive Open Online Course. These courses are fully online and have unlimited enrolment so they often have very large numbers of students on the course.

Open Education is the general outlook that educational resources and knowledge should be made freely accessible to all, and that we should aim to eliminate any barriers to achieve this goal. Promoting collaboration is a key feature of open education.

Phenomenography is a qualitative research methodology, usually based on interviews that aims to investigate the way people think or experience something. It emphasises the interviewee's refection and description of experiences.

Pinterest is a visual social media service that allows users to share videos and images. Images are called 'pin's and they are put onto 'pinboards' which can be customised according to different themes and then followed by others.

Podcasts are a series of digital audio recordings that listeners can download or streamed to their device.

Snapchat is an app for sharing photos, videos and messages. Its distinctive feature is that once the message has been received via Snapchat it is automatically deleted.

Tag is a keyword or phrase added to a social media post with the purpose of relating it to a category or collection.

Twalk is a structured walk augmented by the use of social media (usually Twitter). Participants will walk around a specified route, discussing a nominated topic(s) and use Twitter to enhance the discussions or debates.

Tweet Wall is an app or platform that displays tweets which include a specified hashtag. They are often displayed on a large screen within a populated area, such as a conference or classroom.

Twitter is a service that enables its users to publish short messages (up to 280 characters) called tweets. These tweets enable users to communicate with one another, share links/photos/videos and publicise events.

Twitter chat (or tweetchat) is usually a live event focused around a specific topic. The chat is usually based on a single hashtag.

Visitors and Residents is a simple way of visually plotting users' engagement in online environments. It maps their engagement with online tools on a continuum from visitors to residents depending upon their level of activity.

VLE is a virtual learning environment, it is an online space where learning materials and teaching/learning tools are hosted. Examples include, Moodle, Blackboard and Canvas.

WhatsApp is a messenger app, similar to a text messenger service, which allows the user to send messages, audio, images and videos. It also has features like group chatting and voice messaging.

WordPress is open source software that is often used as a blog.

List of Illustrations

Chapter 3

Chapter 4

Chapter 5

Chapter 6

Chapter 8

Chapter 9

Chapter 11

Chapter 13

Chapter 15

Chapter 17

Chapter 19

Chapter 21

Index

This book need not end here...

Share

All our books—including the one you have just read—are free to access online so that students, researchers and members of the public who can't afford a printed edition will have access to the same ideas. This title will be accessed online by hundreds of readers each month across the globe: why not share the link so that someone you know is one of them?

This book and additional content is available at:
https://doi.org/10.11647/OBP.0162

Customise

Personalise your copy of this book or design new books using OBP and third-party material. Take chapters or whole books from our published list and make a special edition, a new anthology or an illuminating coursepack. Each customised edition will be produced as a paperback and a downloadable PDF. Find out more at:

https://www.openbookpublishers.com/section/59/1

You may also be interested in:

Open Education

International Perspectives in Higher Education
Patrick Blessinger and TJ Bliss (eds.)

https://doi.org/10.11647/OBP.0103

Digital Humanities Pedagogy

Practices, Principles and Politics
Brett D. Hirsch (ed.)

https://doi.org/10.11647/OBP.0024

Delivering on the Promise of Democracy

Visual Case Studies in Educational Equity and
Transformation
Sukhwant Jhaj

https://doi.org/10.11647/OBP.0157

Printed in July 2019
by Rotomail Italia S.p.A., Vignate (MI) - Italy